The Hustle

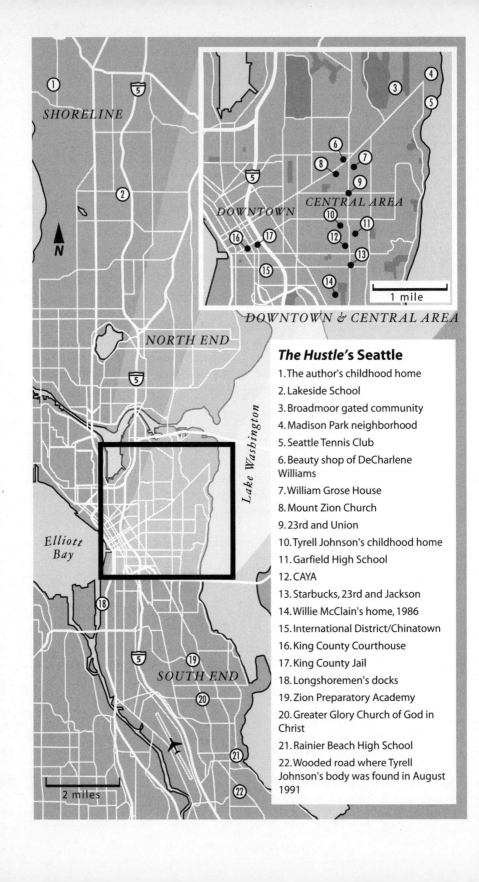

The Hustle's Seattle

1. The author's childhood home
2. Lakeside School
3. Broadmoor gated community
4. Madison Park neighborhood
5. Seattle Tennis Club
6. Beauty shop of DeCharlene Williams
7. William Grose House
8. Mount Zion Church
9. 23rd and Union
10. Tyrell Johnson's childhood home
11. Garfield High School
12. CAYA
13. Starbucks, 23rd and Jackson
14. Willie McClain's home, 1986
15. International District/Chinatown
16. King County Courthouse
17. King County Jail
18. Longshoremen's docks
19. Zion Preparatory Academy
20. Greater Glory Church of God in Christ
21. Rainier Beach High School
22. Wooded road where Tyrell Johnson's body was found in August 1991

The Hustle

One Team and Ten Lives in Black and White

Doug Merlino

BLOOMSBURY
New York   Berlin   London

Published by Bloomsbury USA, New York

All papers used by Bloomsbury USA are natural, recyclable products made from wood grown in well-managed forests. The manufacturing processes conform to the environmental regulations of the country of origin.

Library of Congress Cataloging-in-Publication Data

Merlino, Doug.
    The hustle : one team and ten lives in Black and White / Doug Merlino. — 1st u.s. ed.
        p. cm.
    Includes index.
    ISBN: 978-1-60819-215-1 (alk. paper)
  1. Basketball—Washington (State)—Seattle.   2. School sports—Washington (State)—Seattle.   3. Basketball players—Washington (State)—Seattle.   4. Lakeside School (Seattle, Wash.)—Basketball.   5. Basketball—Social aspects—Washington (State)—Seattle.   6. Seattle (Wash.)—Race relations.   7. Central District (Seattle, Wash.)—Race relations.   8. Racism in sports.   I. Title.
    GV885.73.S43M47 2010
    796.323'6209797772—dc22
2010023030

First U.S. Edition 2011

1 3 5 7 9 10 8 6 4 2

Typeset by Westchester Book Group
Printed in the U.S.A. by Quad / Graphics, Fairfield, Pennsylvania

For my teammates
In memory of Tyrell Johnson

The color line raises the issue of identity. Theirs. Yours. Mine. Will we blend, change, survive, or is the color line one more measure of the limits of our collective imagination, our cultural graveyard of either/or terminal distinctions: black/white, male/female, young/old, good/bad, rich/poor, spirit/flesh? Is it possible to imagine ourselves other than we are, better?

—*John Edgar Wideman*

Contents

Part One

The Season

Basketball is one of those vigorous team activities which will help the youth reach the highest level of human efficiency. Activity leading to further activity, guided by intelligent and sympathetic leadership to achieve the fullest development of latent powers and capacities, is the immediate aim and need of society. The quality of the development will be judged by society in terms of powers and capacities which make for complete living.

—*From the introduction to* Basketball: A text-book for coaches, players, recreation leaders, students and teachers of physical education, *published in 1929*

Spring 1986
Front row: Eric Hampton, Damian Joseph, Myran Barnes, Willie McClain Jr., Tyrell Johnson
Back row: Assistant coach Joe Miller, Doug Merlino, Maitland Finley, Tony Simmons, Sean O'Donnell, John Thompson, head coach Willie McClain

One for All

The brown Dodge van bumps and shakes along the freeway. Willie McClain gives it some gas and a groan comes from under the hood. McClain's hair, a mass of jheri curls, juts above the driver's seat. He's punched in the news station on the radio, and the announcer's voice drones from the speakers in the van's doors, talking about a showdown between Ronald Reagan and Muammar Gadhafi in Libya. We sit on the shag carpet in the back, rocking from side to side, bouncing with every jolt and leaning into every turn.

"Come on, Mait," urges Tyrell, flashing an elfin smile.

A few stifled giggles, and then expectant eyes. "I don't know," Maitland mumbles. He stares at the van's carpet. Under his shaggy, sandy brown hair, he looks like a cherub, with blue eyes, pink lips, and a plaster-white face.

"You can do it, Mait," says JT. While Tyrell's voice carries edges of urgency and challenge, JT's is reassuring.

Mait keeps his eyes cast down. We look to Eric, who, as usual, has been silently observing. Sometimes I steal a glance at Eric and try to figure out what he's thinking. I never can. You can say about anything to Eric, but nothing will break his poker face.

Everyone knows that Eric will settle this. He's the arbiter, the only one in the van who knows both sides of the team. He's black, and has grown up in the same neighborhood as the other black kids, but he also goes to school with the white guys. If he waves Tyrell off, everyone's attention will turn from Mait in an instant. But Eric seems to have processed the whole interaction and considered its particular dynamics and ramifications. He nods his head. "It's all right, Mait," he says in his soft voice.

Mait looks up, balls his hand into a fist, puts it up over his mouth, takes a breath, and begins to blow.

Puh-ha-ha, Puh-ha-ha, Puh-ha-ha, Puh!
Puh-ha-ha, Puh-ha-ha, Puh-ha-ha, Puh!

Unrestrained laughter bounces off the sides of the van. Myran rolls over on his side, Tyrell next to him, both holding their hands over their mouths as they giggle. Sean, next to me with his back resting against the side of the van, looks around and chuckles, his blond hair flopping down on his forehead. Even Coach McClain—along with his son, Willie Jr., who's riding shotgun—is busting up. While our laughter is the contralto titters of fourteen-year-old boys, Coach McClain's seems to get stoked somewhere deep inside before it climbs up and shakes his whole frame as it booms out. His shoulders rise up and down in his navy blue track suit.

Maitland looks up and smiles. His face shows relief, and maybe something else. In this moment, he fits in. The separation between him and everyone else has diminished. He's reduced the distance between all the kids in the van. We've all seen something no one else can ever say they've witnessed: We were there when Maitland beat-boxed.

His model is, of course, the Human Beat Box, of the Fat Boys, a trio of obese rappers whose rhymes are odes to gluttony. They are third on the list of rappers everyone listens to, following Run DMC and LL Cool J.

Damian can get the authoritative tone of Run DMC:

I'm the King of Rock,
there is none higher,
sucker MCs should call me sire,
to burn my kingdom,
you must use fire,
I won't stop rockin' til I retire!

And Tyrell, a self-styled ladies' man, has LL Cool J (short for Ladies Love Cool James):

My radio believe me I like it loud,
I'm the man with the box that can rock the crowd,
Walkin' down the street to the hardcore beat,
while my JVC vibrates the concrete.

And now Maitland has cornered the Fat Boys.

"Oh, man, Mait was *beat-boxing*," Damian says, still laughing, as if he can't believe what he's seen and saying it out loud will make it real. Maitland's shoulders relax, and he looks around at the rest of us with the hint of a sly smile. In the four years I've known him, since fifth grade, I've hardly ever seen Mait look at ease. It's as if he's just exhaled in one long breath. I suddenly wish we could freeze and hold this moment, just to keep that look on his face a little longer.

We wear sweatpants, T-shirts, and sweatshirts over our bumblebee-yellow uniforms, which are made from some ungodly blend of synthetic fabric and perforated with tiny holes that are theoretically supposed to ventilate our perspiration. My shorts—and they are short—ride up my thighs and hug my butt in a way that is not comfortable. My jersey chafes me around the shoulders. I wear white and purple high-tops about the size of ski boots. They are Avias, never to be mistaken with anything remotely cool.

Everyone covets Air Jordans, black with a bold red Nike swoosh. The truth is, I actually have a pair of Jordans, but only wore them to school once. One of my friends ridiculed me for trying to "act black." I was so embarrassed—the fact was, he was right—that I retired them to my closet and only occasionally put them on to shoot on the hoop in our driveway at home, if merely to justify for my mom the expense of buying them.

There are no quiet moments during the ride. If nothing else, someone will always start a capping battle.

"You're so ugly that mirrors have to get insurance in case you look in them."

"You're so black, if you were walking down the street at night and closed your eyes, you'd be invisible."

"Your mama's so fat, when she sits around the house, she *really* sits around the house."

The goal is to come up with the most outrageous insult, one that will reduce the whole van to hysterics. The black guys—especially Tyrell, Myran, and Damian—are the teachers and the masters. It sometimes seems like the first words they ever said must have been caps. The rest of us act as a panel of judges, deciding who got in the best rip, our votes tallied by how hard we laugh. With no experience at playing the dozens, I usually sit silent and hope to go unnoticed. Not this time.

Myran jumps in. "Doug, your nose is so straight, it looks like a pencil."

I look at Myran, who's looking at me, waiting for a response. I calculate the ways having a straight nose might be a bad thing. It seems low on the scale of life's catastrophes. I have plenty of weak spots—my lack of skills on the basketball court, for example, or my nearly total inability to utter anything coherent around a girl (Tyrell got at that when he capped on me: "Doug, you haven't been in a woman since you came out of your mama")—but my nose has never really concerned me.

Myran continues. "You're so white, Casper the Friendly Ghost sees you and gets scared."

My instinctive reaction, which I hold in, is to blurt out, "I am not that white!" I realize that saying it would only prove his point.

I feel my mouth hanging open. Myran loves to rank. Eric and Damian have been prepping me, telling me that I should have some caps ready to get him back if he goes after me. Eric—who usually sits just as silent as I do—has even helped me make up caps so I don't have to think of my own. Most relate to Myran's lips. Everyone goes at Myran for his lips. Their size is a van-ride leitmotif. As I sit there mute, I have Eric's ready-made caps on my own lips, but I hesitate.

I consider Damian and Eric's suggestions that I go back at Myran. Both of them are always watching the angles. A few weeks earlier, between games at a tournament when the team headed out of the gym to get lunch at McDonald's, Damian—a skinny guy with a strut and ears that stick out from his head—stopped near the door, climbed up into the stands, and sat down among a bunch of players on a team from one of Seattle's wealthiest suburbs. The rest of us kept walking toward McDonald's. Five minutes later, Damian caught up, a bag of Skittles in one hand and a can of Coke in the other as a result of his efforts. "They just gave them to me," he explained.

Eric specializes in sizing people up. It's part of what makes him such a good basketball player. A quarter or two into a game, he'll have his opponent figured out and know how to exploit his weaknesses. If the guy goes for Eric's head fake, then Eric will throw that at him until he can stop it. If the guy dribbles only with his right hand, then Eric overplays until he has to go left.

Both seem to know more about human nature than I do. Maybe they are showing me a way to be accepted, like Maitland with the beat-boxing. Or they could be setting me up. More than anything, I worry about standing out. I don't want to start anything with Myran. All I really want to do is keep my head down and fit in with the group.

Myran is waiting. I begin to open my mouth. Nothing comes out. Maybe ten seconds pass. And then Myran moves on, and the natural flow of the ranking returns.

The back of the van is our own world. Coach McClain usually lets us be, content to pilot his raggedy old van down the freeway and let us go on talking about our usual subjects: the games we just played; everything and anything about girls; who's better—Magic, Jordan, Isiah, or Bird?

Sometimes, though, the balance wobbles. Usually it's Myran who starts it to rocking, such as when—treading dangerously close to his own weakness—he begins to make fun of *Maitland's* lips. Once Myran gets warmed up, only a display of greater force will stop him.

McClain, drawing from a lifetime accumulation of caps, finally takes control, breaking in from the driver's seat:

"Myran, Myran, it's such a shame, cuz you don't even know your daddy's name."

The back of the van explodes with guffaws. Guys are rolling on their sides, hands on their foreheads. "Oh, Coach, that was *cold*!" Damian says.

It will be many years before I realize how desperately McClain wants the team to work out and how nervous he is that one of his guys will blurt out something that can't be taken back.

Myran sits silent. Hidden behind the bravado is a boy who is more adrift than any of us ever knew.

The gym looks the same as every other one we play in: collapsible wooden bleachers that stack up and roll out with a grudging rumble; the banners of all the schools in the conference hung on the cream-colored, cinderblock walls; an American flag, sagging just a bit in the middle, tacked up behind a hoop; the shiny maple floor that squeaks when the soles of your sneakers drag across it; over the door, a clock protected from stray balls by a metal grille; above the clock, a scoreboard with a timer and sides labeled "Home" and "Visitor."

We walk onto the floor after the two-hour van ride. With no windows and fluorescent lighting, there is a twilight feeling inside the gym. It smells like basketball, a blend of sweat and dust.

We are north of Seattle, just a short drive from the Canadian border. Spectators meander from the stands to the concession stall, coming back balancing hot dogs, bags of popcorn, Red Vines, and soft drinks in Coca-Cola cups, all of it packed into flimsy cardboard carry boxes.

We strip off our sweatpants and T-shirts, stuff them in the bags we carry, and toss them behind the bench. This method means that we will not have to change in front of each other. It also looks kind of cool—or so it seems to me—like when NBA players brusquely rip off their warm-up gear before entering a game. Our tube socks ride high, pulled up three quarters of the way to our knees. Sean and I both wear white T-shirts under our uniforms, a look inspired by Patrick Ewing of the Georgetown Hoyas. I think it makes me look tough. Tyrell goes one better, wearing a yellow T-shirt—which matches our uniform tops in color—under his jersey. He also has a yellow sweatband perched halfway up his left forearm and a gold necklace that he absentmindedly flips in and out from under his shirt. The other guys wear our butt-hugging uniforms without adornment.

As we take the court, Randy Finley, our organizer and financial backer—and Maitland's father—sits one row behind Willie McClain and chatters in his ear. Finley is a six-foot-two white man with a big belly contained under a tan flannel shirt that he's tucked into his jeans, and a bushy head of salt-and-pepper hair with a thick mustache to match. McClain, with his muscular frame and scowl of concentration, looks a little scary to me—less like a basketball coach than someone who could play linebacker next to Mike Singletary on the Chicago Bears.

I've always had a hard time relating to coaches. On TV and in sports movies, they are always stern but wise, demanding but kindhearted. In my own experience, they are more likely to be commandeering, clipboard-toting strutters in nut-hugging sweatpants, consumed with dreams of glory. McClain, though, is absolutely restrained. If you mess up in practice, he'll yell, but without anger. He expects you to do as he says, because you don't want to find out what will happen if you don't.

We form two lines near midcourt and begin the drill nearly all basketball teams start with: From the right side, one player dribbles toward the basket and lays up a shot off the glass backboard. From the left, another waits for the ball to drop through the net, grabs it, and then fires a pass out to the next player approaching the hoop. Each player goes to the end of the opposite line, and the drill forms a perfect sequence, like a perpetual-motion machine. Here, it's all about showing off: Sean, who is mostly spindly legs in his uniform, weakly thumps the palm of his hand against the backboard as he lays it in; Tyrell comes under the hoop and puts in a reverse; Eric stutter-steps and then nonchalantly banks it off the glass; I imagine I am an NBA player striding toward the basket and then flipping the ball up like it's an afterthought. Maitland and JT are the only two players who don't try any moves. The gym reverberates with thumping basketballs.

The scorekeeper, seated at half court, hits a button on a black metal box on the table in front of him and a shrill buzzer squawks. We gather in a circle around Coach McClain, who kneels down and goes over his usual instructions: Stick to your man. Work to get open. Attack the basket. Look for the open player. When he finishes, we pile our hands one on top of another and slowly raise them.

McClain says: "OK, ready . . . one, two, three . . ."

As the tangle comes down, we yell: "All for one, one for all!"

Our starting lineup—Sean, Maitland, Eric, Tyrell, and Willie Jr.—takes the floor. I sit on the bench with Damian, JT, and Myran. Myran and I see very little playing time, usually subbing in once a half to give one of the starters a few minutes of rest, or at other times if one of them has screwed up so much that McClain wants to make them sit a little while to think things over.

All the other teams we play are from outside Seattle, and their lineups are always nearly all white. A lot of opposing players look like farm boys, with feathered hair or mullets, muscular enough to toss a bale of hay. They look like the type of guys who carry brightly colored plastic combs with handles that stick out of the back pockets of their jeans.

In our first game of the tournament, things go according to McClain's plan. We run a full-court trap, with our quickest players, Eric, Willie Jr., and Tyrell, constantly pressuring their ball handlers, harassing them from the minute they inbound the ball. If one of them doesn't cough up it up, JT or Damian will be lurking at midcourt to intercept a rushed pass. It's a fast-paced style of basketball. Most teams from outside Seattle haven't seen full-court pressure like this and tend to panic. When that happens, we can pile on the points, turning a close game into a blowout. For Maitland, Sean, and me, the role is to wait down on the other end as a last resort, in case our opponents manage to get the ball past the pressure points.

On the bench, Myran keeps up a string of patter, nicknaming players on the other team: Stickboy (too skinny), Molasses (too slow), No-Shot (can't shoot). JT is the team cheerleader, clapping and urging everyone on. When someone makes a good play, JT puts his left hand over his mouth and hollers through it like a megaphone while he pumps his right fist in the air. Damian and I both lean forward, hands on our chins, taking on the role of basketball analysts. McClain shouts from the bench, above all liking to ride Sean, who he sees as too passive on the court: "Come on, Sean! Let's get after it now!"

Eric has one move that almost never fails. He gets the ball out beyond the top of the key and dribbles with his right hand. He begins to drift to the left, as if he's floating. Suddenly he breaks right and darts past the flat-footed defender, driving the lane and shooting or dumping the ball off to a teammate. Sean and Maitland stand near the basket, two gawky figures with their arms up, waiting for a pass. Willie Jr. is the point guard, a surrogate for his dad on the court, directing everyone to their positions with his left hand while he dribbles with his right.

When I get my chance for a few minutes at the end of the first half, I mill around outside the key and occasionally wave my arm in the air. Tyrell and Willie Jr. will not pass the ball to me unless they are in dire trouble. I am not tall enough to post up under the hoop but lack the ball-handling skills to play on the perimeter. The one thing I can do fairly well is shoot the outside shot—the product of innumerable hours practicing by myself on the hoop at home—but whenever I actually do touch the ball, I get so nervous that I'll screw up that I pass it right away, always looking to give it back to Eric.

The game isn't close—the other team is outmatched by our speed and full-court press. We're cruising toward a win. Myran nails a jump shot from way outside. Sean posts up, takes a pass from Willie Jr., and then spins and banks it in. JT sneaks around our opponents and steals a rebound.

Then a member of the other team misses a shot. Maitland grabs the rebound and whips it out to Tyrell, who takes off downcourt on the fast break. He drives toward the hoop from the left side of the key. A player from the opposing team comes in to cut him off. Tyrell, a few feet from the hoop, picks up the dribble, transfers the ball from his left hand to his right, and holds it out to the kid like a waiter offering a tray of appetizers. The defender freezes up—his jaw drops and he stares at the leather sphere floated right under his nose. The din of the game—parents chattering, shoes squawking, coaches yelling—subsides. And then the moment passes. In one seamless motion, Tyrell slides the ball back to his left hand and lays it in. Those of us on the bench fall over ourselves whooping and laughing.

Things go bad in our second game. Our opponents, who must have scouted us, easily pick apart McClain's trapping defense, moving the ball upcourt with sharp passes before we can lock in on them. McClain cajoles from the bench to no avail. The referees make a few questionable calls and Randy Finley loses it in the stands. "Come on, ref! Where was the foul?"

Myran and I languish at the end of the bench as the team comes apart, falling behind by twenty points. Tyrell and Willie Jr. hog the ball, firing up wild shots that are way off the mark. Sean is winded, walking up and down the court, hands on his hips, hanging his head, and sucking air. After he misses a shot, Eric thrusts his head down into his hands, shakes it from side to side, and stomps back up the court before finally looking straight up at the ceiling and muttering in disgust.

I wish that McClain would put me in the game, though I know I could do nothing to change the outcome. Of the other white kids on the team, Maitland gets special attention from McClain because he is Randy Finley's son, Sean because he is six feet two inches tall and McClain thinks he can toughen him up enough to become a force in the middle. I fall through the cracks—a quiet kid without any special skills. I'm here for racial balance.

We get blown out. McClain and Finley both stalk out before us, angry with the team and incensed with the two white refs, whom they believe called the game against us because of our racial composition. I'm surprised at how quickly the other team exposed the inadequacies of our game plan, leaving us with no backup.

We grab our bags, follow into the parking lot in silence, and pack into the van. The ignominy of our defeat soon gives way to jokes, chatter, and capping as we ride back. Eventually we make it to Seattle, where we split up. The white guys head back to their homes in the northern or eastern suburbs; the black guys return to Central Seattle or the South End.

Black Seattle/White Seattle

In the spring of 1986, Willie McClain and his family lived in a small, white A-frame house on a sleepy street in Central Seattle. If you showed up on a weekday afternoon, you'd likely find a scene like this: In the TV room—which wasn't big enough to fit much more than the couch and the McClains' large-screen, projection television—JT might be down on the carpet, playing with Dwayne, the McClains' three-year-old son. Myran, Tyrell, and a kid named James Credit would be sprawled on the sofa, joking and watching videotapes of *The Warriors* and *The Fish That Saved Pittsburgh*. Sometimes they listened to music—that spring, a demo tape put out by an underground Seattle rapper named Sir Mix-a-Lot was getting a lot of play in the house. Upstairs, Damian and Willie Jr. bashed into each other as they tried to dunk a Nerf basketball through the hoop hung on the back of the door of Little Willie's bedroom. Diane McClain, Willie's wife, would be in the kitchen, the largest room in the house, cooking up tacos, hot dogs, or spaghetti. All the boys ate a lot, but Myran had an especially large appetite. After the kids had their fill, JT always made sure to help wash the dishes. As the McClains intended, the afternoons had the feeling of an extended family getting together. "They never fought each other," Diane McClain says of the boys. "Everyone was just really close."

In the late afternoon, Willie McClain Sr. arrived home from work—he'd just gotten a job as a playground supervisor and bus driver for a Christian elementary school for African-American kids. The boys at the house were his guys. He'd started coaching most of them in 1979, when they were seven. He considered himself a surrogate dad for Myran, Damian, and JT, who had no fathers at home. "I told them what they could and could not do, plain and simple," he says.

At thirty-two years old, McClain was pulling his own life together. The need for change had been hammered into him a few years earlier, when he'd showed up to coach a basketball game with a hangover. "I was out of it," he says. "The kids ended up coaching themselves." When JT and Eric asked him what was wrong, McClain found that he didn't have a good answer. The realization hit him: "You got to get yourself together, or you're going to pass on your lifestyle to your sons." He didn't want his boys or the players on his team to waste their talents like he believed he had squandered his.

Church was one thing that kept him grounded. Coaching was another.

McClain's team played in the local community league, formally known as the Central Area Youth Association but universally referred to by reciting its four initials one at a time, C-A-Y-A. The great majority of players in the league were black.

The Central Area, a roughly four-square-mile patch of land tucked between the downtown business district to the west and the waterfront mansions on Lake Washington to the east, was the historical heart of black Seattle. Most of the African Americans in the city—blacks made up around 10 percent of Seattle's population of five hundred thousand in 1986—lived in the neighborhood or those stretching out directly south of it.

Willie McClain loved basketball for the beauty and precision of the game, but youth sports invariably mixed with racial concerns. When CAYA teams played outside the league, it wasn't unusual for every opposing player to be white. McClain had sometimes given up home basketball games and driven his kids out of the Central Area to compete, because coaches from the wealthy suburbs east of Seattle, across Lake Washington, wouldn't bring in their teams to play in the Central Area. McClain knew that it would be useless to appeal—his complaints would go to white league administrators who would just find a way to back up the suburban coaches.

Separation between blacks and whites was nothing new for McClain. Having spent the first years of his life in Mississippi, McClain knew there were places where racism ran much hotter. But like most African Americans in Seattle—which has long prided itself as a place with

smoother race relations than the rest of the country—he found himself
on the periphery of the city's economy.

. . .

From its beginning, in November 1851, when a small group of settlers
led by a twenty-nine-year-old surveyor from Illinois named Arthur Denny
sailed into Elliott Bay, Seattle has been a place where people come to
pursue their passions and economic interests at a remove from the rest of
America. As long as you don't mess with anyone's livelihood or raise too
much fuss, Seattle—out on the wet, northwestern edge of the country—
will likely meet you with a tight-lipped smile, a bit of small talk, and
then get on with things. For its minority populations, says University of
Washington historian Quintard Taylor, Seattle has long presented a
paradox: While much of the city espouses liberalism, that rhetoric has
been "juxtaposed against the reality of discrimination." This is a place,
after all, that named itself in honor of an Indian chief even as the local
tribes were being efficiently—and sometimes violently—removed from
the land.

From its inception, Seattle has ridden waves of economic boom and
bust. Within weeks after trudging ashore, the Denny Party got to work
cutting down trees near the water and shipping the timber on boats
headed for San Francisco, then surging with Gold Rush money. In 1852,
Henry Yesler, newly arrived from Ohio, built a steam-powered sawmill,
and the town—really just a logging camp on the shores of Puget Sound—
was off and running.

Of the handful of blacks who settled in frontier Seattle, the one who
would have the most lasting influence was William Grose, who landed in
the muddy, waterfront village of whitewashed clapboard homes in about
1860. Born in Washington, D.C., Grose had sailed to China and Central
America with the navy, passed through the gold fields in California and
British Columbia, and had worked as a ship's steward before coming to
Seattle. On his arrival, Grose, then in his midtwenties, took a job at the
grill of a saloon lunch counter. At six-foot-four and more than 400 pounds,
he soon became known as "Big Bill the Cook."

For its first few decades, Seattle was a rough-hewn town with an
economy centered on logging and Yesler's sawmill. Most of the business
was controlled at the top by the pioneer families, who had divvied up the
choicest land among themselves when they founded the town. It was a

live-and-let-live kind of place—for example, even though he was a religious teetotaler, Arthur Denny managed to look past the numerous local establishments that gave workingmen the chance to booze, whore, and lose their money gambling.

Amid all this, blacks in Seattle had more freedom than in most other parts of the United States, even in the West. Oregon, at the time, denied blacks voting rights and prohibited them from settling. While other western states passed laws that prohibited interracial marriage, Washington Territory did not enact any overtly discriminatory statutes. But while blacks did not face a lot of outright harassment, neither did they have much political or economic power. Barred from labor unions, African Americans found themselves at the bottom of the job market, working as janitors or laborers, or, on the more prestigious end of the scale, cooks, porters, chauffeurs and, in several cases, barbers. Robert Dixon, for example, a black barber from Virginia who arrived in 1865, opened a shop downtown where he cut the hair of city fathers such as Arthur Denny (black barbers often did not serve other blacks during business hours for fear of putting off their white customers).

Part of the reason for the city's relative tolerance was that there just weren't very many blacks around to discriminate against. In 1880, African Americans numbered just nineteen of thirty-five hundred people in the town. At the time, the primary targets of racial animosity in Seattle were American Indians and Chinese. Indians, who had lived in the region for centuries, were generally viewed as savages. Hatred of the Chinese, who were recruited to the Northwest to build the railroads, exploded in February 1886, when unionized white workers—who accused the Chinese of undercutting salaries—rampaged through Seattle's Chinatown and forced Chinese to the docks, where two hundred were loaded on a steamer and sent to San Francisco. Within a month, almost all of Seattle's Chinese had been deported.

During this time, William Grose did well. In 1876 he started a restaurant downtown called Our House, and later opened a barbershop and a three-story hotel near the waterfront. An amiable man, he was well known in town—a magazine drawing of a crowd at an 1882 lynching of three accused white murderers shows Grose standing near sawmill owner Henry Yesler. That same year, Grose, whose businesses made him Seattle's wealthiest African American, paid Yesler $1,000 for twelve acres of land in the northeastern section of the city, a couple of miles from the waterfront. At the time, the land, along East Madison Street, was a wooded area still populated by bears. After Grose started a farm and built a home on the property, he began to sell off parcels to other African Americans. By the 1890s, the area was developing as the center of Seattle's "respectable," middle-class African-American population, gaining it the disparaging nickname "Coon Hollow."

William Grose died in 1898, and Arthur Denny followed the next year, both having made their fortunes. By this time, Seattle had established itself as the primary city on Puget Sound. As the town's residential patterns began to emerge, wealthier whites moved away from the area downtown to outer neighborhoods. Near the waterfront around Jackson Street—what is today known as the "International District" or simply "Chinatown"—lived Asians and poorer blacks, in the city's red-light neighborhood, home to brothels and residential hotels. Over the coming decades, the Jackson Street area and the East Madison neighborhood—two communities separated by a couple of miles and a class barrier—would grow toward each other as more African Americans arrived in the city and filled in the middle, forming the Black Central Area.

In 1900, African Americans made up 406 of Seattle's population of eighty thousand, a minuscule but unsurprising number. Most African Americans at the time—7 million out of 8 million—lived in the South. The majority worked in the fields, as hired hands or sharecroppers, tending cotton and sugarcane. The federal government's post–Civil War Reconstruction efforts had been beaten back, replaced with Jim Crow segregation, the Ku Klux Klan, the loss of voting rights, and economic subjugation. Lynching became a popular entertainment for white southerners, with large crowds of spectators coming out to gape and enjoy themselves as black men—"strange fruit," as Billie Holiday later sang—hung from trees. In 1896, the U.S. Supreme Court stamped its approval on the separation of blacks and whites, ruling that laws permitting segregation "do not necessarily imply the inferiority of either race to the other."

In response to the postemancipation plight, the seminal black scholar W. E. B. Du Bois wrote that being African American meant living with the "double consciousness" of being both black and American, of trying to survive in a society that views you as inferior because of your color. "The history of the American Negro is the history of this strife—this longing to attain self-conscious manhood, to merge his double self into a better and truer self," Du Bois wrote. "He simply wishes to make it possible for a man to be both a Negro and an American, without being cursed and spit upon by his fellows, without having the doors of opportunity closed roughly in his face."

Du Bois grew up in Massachusetts and graduated from Harvard. A founder of the National Association for the Advancement of Colored People, he believed that civil rights legislation and political action were needed to advance the place of African Americans. He thought that a black vanguard—the "Talented Tenth," in his words—could set an example. As Du Bois saw it, the success of the Talented Tenth—really, the educated, black elite—would pave the way into society for the rest of black America to follow.

Du Bois's beliefs ran counter to those of Booker T. Washington, the country's most influential African American. Washington, who had been born a slave, headed the Tuskegee Institute in Alabama, a vocational school that taught blacks skills in trades such as agriculture and carpentry. Instead of demanding rights from whites, Washington advocated that African Americans focus on themselves first. "It is at the bottom of life we must begin, and not at the top," he said in an 1895 speech that became known as the "Atlanta Compromise." "The wisest among my race understand that the agitation of questions of social equality is the extremist folly, and that progress in the enjoyment of all the privileges that will come to us must be the result of severe and constant struggle rather than of artificial forcing."

Washington, in effect, endorsed segregation: "In all things that are purely social we can be as separate as the fingers," he said of blacks and whites, "yet one as the hand in all things essential to mutual progress."

Du Bois attacked Washington's approach, arguing that accommodation without civil rights and a path to higher education would cement the status of African Americans as an inferior class. It was a battle of ideas that would set the framework for arguments about black advancement in American society for the coming decades—whether to demand rights through the political process, or to look inward and concentrate on self-improvement within the black community without regard to white America. More than a century later, as I would learn when speaking with my black teammates, the tensions between the two positions remain unresolved.

Just as Seattle's first black community was coalescing around William Grose's land in the East Madison neighborhood in the 1890s, my great-grandfather Giovanni Merlino was conscripted into the Italian Army. When my grandfather was a kid, Giovanni used to show him the scars from bullet wounds in his shoulder and his side he'd gotten after he was sent to fight in Ethiopia. One day, the Italians—about twenty thousand troops in my great-grandfather's telling—met a massive force of Ethiopians, who attacked from all sides. Before long, the Italians were in a panicked retreat. My great-grandfather survived only because his comrades carried him off the battlefield after he'd been shot. It's impossible to say for certain, but given the details and the time he was in Ethiopia, Giovanni was probably describing the Battle of Adowa, which happened on March 1, 1896. The Ethiopians routed the Italians that day, derailing (for a time) Italy's ambitions to conquer their country and keeping it the only nation in Africa free of colonization.

If Giovanni thought about his role in the larger history of European adventures in Africa, he didn't mention it to my grandfather. He returned home to his village in the mountains of southern Italy and found there was no work. His brother had already left for America, one of several men from the area who had sailed to New York and then headed across the country, drawn by the promise of jobs in the coal mines outside Seattle. Giovanni followed, arriving in 1898.

The brothers had good timing. In the late 1890s, with the Klondike Gold Rush in full swing, Seattle was in the midst of one of its occasional economic booms. Thousands of prospectors, dreamers, and drifters poured money into the city as they geared up for the journey to Alaska. Giovanni went to work as a miner while Angelo opened an Italian grocery. In 1908, Giovanni returned to the village in Italy and asked a girl he knew to marry him. When they came back, my great-grandmother told him she had no desire to live in a mining camp, so they moved to Seattle, where he took a job in an iron foundry.

The Italians lived in the Rainier Valley area of Seattle, just south of the Central Area. "Garlic Gulch" was full of "wops" who, like Giovanni, grew tomatoes and zucchini in their backyards, kept chickens and rabbits, and fermented homemade wine—known as "Dago red"—in their basements.

As their numbers began to grow, the Italians settled in on Seattle's economic ladder about one notch above blacks, a status that led to competition for menial work. One such job was shoe shining. At the turn of the century, Italians in Seattle had organized to the extent that they could buy the "rights" to set up shoe-shine stands on the sidewalks outside of downtown businesses. Blacks set up for free in alleys and side streets. After the Italians complained, the City Council passed a motion that required shoe shiners who operated on public property to pay for their spaces. The language of the law was race-neutral, but the effect was to shut down the black competition and give the Italians—on the cusp of being considered full-fledged "whites"—a leg up. It's a small example that shows the difficult compromise behind Booker T. Washington's theory of advancing through self-improvement: Without equal protection under the law, blacks could never know how secure their futures were.

Seattle's preeminent black family in the early 1900s was that of Horace Cayton, publisher of the *Seattle Republican*, the city's second-largest newspaper, and his wife, Susie Revels, the daughter of the first black U.S. senator, Mississippi's Hiram Revels, who served during Reconstruction. In 1909, when Booker T. Washington came to visit Seattle for the Alaskan, Yukon, and Pacific Exposition, the Cayton family had the honor of putting him up and showing him the city. One night at dinner, Horace Cayton confronted Washington about his insistence on staying in the South and accepting segregation. As Cayton's son, Horace Cayton Jr., recounts in his autobiography, *Long Old Road*, his father told Washington that he had been swayed by the arguments of W. E. B. Du Bois that blacks did not need to compromise but should make a stand for their freedom. "Here in the Northwest, we are striking out in every direction," the elder Cayton said. "Negroes in this town have become small businessmen or skilled mechanics and live a good life. Their children are getting good educations and will be able to stand up and compete with other men."

Washington answered calmly. "The Negro is not in a position to make a bid for his freedom at present, Mr. Cayton," he said. "The South was defeated, not destroyed, today it is influencing more of the country than you are perhaps aware. You speak of the insanity of the South in regards to the Negro. I sincerely hope, Mr. Cayton, the insanity of the

South does not overcome you here in the relative freedom of the North-west. I hope that the infection of Negro prejudice does not spread to this part of the country. If it does, you may find that you have been living in a fool's paradise."

The warning was prophetic. Seattle's black population grew markedly during the first decade of the twentieth century—many African Americans came to Seattle after being recruited to break strikes in the coal mines east and south of the city, where my great-grandfather had first worked. By 1910, twenty-three hundred African Americans lived in the city, a little less than 1 percent of the overall population. Over the next decade, segregation and discrimination in Seattle—following a trend across the country—began to harden. As more African Americans came to Seattle, Horace Cayton gradually included more "black" news in his paper, which led to a slow loss of white subscribers. In 1917, Cayton ran a front-page story that detailed a hideous lynching in Mississippi. The story shocked and offended many of his white readers, and the paper began to bleed subscribers and advertisers. Within three months, the *Seattle Republican* went broke. "With the new immigration the pattern [of race relations in Seattle] was beginning to change," writes Horace Cayton Jr. of the time. "There was no longer a place for an in-between group, and everyone became identified either as a Negro or white. We were, to my knowledge, the only Negro family to feel so dramatically the impact of those social forces, and our fall from our unique position was swift and, for us, painful."

The start of World War I in 1914 abruptly ended the great wave of immigration from southern and eastern Europe that had begun in the 1870s. Suddenly, with the nation gearing up for war, there was an acute shortage of workers for the factories and mills in cities such as Detroit, Chicago, Pittsburgh, St. Louis, and New York. As it happened, the country had a large population of able-bodied men who were underemployed and waiting around for a chance for better jobs. Agents from northern factories traveled south to recruit workers, giving free transport tickets to young black men willing to move. This was the start of the Great Migration, which saw one million black Americans migrate north by the onset of the Depression in 1929. For African Americans it was a profound adjustment, the beginning of a change from being a mostly rural to a mostly urban people. In New York, the Harlem Renaissance birthed an explosion of artistic talent that introduced black culture to white America.

Seattle's black population hovered at about a few thousand between 1910 and 1940. Though there had been advances in integrating the longshoremen's and ships' stewards' unions—following violent clashes with whites after blacks workers were brought in as strikebreakers—most blacks were still relegated to menial jobs. In 1930, there were 1,405 black men working in Seattle; 62 percent were laborers, bootblacks, janitors, waiters, or servants. Of the 487 black women working in the city, 287 were domestic servants. There were 4 black attorneys, 3 physicians, 3 dentists, and 2 foot doctors.

African Americans only really headed west in large numbers at the start of World War II. Shipyard jobs pulled blacks to cities such as Oakland and Portland that until then had small black populations. In Seattle, Boeing, which had been founded in 1916, ramped up its production of bombers; another local company built Sherman tanks; and some thirty shipyards in the region fired up to round-the-clock production, with an overall capacity to employ 150,000 workers. Between 1940 and 1950, the number of blacks in Seattle rose from 3,789 to 15,666.

As Seattle's black population grew, it developed institutions, including churches, local chapters of organizations such as the Urban League and the NAACP, and even a short-lived Negro Leagues baseball team, the Seattle Steelheads. A boisterous jazz and nightlife scene centered around clubs on Jackson Street even drew a seventeen-year-old piano player from Florida named Ray Charles, who arrived in 1948, gave lessons to an even younger local kid named Quincy Jones, and tore things up for a couple of years before heading on to Los Angeles. It was something of a golden era, with plentiful defense contracts leading to a booming labor market and decently paid jobs. The increasing numbers of African Americans also brought overt displays of discrimination. Around town, signs went up on restaurants, hotels, and theaters reading "Whites Only" and "We Don't Serve Colored."

There also were cultural differences between the new migrants from the South and old-school Seattle African-American families. "I was quite ashamed of them," LeEtta King, a longtime black Seattle resident, told a historian of the 1940s influx. "They looked so bad. . . . Their big shapes—and their heads tied up with a handkerchief. . . . And they were noisy. I just tried not to see them."

Willie McClain was born in 1953 in Gulfport, Mississippi, on the Gulf Coast right across the water from New Orleans. At the time, his family didn't live much differently than it would have fifty years earlier—they hauled water from the well, made medicine from plants when they were sick, and lit their home with kerosene lamps. The family, including Willie's mom, stepdad, and six siblings, lived in an area called "The Quarters"—the old slave quarters—crowding into a one-bedroom shanty in a U-shaped set of houses centered on a courtyard where chickens pecked in the dirt. The tin-roofed homes were built on four-foot stilts, so that when the rains flooded the river, Willie could jump from his front door into the overflow.

"It was completely segregated," McClain says of Gulfport. "Totally." Willie's mom told him never to cross the railroad tracks, the line that separated blacks from whites. At the time of McClain's birth, it would still be a year until the Supreme Court ruled that segregation of the public schools was not acceptable; two years before Rosa Parks refused to give up her seat and Martin Luther King Jr. began the Montgomery bus boycott; and also two years before Emmett Till, a fourteen-year-old black kid visiting Mississippi from Chicago, was tortured, killed, and dumped in the Tallahatchie River, three hundred miles to the north of Gulfport. Till's killers—they later described the murder to a magazine reporter—were acquitted by an all-white jury after an hour of deliberation. Till's alleged crime was whistling at a white woman behind the counter of a grocery store.

In 1960, when Willie was almost seven, his mom told the kids they were going to take a trip. Her sister, always the go-getter of the family, had already moved to Seattle. She had gotten a nursing job, and her husband had found work as a galley cook in the merchant marine. Willie's aunt promised that if the rest of the family came, she would help them get settled. There wasn't much to pack—the family, for example, used wooden pallets as beds. Willie's mom prepared a whole bunch of food—blacks weren't welcome in many restaurants along the way—and they boarded a Greyhound bus to start the three-thousand-mile journey. As he sat at the back of the segregated coach as it pulled out of Gulfport, Willie had no idea he wasn't coming back.

The decades after World War II marked the start of large-scale migrations out of Deep South states such as Mississippi, Alabama, and Georgia as the mechanization of cotton picking demolished the demand for unskilled labor. Overall, some five million African Americans left the South between 1940 and 1970. This was the Second Great Migration. During that period, Seattle's black population climbed from thirty-eight hundred in 1940 to thirty-eight thousand in 1970.

That's also when the families of most of the black players on our team arrived. In the 1950s, Myran's grandmother, the daughter of a steel-mill worker who had migrated from Arkansas to St. Louis himself, packed up and headed to Seattle with her sister. Damian's grandmother and great-aunt left Louisiana's Cajun Country and landed in Spokane, three hundred miles east of Seattle. JT's mom was born in Seattle right after her parents came out from Monroe, Louisiana. When he was thirteen, Tyrell's father was sent from Chicago to Seattle, where he moved in with his grandmother, who had come from Decatur, Alabama, and found a job cooking and doing laundry in a sanatorium.

In 1960, the Central Area was home to four out of five blacks in Seattle. Of the rest, many lived in public housing developments sprinkled throughout the city's South End. The reality was that black people had few options other than the Central Area. From the late 1920s through 1948, many property deeds in other parts of the city included restrictive covenants that barred sale to blacks, Asians, Native Americans, and, in some cases, Jews. The North End of Seattle was almost exclusively white. After the Supreme Court ruled in 1948 that restrictive covenants could not be enforced, custom and active hostility kept blacks out of white neighborhoods for decades to come. In 1964, Seattle voters overwhelmingly rejected an "open housing" ordinance that would have made it illegal to discriminate on the basis of race when selling or renting a home.

Willie McClain's family moved into the High Point public housing development in West Seattle, a bulge of land that juts into Puget Sound south of downtown Seattle. High Point had been built during World War II for defense industry workers. In 1960, as Willie remembers it, the vast majority of High Point's residents were black. The kids had a fairly idyllic life as long as they stayed within the projects—they played tetherball, basketball, and capture the flag on the playfield, rode their bikes down a steep dirt hill, and hunted for frogs in the wetlands. If they ventured from the development, though, it was different. McClain remembers walking down the street with his friends and white people yelling at them, "Go back to the projects!" and "You're in the wrong part of town!" When the kids tried to walk to a big public park nearby, the police stopped them and told them to go back to High Point. "In Gulfport, you were liable to get hit, shot, killed, and disappeared," McClain says. "Here, I guess you could say it was open and blatant, but not life-threatening. It was more of a threat: 'You better get yourself back up there before we do something to you.'"

In November 1961, Martin Luther King Jr., then only thirty-two years old, made his only visit to Seattle. Thousands of people came out to the University of Washington, a downtown auditorium, and Garfield High School in the Central Area, where he gave speeches calling for an end to segregation. Carrying on the intellectual tradition established by Du Bois, King pressed for the full legal, economic, and social integration of blacks into American society. In New York, Malcolm X represented another prong of the movement. He led the Nation of Islam's Mosque No. 7 in Harlem and used his position to deliver blistering indictments of white treatment of blacks in America. Picking up on the strand of black intellectual thought that flowed from Booker T. Washington through Marcus Garvey, who led a Harlem-based movement in the 1910s that called for blacks to repatriate to Africa, Malcolm X advocated the establishment of a separate homeland in the South for African Americans. In probably his most famous quote, he insisted that blacks should achieve freedom "by any means necessary." At the same time, King and Malcolm X, though very different in philosophy, worked somewhat in tandem. "If the white people realize what the alternative is," Malcolm said, "perhaps they will be more willing to hear Dr. King."

In the early 1960s, after a few years in public housing, Willie Mc-Clain's family moved into a home in the Central Area. At the time, the neighborhood was brimming with new arrivals from the South—between just 1960 and 1967, the number of African Americans living in the Central Area shot up from 20,800 to 32,400. Seemingly overnight, the city developed a "ghetto." In 1950, the median income of blacks in Seattle was 73 percent that of whites; by 1967, the median income for blacks living in the Central Area was 54 percent that of Seattle's white population. Blight spread as banks and insurance companies redlined the neighborhood, refusing to insure or provide loans to property owners there. Black enrollment at some neighborhood schools topped 90 percent, while black unemployment in Seattle ran at up to triple that of the city's overall rate during the 1960s.

Gradually, the local media began to venture into the Central Area to see what exactly was going on there. In 1965, *Seattle* magazine ran an article titled "The World That Whites Don't Know," warning that the neighborhood was "seething with unrest and bitterness" over job and housing discrimination, and police brutality. The article profiled David Garner, a young migrant from Louisiana who had newly arrived with his family. He'd found work as a janitor at a building downtown, starting his shift in the evening after the office workers had left and finishing before they arrived the next day, all but invisible to white Seattle. "I feel like a visitor from Mars," Garner said. The author, a white man, wrote, "Somehow, the white masses in Seattle have developed a tradition—or a talent—for looking right through black skin, as if they thought that Negroes were a form of non-people."

Willie McClain—who was known to his friends by his nickname, "June Bug"—found the Central Area to be a safe haven, but also a boundary. His main contact with mainstream Seattle as a kid came through an older man Willie and his friends knew only as "Coach." He was a white man who came to watch them play baseball and then picked them up on weekends and drove them in his station wagon on excursions to the beach, the movies, and an all-you-can-eat restaurant in a wealthy white suburb. McClain compares Coach's role in their lives to the one the organizer of our team, Randy Finley, played in those of my black teammates. "He never did anything inappropriate," McClain says. "He just seemed to have an interest in exposing us to things outside the Central Area." If they left without Coach, the reception was different. When they rode their bikes to the all-you-can-eat restaurant by themselves while in middle school, the police told them to head back to Seattle. McClain remembers that white shopkeepers would wipe the counters after black customers touched them and spray air freshener as they were leaving.

The civil rights movement saw its greatest successes in the middle of the sixties. The Civil Rights Act of 1964 outlawed discrimination and segregation in public places, employment, schools, and housing. The next year the Voting Rights Act gave the federal government the power to end disenfranchisement in the South.

Martin Luther King Jr. believed it was just the start of a process of redressing the damage inflicted by racial subjugation. The "second phase" of the civil rights movement, he insisted, would move past racial discrimination and take on poverty and inequality, a message more often than not now overlooked in the yearly tributes around his holiday that almost always focus on his "I have a dream" speech. "White Americans would have liked to believe that in the past ten years a mechanism had somehow been created that needed only orderly and smooth tending for the painless accomplishment of change," he wrote. "Yet this is precisely what has not been achieved."

In Seattle, the industrial base simply did not absorb the new black migrants from the South, even as the city underwent a Boeing-led economic boom in the mid-1960s. At the height, in 1967, employment at the airplane manufacturer ballooned to 150,000 workers, of whom 5,400 (3.6 percent) were black. Three years later, after layoffs had begun, only 1,500 black employees remained at Boeing, 1.4 percent of the workforce. Even in the best of times, unemployment rates for blacks in Seattle remained well above those of whites, even for unskilled jobs. Many construction unions, for example, blocked black membership until well into the 1970s; they started to integrate only after African-American protesters began to shut down construction sites.

A new generation of activists, intellectual descendants of the slain Malcolm X, was losing its patience with nonviolence and negotiation. By 1967 there had already been several long, hot summers, when urban violence—"riots," "rebellions," or "uprisings," depending on who's talking—had sparked in Harlem, Detroit, Los Angeles, and elsewhere. That April, a young King protégé named Stokely Carmichael came to speak at the Central Area's Garfield High School. A year earlier, Carmichael had coined the term "Black Power" to describe his more radical approach to civil rights, which included cultural pride, economic independence, separation from mainstream America, and—if necessary—violence.

Garfield High School, the alma mater of musicians Quincy Jones and Jimi Hendrix, had become the center of the black community—more than half of its students in 1967 were African American. If you wanted to take a message to black people in Seattle, the school's auditorium was the place to do it.

Carmichael lit up the crowd of four thousand. Tall, skinny, and clean-cut in a black suit, white shirt, loosened tie, and a button that read KEEP THE FAITH, BABY, the twenty-five-year-old gave an incendiary seventy-minute speech, his voice oscillating between a roar and a whisper. "We are the victims and white people are the executioners, and they have kept us down by force and by violence, and that if we are violent, it is just that we have learned well from our teachers," he said. "They have bombed our churches, they have shot us in the streets, they have lynched us, they have cattle-prodded us, they have thrown lye over us, they have dragged our children out in the night. We have been the recipients of violence for over four hundred years. We've just learned well how to use it today. . . . So don't you get caught up in no discussion about violence. We just making it crystal clear to the honky today that if he try to shoot us, we gonna kill him 'fore God gets the news. Period!"

Martin Luther King Jr. had written sympathetically about Black Power, saying that he understood the movement was sparked by frustration with the lack of progress toward full equality. But King criticized Black Power advocates for stoking anger while failing to offer hope or any realistic political program for change; King argued that it was impossible for blacks, at a bit more than 10 percent of the population, to separate themselves culturally and economically from the rest of the country. Still, Carmichael's words resonated with African Americans who had not been able to capitalize on the breakthroughs of the civil rights movement. As King acknowledged, "What does it profit a man to be able to eat at an integrated lunch counter if he doesn't have enough money to buy a hamburger?"

Seattle's civil rights leadership had been drawn from the middle class and was primarily concerned with issues of open housing, integration, and access to jobs; the Black Power movement drew on the anger and disenchantment of poorer, unskilled blacks. It was a division as old as the one between the "middle class" blacks who lived in the community established by William Grose around East Madison Street and the working classes who had settled to the south, in the Jackson Street area. The difference in the 1960s was that rapid migration had tilted the numbers even farther away from the middle class. The two factions in Seattle—as with African-American groups across the country—had been able to maintain common cause when united around issues such as outright discrimination. Once some basic political concessions were won, the coalition could not hold.

Carmichael's speech stoked feelings of black nationalism in an eighteen-year-old Central Area resident named Aaron Dixon. "Things began to change then," says Dixon, whose parents had moved out from

Chicago for better opportunities. "For a lot of young black people, we for the first time began to feel our anger, and that we had a right to be angry at white people, even white people we had been friends with." In early 1968, Dixon founded the Seattle Black Panthers with his brother Elmer and a few others. It was the second chapter in the nation after the original in Oakland, which was then calling for the overthrow of the U.S. government.

The Seattle Panthers organized actions such as a sit-in at a high school after two black girls were sent home and told to "straighten" their Afros. They demanded that the school offer African-American history classes and hire a black principal or vice principal. Larry Gossett, a black student leader at the University of Washington who led the high school protest with Aaron Dixon, says, "Seattle just didn't understand. They said, 'Sit-ins happen in the South where they're not nice to their coloreds. Up in Seattle, we're nice. We don't have those problems. No need for anybody to want Black Power in Seattle.' That's how the white power structure saw our city."

Willie McClain, fourteen at the start of 1968, was wide-shouldered, muscular, and on his way to becoming captain of the basketball team at Garfield. He looked to the Panthers as role models—they seemed like strong men who could express themselves and get what they wanted. "Black Power hit like a wave," he says. "It began to give young men a sense of belonging, of power, authority, and strength within numbers." He was also developing what he later—going one better on Du Bois's famous formulation—called a "triple personality." There was an "academic guy" who showed promise in school. There was an "athlete in the upper echelon talentwise, a budding football and basketball star." And there was "a nasty little bugger who wanted to do violence and harm to everybody."

On April 4 that year, Martin Luther King Jr. was assassinated on a Memphis motel balcony, sparking anguish and unrest in cities around the country. A full-scale riot was averted in Seattle, but that summer—which saw Bobby Kennedy's assassination, the continued escalation of the Vietnam War, and riots on the streets of Chicago during the Democratic National Convention—the situation in the Central Area grew increasingly tense.

In a report written in the spring of 1968, the Seattle Urban League warned about the mounting effects of cramped and dilapidated housing in the Central Area, black unemployment, poverty, and frustration over lack of opportunity for education. The inability to move out of the Central Area—only 4 percent of blacks in Seattle lived in integrated neighborhoods—was leading to a feeling of being trapped, and the situation was deteriorating. "The rise of new militant leaders, many constructive, some destructive, may take us forward or lead us into a holocaust," the authors cautioned. "There is increasing hostility to an oppressive society—to the police particularly. . . . Open distrust, contempt and hatred towards Caucasians is no longer contained."

On the first day of July, Larry Gossett, Aaron Dixon, and another protester who had led the high school sit-in were convicted of "unlawful assembly" and sentenced to six months in jail. That night, several hundred African Americans gathered at Garfield High School to protest.

Willie McClain was hanging out with his friends in front of the school, which faces Twenty-third Avenue, one of the city's main arteries. As he remembers it, a white guy in a convertible pulled up to a stoplight. Words were exchanged. Someone threw a rock. At that point, McClain didn't need any prodding. "I was there with the rioting, I was there with the pillaging, I was there with the late-night destruction," he says. It heated up faster than McClain could believe. "It started with what I call mischievous youth—boys who were fifteen and sixteen years old—who were out throwing rocks, not gas bottles, just doing what I call elementary rioting, but it got real serious to the point where the police were starting to shoot at people," he says.

Kathy Jones, a seventeen-year-old African American who was on the streets near Garfield that night, told the *Seattle Times* decades later that when the riots started, she thought, "We've been trying peacefully for three years to get you to listen to us. . . . Maybe there's another way. Maybe then you'll listen." Willie McClain remembers thinking about the indignities he'd suffered as a black in Seattle and feeling a rush of adrenaline as the destruction started: "All these different things that have always been there pop up and you have a rage that comes over you and says, *This is what you can do about it.*"

The outpouring of anger continued for two nights, with passing cars getting pelted with rocks and bricks. The police used helicopters and tear gas. Fifteen people were sent to the hospital. Street violence flared periodically for the rest of the summer. The cops basically put the Central Area on lockdown.

In August 1968, the Reverend Samuel McKinney, leader of the Central Area's influential Mount Zion Baptist Church, called for a "black united front" that would join Seattle's African Americans across economic classes to work for common cause. "The basis of unity is not fear or coercion, but that the commonality of our blackness demands that we work together or hang separately," he said. A few months later, a civic commission tasked with looking into the causes of the summer's "disorders" offered, "Only when we begin to solve the overriding problems of race and poverty which exist in our community will we begin to achieve racial harmony."

But it was too late for the civil rights movement to regain accord. Even as the Black Panthers seized the national headlines in 1968, Richard Nixon won the presidency while employing the "Southern strategy," purposefully playing to white fears of economic change and disorder, whether of blacks taking their jobs or hippies baking their brains on acid.

Willie McClain's personal life, mirroring the times, became increasingly unhinged. He would come to see that period as the beginning of a time of confusion and struggle. "There was a big gap," he says. "The authority left my life. I became the authority, did whatever I wanted when I wanted, as crazy as I wanted, as often as I wanted."

In March 1972, Willie and Diane McClain had Willie Jr., their first child. By then, the civil rights movement had dispersed into efforts for abortion rights, equality for women, affirmative action, school desegregation, and the environment. The national leadership of the Black Panther Party dissolved, plagued by both internal bickering and the efforts of the FBI to destroy it.

Seattle, too, fell on hard times. During the 1971 "Boeing Bust"—caused by federal cutbacks in outlays for warplanes—local employment at the airplane manufacturer plummeted to under forty thousand, less than a third of what it had been four years earlier. In an article titled "City of Despair," the *Economist* magazine reported that Seattle was seeing perhaps the worst economic decline in America since the Depression: "Today, food and shelter have become a prime concern of a large proportion of the unemployed. The most desperate are those in the slums of the city's center, which contain the racial minorities and those whose hold on jobs is tenuous, even in good times. Here one recent count found 48 percent out of work."

By the middle of the decade, Aaron Dixon and his brother Elmer, the Seattle Black Panther founders, still operated under the Panther name but were concentrating on running a center that provided schoolkids with free breakfasts. Larry Gossett, the student radical at the University of Washington, became the administrator of the school's newly created Black Student Division; in the late 1970s, he took a position in the administration of a liberal Seattle mayor. But the position of the majority of blacks in Seattle remained on the outside looking in at the economic mainstream. In 1979, Elmer Dixon told a newspaper reporter that he saw things sliding backward. "There's more apathy now, the job situation is worse, and unemployment figures don't reflect true unemployment," he said. "The only benefits have been for a few on an individual level."

· · ·

This was the uneasy situation in the early 1980s, when the members of our team were in grade school.

By then, Garlic Gulch was long gone. In the late 1960s, open housing became a federally mandated reality. With the Central Area hemmed in to the west, north, and east by wealthy neighborhoods, the only choice for African Americans who wanted to leave the Central Area's overcrowded and substandard housing was to move south, into the Rainier Valley, home to much of the city's white working class. During the 1970s, thousands of African Americans did just that. This helped to relieve some of the tension in the Central Area. It also hastened the departure of the remaining Italians in the old neighborhood. "Little by little the blacks moved in and the whites took off," an old Italian woman told a reporter in 1978. As a kid, I had no idea there had ever been an Italian area of Seattle. My family had long before moved to the North End.

Occasionally I rode through the Central Area along Twenty-third with my parents. We kept the windows rolled up and the doors locked. The businesses that were there—places like nail and hair salons and soul food restaurants—were not geared toward suburbanites. I peered out of our station wagon at the surroundings. Black guys hung out on corners, the cars tended to be old and junky, and there were way more boarded-up and dilapidated houses than I had seen in other parts of the city.

The one time I went to the Central Area as a destination, it was for sports. I was in the seventh grade and in my first year as a football player on a team in the northern suburbs. We were scheduled to play a CAYA team at Garfield. It was not a road trip we looked forward to. In the last practice before the game, our coach told us we were going to have to be careful because the black kids would grab and twist our nuts during plays. We had better not mess around, he warned—if we didn't take it to them, they were going to beat the crap out of us.

That Saturday, as usual, we met in the parking lot of our practice field and carpooled to the game. We strolled onto Garfield's rock-strewn, nearly grass-free field in our baby blue uniforms. During pregame drills, a few players on my team, rough kids at the best of times, went into a rage. The meanest kid on our team—he had already broken a helmet by spearing it into an opponent—was almost frothing at the mouth, screaming at the rest of us that we had to "beat these niggers!"

I started to freak out. I didn't like my teammate, and now, seeing a hate-fueled fury overtake him, I feared him. I knew where his venom was coming from. His mom, of whom my own mother actively disapproved, stood on the sidelines during our games, smoking cigarettes and screaming profanity at our team and our opponents. Race was not a subject discussed in our house—there were no blacks in our suburb, so there was no reason to bring it up. My most regular exposure to black people was through watching sports on television. I was more curious than anything. Still, when we got to Garfield, I could look around, see the surroundings, and know that the Central Area was different. I also had to process the warnings of my coach, who had told us before playing Rainier Beach, a black team in the South End, to leave our helmets on after the game when we shook hands or they might hit us in the face.

By kickoff time, my sole hope was to get through the next four quarters uninjured. Some of the CAYA players tried their best to intimidate us. As I lined up on the offensive line, the kid across from me taunted, "Hey, white boy!" At the end of the play, after the whistle had blown, another kid drove his helmet into my ribs from the side, leaving me feeling like I was going to puke. He pointed at me and laughed: "I got you! I got you!" In the meantime, my teammate was fuming in the huddle, spittle flying from his mouth: "Let's kill them!" I looked around at the other players on my team. Most seemed to be as frightened as I was. We were caught between my teammate and a few others who followed his lead, and a bunch of black kids who supposedly wanted to rip off our balls. I only noticed late in the game that some of their players seemed uncomfortable, too. They stopped when the whistle blew and quietly went back to the huddle. Both of our teams, I realized, had been hijacked by the most extreme elements. The rest of us were caught up in their drama, too cowed to do anything but go along.

A little more than a year later, in March 1986, Willie McClain's players gathered at his house. The team climbed into the brown Dodge van, the same as they always did when going to a game or practice. This time, though, McClain drove to the freeway. As the van merged with traffic and rumbled north, the players began to wonder what was up.

"Where are we going?" Myran asked.

McClain answered, "We're going to try something new this year. We're going to join up with some players from up north."

"Up north? What do you mean? There aren't any players up north!" Willie Jr. protested.

"Listen," McClain told them. "We're going to have a mixed team this year. We're going to play with some white players. It might be a culture shock, so I want you to be ready. A lot of things are going to be different. But you remember what I've been telling you about opportunities? This could be something really good for you guys."

By that time in his life, McClain regretted his earlier days on the streets. He regretted rioting in 1968, he regretted dropping out of community college and ending his sports career, and he regretted the years after that when he dabbled in drug dealing and whatever other hustle he could put over to get some money. "It wasn't me. It wasn't in my heart," McClain says. "But my disappointment of not being successful in athletics and coming to the realization that my athletic career was over, that there was nowhere else to go, all of a sudden—'urk,' stop, nothing. I tried to play some semipro football but all I got was a broken finger out of that. One thing led to another—I didn't have that direction."

In the end, none of it had gotten him anywhere. It was his aunt, the first member of the family to move out from Mississippi, who really gave him a break in 1976, when she sold him a house for only $5,000. Mc-

Clain soon landed his first "straight" job, working as a trainee cashier at a Goodwill store. Although a lot of people would have seen thrift-store work as pretty far down, Willie was happy to have it. It was, in his words, a "humble beginning." He'd worked his way up from there, including a job as a bank teller and another as a furniture salesman before landing at the African-American Christian elementary school in 1984. By then, McClain saw that he had wasted his athletic potential as well as his chance for higher education. He didn't want his players to do the same thing.

A twenty-minute drive later, they arrived at Lakeside Middle School, just shy of the city's northern boundary, and eleven miles north of Mc-Clain's house. The ivy-covered brick building didn't look like any school the kids had ever seen. Willie Jr. looked around and thought it was a college. His dad parked the van outside the gym, and they climbed out into the night. They walked through the door, a handful of thirteen- and fourteen-year-old boys in sweats, trying out their most affected struts. First thing, they were going to make it clear to these white kids who could play.

You'll All Work for Us Someday

Four years before Willie McClain and his players rolled up in their van in 1986, I arrived at Lakeside, a chubby kid decked out in a bowl cut, no-brand clothes, a digital watch, and Velcro shoes. Where I came from, the convenience of Velcro was appreciated; at Lakeside, it singled you out as a moron who couldn't tie your shoelaces.

I was nervous but happy to arrive at Lakeside, as public school had not been going that well. If not for my enthusiastic participation in baseball and basketball, I might have been totally ostracized. At the start of fourth grade, the year before I enrolled at Lakeside, my teacher, Mr. Coyle, a man who entered our class every day with the air of a suburban Sisyphus, introduced a scheme that was supposed to encourage us to read. Each kid got a piece of paper on the wall with a little pie chart. The twelve slices of the pie stood for a different reading subject area, such as history, classics, music, and sports. After you read a book and wrote a few bare details about it on a form, you got to color in one of the sections. Encouraged by my mom, who shuttled me back and forth from the public library, I completed the chart in about six weeks, plowing through books such as *A Tale of Two Cities* and a history of the Third Reich. With each book, Mr. Coyle resignedly removed my piece of paper from the wall and let me ink in another slice while my classmates rolled their eyes. It did not lead to great popularity.

I spent a lot of recesses in the library, holed up with books on great sports teams, the history of World War II, and Westerns. I read dozens of Louis L'Amour potboilers, which my mom bought for me from the rack near the checkout at the supermarket. I identified with his standard hero, a tight-lipped cowboy who camped out on the range next to a lonely fire and found love only after a strong and independent woman recognized the bravery behind his stoic demeanor, and the bad guys had pushed him so far that he was forced to teach them a lesson with his six-shooter.

My mom decided to look into Lakeside after she heard about it from a friend. The day she brought me to visit, we walked through the ivied entrance, climbed the stairs to the office to sign in, and, it seemed, entered another reality. I was paired with a student guide, who initiated me into the ways of this new world: teachers who dressed in tweed jackets like college professors; classes that ended after forty minutes, sending students into the halls to go to their next ones (at public school, Mr. Coyle taught every subject besides music and PE); kids who wore Oxford shirts, corduroy pants, Top-Sider boat shoes, and Vuarnet sunglasses that hung around their necks on nylon cords. There were no recesses, just "free" periods, where students would sit on the floors in the halls and study. The hipper seventh- and eighth-grade boys gathered on tattered couches in the "student lounge"—a stage along one side of the cafeteria—where they cranked bands like the Clash and the Kinks through a boom box. There were no decorations on the walls, like in public school—no big swaths of paper covered with student paintings or blandishments for school spaghetti night. It would have disrupted the seriousness of purpose.

At lunch, a group of teachers queried me about my interests. A few weeks later, my mom brought me down to take an all-day aptitude test. Before long, my parents received a letter welcoming my family to the "Lakeside Community." In exchange for the $5,000 tuition, I would be one of thirty-two students in the incoming fifth-grade class.

Lakeside had been founded in 1923 by a group of Seattle businessmen who wanted to ensure that their sons received educations like those imparted in the best boarding schools back east. First housed in a building on the shores of Lake Washington (hence the name), the school moved in 1930 to a newly built campus on the northern boundary of Seattle, not far from the Highlands, a gated community that was an enclave for the city's elite and a source of many of Lakeside's students. Its aspirations were visible in its design, which featured a cluster of Colonial-style, redbrick buildings with white trim arranged around a grass quadrangle, modeled

after New England boarding schools Phillips Exeter and Phillips Ando-
ver. By 1950, it had a student body of two hundred. A school brochure
from the Eisenhower era showcases photos of boys on the school rifle
range, lifting weights to condition for skiing, and eating lunch in jackets
and ties. It reported that graduates in the class of 1954 had gained admission to Harvard, Princeton, MIT, Yale, and Stanford.

The student who would do the most to secure the school's future
reputation enrolled in 1967. A skinny seventh-grader with size 13 feet,
Bill Gates found that he loved Lakeside. During his first year, the administration decided it wanted to give students access to computers, something few schools in the country had. Because of the price and size of
computers at the time, the school bought a teletype machine, on which
students typed commands to be sent to a mainframe computer in downtown Seattle. Gates joined a group of boys who spent their free time writing programs. He became close with a fellow student, Paul Allen, and by
the time I went to Lakeside the stories about how the pair spent nights
sleeping in the computer room were school legend. Gates graduated in
1973 and dropped out of Harvard two years later to found Microsoft with
Allen. Gates has said that if he had not gone to Lakeside, Microsoft would
not exist.

Gates is only the most prominent in a network of alumni that is
deeply rooted in Seattle's elite. If you look anywhere where the wheels
of power are turned in Seattle, you'll find someone with a Lakeside
connection—for example, four of the five men who were the principals
in the private corporation that designed and built the Space Needle in
1962 were alums or parents of graduates. Craig McCaw, one of Gates's
classmates, went on to start what is now AT&T Wireless. Other graduates populate Seattle's corporate boards and law firms. More than a few
are property developers. Some are politicians. The scions of the Weyer-
haeuser logging empire and Nordstrom's department stores attended the
school when I was there, as did the twin sons of a local billboard mogul
who also owned the Seattle SuperSonics basketball team (when you
watched Sonics' games on TV, you could always spot the twins right behind the bench). In the early 1970s, Lakeside merged with an all-girls
school to become co-ed. By the 1980s, it was recognized as the most elite
place to educate your kids in the Northwest.

In a *Seattle Weekly* article titled "The Lakeside Mystique" published
in January 1986—just a few months before we formed our team with

Willie McClain's players—a reporter who had been a Lakeside student in the 1960s came back to reevaluate the school, which he labeled "our Exeter, our Eton."

Unsurprisingly, the writer found that students at Lakeside were "competitive, academically aggressive, and they keep their eyes on each other as much as they do on the bottom line of their lives: their grades." But while the school had always been a place for the rich, and the trust funds of some students "could finance small island nations," it was changing along with Seattle. Family name and money still had their place, but a new breed of students was coming from what a Lakeside board member called "the new middle class, the professional class of uninherited wealth." This shift toward academic merit was resulting in an even more formidable kind of Lakeside graduate, according to the writer: "When they squeeze out of the opposite end of the Ivy League tube . . . and into the treasured career slots that lay waiting, they may make the current generation of yuppies look anemic."

The article raised hackles at the school, mainly for a few assertions. One was the quote of a parent of a recent graduate, who said, "You can pick out a Lakeside student. . . . They have a sort of arrogance, a sort of power that other kids don't have. They are aloof and snobby. They are not real gentle, kind people."

Another was the one the reporter used to close the article: "These natural aristocrats are not above rubbing it in," he wrote. "When the Lakeside Lions are losing a football game, which doesn't happen all that often, Lakesiders chant, 'It's all right, it's OK, you'll all work for us someday.'"

When I read it, I knew the scene exactly. The chant, while I was at Lakeside, was always initiated by an upperclassman in the requisite uniform of baggy corduroys, an untucked Oxford shirt worn over a white T-shirt, and shaggy hair. Toward the end of a game we were losing, he would stand, motion to the rest of the class, and lead the mantra. After that he led the "key cheer," in which students took their car keys out of their pockets and dangled them at the kids in the stands on the other side of the gym or the football field. This interlude always stunned me; the message so clearly seemed to be: *No matter what the score of this game, you are the losers.*

The feeling at the school after the article ran was that the cheer had been taken out of context. Parents and teachers pointed out that Lakeside students, through volunteer work, did a lot of good. They said that a chant given at a sporting event wasn't a reflection of the student body as a whole. I never heard anyone refute or take up the actual content of the cheer. It took me years to realize that sometimes awkward jokes contain nuggets of truth that otherwise go unexpressed.

The first Lakeside-related function I attended after my admission was a welcome party for our incoming class, held at the home of one of my new classmates, a mansion overlooking Puget Sound. It was the beginning of a total-immersion course in the sociology of Seattle's upper crust.

I quickly learned that a core group of kids all knew each other. Many had grown up in the Highlands or Broadmoor, a gated community near Lake Washington protected by a ten-foot-high hedge (it's just northeast of William Grose's East Madison section of the Central Area). Broadmoor borders the neighborhood of Madison Park, snug on Lake Washington. Kids who grew up in this area knew each other from day-care, kindergarten, soccer teams, the youth symphony, summer camp, piano lessons, ballroom dance classes, and summers at the Seattle Tennis Club, a short walk away on the lakeshore. Some families had condos in Sun Valley or memberships in the Seattle Yacht Club. The web of Lakesiders' relationships mimicked those of their parents, businessmen and lawyers who saw each other after work at the golf club inside Broadmoor's gated walls or downtown at the Washington Athletic Club, and moms who got acquainted through memberships in charitable organizations and private school parents' associations.

After growing up in a suburban development built in the 1960s, I was suddenly aware of the gradations of wealth. In the suburbs, everything seemed the same—the houses were the same size; the kids all had the same toys; everyone played football or baseball in the cul-de-sac, and rode their dirt bikes on the tracks in the woods; everyone went to the public school a few blocks away except for a few kids in the Christian or Catholic schools.

We lived in a two-level, four-bedroom home that was painted a shade of green very close to the color of a lot of refrigerators from that era. Our front yard was landscaped with rhododendrons, ferns, beauty bark, and a narrow strip of sodded grass. Our neighbors included a veterinarian, two community college teachers, and a Boeing engineer. When we wanted an exotic meal, we got takeout from the Chinese restaurant. Some of my friends went to temple rather than church, but my mom explained that Jews were like us Catholics except for some slight differences, such as the fact that they went to a synagogue, and that they didn't believe in Jesus.

I'd been an awkward, shy, and unpopular kid at public elementary school. I hoped that Lakeside would be a chance to get off on a new foot, but it took less than an hour at the welcome party to realize I wasn't going to easily slide into things. I lacked the language, style, and common points of reference.

Though there were others in the class in the same position I was in, the group of interconnected kids quickly established themselves as the tastemakers. The rest of the kids, from disparate parts of Seattle and its suburbs, had a few choices: the more socially nimble adopted the preppie style and melded right in; a group of bookish kids banded together and formed their own nerdy subculture; a third group, which included me, fell outside the other two groups and so made up a separate lunchroom tribe: the misfits' table.

Another regular at the table, Eric Hampton—the only black kid in our class—inarguably had the biggest social adjustment to make upon entering Lakeside. In the early 1980s, the school was actively trying to recruit more black students, though it had no real plan on how to go about it. Lakeside had started to admit blacks in 1965, launching a summer program for minority kids from the Central Area. The Lakeside Educational Enrichment Program, or LEEP, aimed to give eighth and ninth graders remedial instruction and to boost their academic confidence. Backed by federal funds, it was one of several similar programs across the country, all aiming to increase the enrollment of black students at private schools at a time when such schools were coming under attack as racist and elitist. At Lakeside, three of the sixty boys in the program were chosen to integrate the school and given scholarships.

Since then, a trickle of black students had entered the school. The first year Lakeside actually kept track of its enrollment by racial categories was 1980, when it tallied 21 African-American students out of a student body of 627. Recruitment consisted primarily of skimming the standout summer LEEP students. Ronnie Cunningham, for example, the first black student to make it through Lakeside from fifth grade all the way to graduation, started in 1979 after he had tagged along with his older sister to LEEP. Ronnie was asked to enroll after the counselors noticed him doing math problems faster than the kids actually in the program. It happened that Ronnie's mother knew Eric Hampton's dad, and she told him about the school.

Charlie Hampton was born in Lake Providence, Louisiana, right on the Mississippi River, the son of an army serviceman and a mother who worked as a domestic. The family moved around a lot, following Charlie's father as he was posted to army bases in North Carolina, Texas, West Germany, south of Seattle in Tacoma, and finally back to Louisiana. Charlie studied engineering at Southern University in Baton Rouge and became the first in his family to graduate from college. In the late 1960s he took a job at the Hanford Nuclear Reservation in Eastern Washington, where he worked on a project to condense and solidify nuclear waste. When he figured out the job at Hanford wasn't for him, he moved his family—Eric and his older brother had already been born—to Seattle. Charlie studied business at the University of Washington and ended up managing real estate for the city of Seattle.

The Hampton family lived in the "middle class" Madrona neighborhood in the Central Area, an area southeast of William Grose's property. When he was nine years old, Eric started to play on Willie McClain's CAYA basketball team. On days when they weren't over at the McClain's, it was more than likely that Damian and JT were at the Hamptons. "They spent almost as much time at my house as they did at their own, eating, sleeping, and everything else," says Charlie Hampton, a compact, energetic man with a thick mustache and a boisterous laugh. "We were the quote 'rich folks on the block.'"

Eric went to the public elementary school down the street, where he'd been tracked into the "gifted" program. After Charlie Hampton went out to have a look at Lakeside, he figured there was no reason not to try to get his son the best education Seattle had to offer, telling Eric, "These same snotty-nosed rich kids you see around here will be the same people running this country in thirty years. Maybe it's your break in life, or maybe it's not your break in life, but you'll know how the rest of the world lives. You won't have to fear anybody, you know what you got is as good as what they got, you know that you're just as smart as anybody."

Eric had other ideas. "In the morning, I used to cry, 'I don't want to go to this school!'" he says. "I remember just feeling isolated. I was the only little black kid. I didn't know anybody, really. So I kind of isolated myself, just on the assumption that I didn't know these people and they weren't going to be nice to me." Eric was a skinny kid who said very little. When he spoke, it was in a voice so subdued that it was hard to hear what he was saying. If a teacher called on him in class, he tended to look down at his desk and mumble his answers. One day not long after the school year started, he refused to return to Lakeside.

The school administration scrambled to get him back, conferencing with his parents. One of our more amiable classmates was dispatched to go to the Hampton house and play with Eric. Eric heard his mom and dad shouting at each other—his dad wanted him to go back, while his mom said he should be allowed to make his own choice about where he wanted to go to school. Finally, it was agreed that Eric would give Lakeside another try.

No one among the students at Lakeside said anything about Eric's absence. Our English teacher, Mr. Bayley, finally broke the silence, telling us at the end of a class period that there was something he wanted to talk about. Our small class sat around the perimeter of four long oak tables that had been arranged to make a square as Mr. Bayley—who, like every single teacher at the school that year, was white—stood up in his brown cardigan sweater with a look of disappointment on his face. He sucked in a long, deep breath and began to speak very deliberately.

"I'm sure that you've noticed that Eric Hampton has not been in school," he said. "We've been talking to his parents, and he'll be coming back tomorrow. He's had a hard time adjusting here. You should treat him like you treat anyone else. Just because he's black doesn't mean that there is anything different about him. Please make an effort to make him feel comfortable. I want you to go home tonight and think about it."

We collected our books and filed out silently, hanging our heads in the exaggerated way kids do when they're expected to look contrite. I felt guilty but didn't really know why. The first few weeks had been a disorienting battle to be accepted. Eric's isolation came largely from his own shyness, which was compounded by his one obvious difference from everyone else. You wanted to be friends with him but didn't know what to say—his race was something you registered but also tried to ignore. The easiest thing to do was to stay quiet.

To get to school throughout his years at Lakeside, Eric caught the bus and rode downtown, where he usually met up with "the other little black kids from Lakeside." They transferred to another bus that took them up to the North End. They were, both literally and figuratively, traveling away from a public school system that had been in disarray for years.

As Seattle's black population grew throughout the 1950s and 1960s, its public schools became increasingly segregated. Garfield High School, for example, went from 4 percent black enrollment in 1940 to 75 percent in 1972, the year Willie McClain graduated. By then, black and Asian kids also made up the majority enrollments of several elementary and middle schools in the Central Area; schools in the North End were almost entirely white.

In the 1970s, school desegregation became a civil rights battleground across the country. Activists, looking for ways to implement the legislative and legal victories of the previous decades, began to file lawsuits against school districts that had not integrated. In Boston, where a federal judge in 1974 ordered a mandatory busing plan, whites rioted and threw bottles and rocks at buses full of black students. Seattle by then had already tried voluntary desegregation, which had failed after too few families took up the offer. With civil rights groups threatening litigation, the city had to take action. It came up with its own mandatory busing plan, which went into effect at the start of the 1978 school year.

As you would expect in a town that takes pride in its politeness, the implementation of the program was orderly. That didn't mean it was popular. "No one should be lulled into believing that because schools opened peacefully, without violence, that there is support for this crazy busing nonsense," the president of a group working to overturn the plan told the *Seattle Times* in 1978. "This only means that Seattleites are law-abiding and have faith in our democratic system." A referendum the group put on the city ballot to end mandatory busing passed with 61 percent of the vote but was ruled unconstitutional by the courts.

Instead, whites simply deserted the Seattle public schools. In 1976 there were 41,600 white students in the Seattle public schools and 10,800 African-American students. Four years later, the number of black students in the system was nearly unchanged; white enrollment had plummeted 34 percent, to 27,300.

When I was one year old, my family moved from Seattle to a suburb five miles north of the city's boundary. Later, when I asked my mom why we left Seattle proper, she said, "For the schools. I didn't want you to be bused." According to statistics kept by the state, my public elementary school had 327 students when I began fourth grade in 1981. Of those, 315 were white, 9 were Asian, 1 was Native American, and 2 were black.

By 1986, when our team played together, a major issue in the Seattle schools was "disproportionality"—African-American and other minority students were getting lower grades than white students and getting kicked out of school at much higher rates. For example, in the 1984–1985 school year, 56 percent of African-American high school students in Seattle had a D average or below, compared to 24 percent of white students. In the same year, 35 percent of black middle and high school students were suspended or expelled, opposed to 15 percent of white students.

Though busing had taken some of the edge off the dramatic segregation of the early 1970s, there were still huge imbalances between schools in the northern and southern parts of the city. As a kid, Damian saw them firsthand when he was bused to an elementary school in the North End, where he was one of a few black students in his classes. "The schools were way better," Damian says, looking back at the experience. He saw the difference not only in obvious things such as the North End schools having art supplies and other extras, but also in the standards the teachers set for the students.

The contrast really struck Damian a few years later, when he was assigned to middle school in the South End. In the mornings, the seventh- and eighth-grade kids rode the bus with high school students. Some of the older kids openly smoked pot during the ride, but the drivers never disciplined them—Damian thinks they were afraid to say anything. Students were issued books with the covers torn off, and the bathroom stalls were missing doors. Expectations were minimal. As long as you didn't do anything egregious, you would sail right through. "Teachers weren't there half the time, kids fighting, people skipping class, people shooting dice at lunchtime, getting high, messing with girls and boys in the bathroom, oh man, it was crazy," Damian says. For guys like Damian, Willie Jr., and Tyrell, it meant that school was fun. Without any homework, there was a lot of time just to fool around. Myran had a harder time. He would get by for a while, but then—displaying a troubling moodiness that he tried and failed to contain—he would get in a fight or otherwise act out. He was kicked out of one school after another.

At Lakeside, parents—usually moms—prowled the halls every day, buttonholing teachers and administrators. If they were not happy with something, they raised hell. During my time from fifth to eighth grade, parents mobilized to get three teachers they considered not up to standards fired. There was no formal review, teachers' union to lodge a protest with, or even a process of appeal. The headmaster made the decision and, at the end of the year, the contracts of the teachers in question were not renewed. Lakeside parents expected to be heard and obeyed. With only the father working in most cases, they had more time to pay attention to everything that happened at the school.

After school and on weekends, my Lakeside classmates participated in structured activities that almost always cost money: tennis, violin, soccer, skiing, summer camp, gymnastics, ballroom dancing, French. My mom subscribed to the Seattle Children's Theatre, which she clawed my younger brother and me away from our Saturday morning cartoon regimen to attend. Each time we went, I sat resentfully until about fifteen minutes into the play, when I started to enjoy the story despite myself. After the play, the actors came back out on the stage to talk to the kids about their characters and how they played them, which intrigued me.

Damian and the other kids from Willie McClain's team often headed to a local playground, where they scrapped in games with other kids, older boys, and even men, the winners staying on the court to take next game, losers sitting out. I would have traded the theater for the basketball court in a second, but, of course, all of us were already being socialized to operate in very different spheres.

My performance in my first few years at Lakeside was completely erratic: I sailed through some classes and bombed others. In sixth grade I got in a couple of playground fights—won one, lost one—with a popular preppie from Madison Park (with his pink Oxford shirts and bouncy blond hair, he looked like he had walked off the screen from a John Hughes movie). In the summer before seventh grade, the school headmaster threatened me with expulsion and instructed me to write an essay explaining how I planned on doing better in the coming year.

Most of my capricious behavior flowed from a fault line between my parents that Lakeside exposed. My dad, at best, was ambivalent about my attendance at the school. He had gone to Catholic schools and didn't see the need for Lakeside. He'd taken over our family business leasing coin-operated washers and dryers to apartment building owners, which was financially lucrative if not especially glamorous. He still hung out with the same friends from high school and college, and showed no interest in joining a golf club or anything else that might indicate social climbing. At one parent meeting he went to right after I started at Lakeside, every other father was wearing a tie; he felt that they looked down on him when they heard what he did for a living.

My mom was the daughter of an engineer who had moved west during World War II to work on the Manhattan Project at the Hanford Nuclear Reservation in Eastern Washington—the same place where Charlie Hampton took a job twenty-five years later. Richland, the town where my mom was born, was essentially built by the government to house the nuclear workers; those with higher social standing, such as engineers, got better housing. From this, my mom grew up with an ingrained—and not unfounded—belief in the role of education as the engine of upward class mobility. She was proud that I was going to the best school in Seattle.

In contrast to my experience at public school, classes at Lakeside generally allowed for creative problem solving and student initiative, and I enjoyed them. But another part of me felt that if I did too well, I would be selling out to the snobs. All that mixed with a begrudging fascination I had with some of my classmates, especially the poised self-assurance that many of them projected. I made efforts to fit in, adopting fashion symbols such as Stan Smith tennis shoes; but I also got deeply into heavy metal—from Metallica to Ratt to Iron Maiden, the more bombast the better—which was far from the music of choice at Lakeside.

In the meantime, Eric Hampton had a separate struggle to fit in, which he sums up succinctly: "I wasn't wealthy and I was a minority."

After his brief disappearance at the start of fifth grade, Eric—who was quiet but had a gently scathing sense of humor—had become an accepted, if not overwhelmingly popular, part of the class. He tried to dress like everyone else and to evince enthusiasm for bands like the Police and Men at Work. At times it flipped, and he became the school's representative of everything "black." For example, after the show *That's Incredible* ran a segment on break dancing just as it was coming into national style, the consensus at Lakeside was that it was "stupid," an opinion Eric pretended to agree with. The next year, though, after break dancing became genuinely popular, Eric was naturally seen as the guy who would know all about it. "Everybody's asking me, 'Can you show me how to break-dance?'" he says with a laugh. "Everybody assumed I could break-dance. I couldn't."

Eric noticed that before school vacations kids would talk about Sun Valley, and he always wondered what they meant. He didn't realize it was a ski resort in Idaho until years later. "You feel inferior because of the simple fact that you're different, but also because you're poor, and that's the biggest thing," he says. "If you have the resources, it makes life easier—you can at least maintain your self-esteem, your self-respect."

It turned out that both of us, quite separately, found the school basketball team to be a space somewhat removed from the rest of the school. For one, most of the "elite" kids at Lakeside didn't play basketball—their sports were tennis, golf, skiing, and swimming (and later, lacrosse, crew, and even, in at least one case, polo). Then there was also just the nature of the sport. Stepping onto the court simplified life down to a few variables: You grabbed the ball, ran the pebbled leather against your hand, turned it to find the seam, squared up to the basket, propelled yourself up off the ground, lifted the ball above your head, and let it fly. Then, instant resolution: The ball goes in or it doesn't.

After our school team started in the seventh grade, Eric established himself as the star from about the first practice. His incredible lateral speed allowed him to make steal after steal on defense and blow by defenders when he had the ball. He scored more than twenty points a game and always seemed to be everywhere on the court. In one tournament championship game, we had played poorly and were down by five points with one minute left. Then Eric decided to drop the pretense that we were a team of equals. In the last minute, he stole the ball every time their guards touched it and scored nine points in a row. When time ran out, the rest of us rushed around him and jumped up and down while he pointed his index finger in the air, let his head drop back, and screamed.

Two of my closest friends at the school also were starters on the basketball team. Maitland Finley, tall and skinny with sleepy blue eyes and shaggy brown hair, was one of the only kids in the class who spoke less than Eric. His family lived way out in the rural suburbs north of Seattle. In public school, before he enrolled at Lakeside, he'd get so far ahead of his classmates that he often ended up to the side reading alone while the teacher attended to everyone else.

Maitland was completely straightforward. If you asked him if he wanted to do something—say, play basketball during lunch period—and he didn't want to, he just answered, with a shrug of his shoulders, "No." As we grew older, Maitland seemed to remain above the fray as other boys became more obnoxious. When a kid made a comment about a girl in our class, something like, "She's a carpenter's dream—flat as a board and never been nailed," Maitland's face flushed and he turned away. He also never seemed to notice or care about the shifting social hierarchy within the school, who was in, who was out.

Sean O'Donnell was, besides Eric, our other weapon, solely because, at more than six feet, he was taller than any other kid in the league. Simply standing near the basket with his arms in the air made him a presence. On the court, unfortunately, Sean resembled a human version of C-3PO, the gold robot in *Star Wars*. He moved in herky-jerky starts and stops and had hands of stone.

The son of a stockbroker from Bellevue, a suburb east of Seattle across Lake Washington, Sean had been sent to Lakeside after his fourth-grade public school teacher told his parents that he was a "calming influence" on the other kids. His parents wondered why the other kids weren't calm. Sean, who had straight blond hair that fell across his forehead at an angle, was more socially malleable than Eric, Maitland, or me, able to fit in across Lakeside's various cliques. He didn't take school all that seriously, more likely to break out his impression of Bill Murray's golf course groundskeeper in *Caddyshack* than to please our teachers. He also was the first person to tell me the urban legend about Richard Gere and the gerbil, delighting in the reaction that spread across my face.

Eric's, Sean's, and Maitland's fathers made up the Lakeside Middle School basketball team's Greek chorus. Sean's dad, the stockbroker, was a constant presence at our games, a talkative man with a balding head, a beer belly, and a bellowing voice, he always seemed like he should be chewing on a cigar and cradling a tumbler of scotch. Eric's father, Charlie, equally loquacious, sat beside him. The last member of the trio, Maitland's dad, Randy, was the most outsized personality of all, yelling encouragement from the sidelines and giving pointers to our coach after the game.

Randy Finley was watching our opposition as well. As we began our eighth-grade season, he made note of two of the best players we faced. He would recruit them onto the separate, integrated basketball team he was about to form.

Dino Christofilis, who went to a Christian school in the North End, was a whirlwind at forward who went after every loose ball like his life depended on it. He had a beautiful jump shot, and valiantly hustled and rallied his teammates. He also was hard to dislike—if you made a good play, he'd come up, slap you on the back, and tell you so.

Chris Dickinson attended the Bush School, another elite private school in Seattle, and was Dino's only rival in intensity. Tall and strapping, he walked like a gunfighter, as if his muscles bulged so much that it was impossible for his arms to fall flush. At power forward he swung his elbows around with a velocity that made you fear for your head.

I had an uncomfortable run-in with Chris shortly before we became teammates. Our Lakeside basketball team was scheduled to play Bush. On a Saturday night, the week before the game, a couple of girls from my German class called me at home. They brought up Chris, whose physique, square jaw, and well-coiffed head of brown hair made him the object of many crushes among girls on the Seattle private-school circuit. Before long, fueled by jealousy, I was elaborating on how Chris was an overrated basketball player. This information quickly made it back to him. I was told on Monday that he hadn't received my comments well.

Over the next week, a fight was rumored for the postgame dance. I wasn't looking forward to any kind of conflict—Chris had at least four inches of height and a lot of muscle on me. We won the game. At the dance, I tried to avoid him while pretending that I wasn't, but the two of us were herded together.

"I heard you been talkin' shit about me," Chris said, puffing out his chest in his polo shirt. I noticed that his hair was damp and neatly parted. It looked like he'd put mousse in it. I was impressed that he'd taken a shower after the game. No one on my team ever did that. It made him seem more mature.

"Not really," I answered, trying to toe the line between confrontation and capitulation.

We stared at each other in hard-guy poses. And we kept staring at each other—neither of us made a step forward or said a thing. Finally, the tension fizzled. I walked away, trying to mask the relief that was washing through my body. I knew the situation had ended about as well as it could have—we had both saved face, and we hadn't had to fight. After we became teammates, neither Chris nor I ever brought up our showdown—it was as if it never happened.

Randy Finley also took notice when a bunch of black kids showed up to watch one of our games during a Christmas tournament, sitting in a group in the bleachers. Every time Eric touched the ball, they began to yell, clap, and holler. Charlie Hampton told Randy that the kids were Eric's teammates from Willie McClain's CAYA team. Randy eyed our two teams—one all white, besides Eric Hampton; the other all black— and asked Charlie Hampton for an introduction to Willie McClain.

More Than Just Running
Up and Down the Floor

The first night of practice, Willie McClain leads his players into the gym. McClain and Randy Finley shake hands. We grab some basketballs and shoot around until McClain calls us to center court.

"I want everyone to introduce themselves," he says, getting his first look at Sean, Maitland, and me, the white kids who are his new charges. Any bluster fades as we go around the circle. Kids look down at the floor and say their names in soft voices. I remember to hold my head up and make eye contact when it comes to my turn. Though I'm as shy as anyone, four years of Lakeside have taught me that.

McClain looks at Randy Finley and then back at us. "OK, let's get started. We're going to jump right into things."

McClain calls out Eric, Tyrell, and Willie Jr. to help demonstrate his full-court press, a "two-two-one." After we score, two of our players stay near the basket to defend the in-bounds pass and try to pick it off or trap the opponent who gets the ball. Two more lurk near midcourt to grab any errant passes. One goes to the opposite end in case the other team gets by our defenders.

There is no standing around. McClain's defense is designed to throttle the other team with constant pressure. That means a lot of running and scrambling. The aim is to rattle the other team into coughing up the ball.

This game plan perfectly fits McClain's team. His players are short but very, very quick, both laterally across the court and vertically toward the hoop. Damian and I, for example, are both about five-foot-eight, but

while I can barely jump high enough to touch the bottom of the backboard, he can get his hand up over the rim, falling an inch or two short of dunking.

It doesn't take very long to see that McClain's players can cover the distance between the sidelines faster than I can even swivel around and figure out what's going on. If I get a good position on Damian for a rebound, he compensates with his superior leap, rising and snatching the ball off my fingertips. JT has an incredible ability to analyze spatial relationships on the court—after someone shoots and the ball is in the air, he takes in where everyone is positioning and the trajectory of the shot, and somehow always seems to place himself exactly where the ball drops. It's as if someone has taken our sleepy little team—which is really just a bunch of average players arranged around Eric Hampton—and decided that we need to do everything at double speed.

As the practice wears on, Randy Finley stands off to the side, his arms crossed and a smile of enjoyment on his face.

McClain walks up and down the sideline, yelling instructions: "Get across the floor! Cut him off! Front up on him! Do not let your man get behind you!"

"OK, stop!" McClain hurries out onto midcourt and positions himself next to Sean. "This is how you square up on defense." McClain demonstrates, bending at the knees like he's sitting in a chair, keeping his legs far apart, both arms spread out with hands open as Sean, a head taller than the coach, mimics his stance, extending his long, gangly arms and waving them around.

Every basketball coach I've had before McClain has structured practices around a series of drills meant to teach certain skills. We might run through give-and-go passes for half an hour, every player going through the drill as the rest of the team watches. Practices are in effect somewhat like classes, where the coach demonstrates one particular concept that the players then repeat.

McClain, on the other hand, is more for trial by fire. He shows us what he wants, and then we begin a full-court scrimmage. He doesn't know my name, so when he wants me to move to a position on the floor he just makes eye contact, points, and shouts, "Over here! Quick now!" Even from the first practice, I notice a tinge of exasperation in his voice when he's giving me instructions.

We spend forty minutes sprinting back and forth, McClain's exhortations nipping behind us. When someone screws up, McClain makes everyone run lines—the court is divided into fourths and you have to run from the baseline to each line, touch it, return to the baseline, and then progress to the next one until you make it all the way to the opposite side and back.

I'm exhausted by the end, soaked in sweat. McClain tells us that he will see us in two days as his players pull on their sweatpants and sweatshirts. Before they file out into the parking lot, Tyrell walks over to Maitland, slaps him five, and says, "Good practice."

• • •

That night, as he drove the van south on the freeway back to the Central Area, his guys chattering in the back, Willie McClain felt relieved. He'd been nervous before the practice. He knew that if the team didn't work out, there'd be plenty of people back in the Central Area who would be ready to tell him it was all a mistake from the start. He had his own doubts, too: What if the white parents didn't want their sons coached by a black man? Would these white kids listen to him? How would his guys act? He dealt with it by going straight into a full-speed practice. He'd always found that as long as he was out on the floor, immersed in the game, he could block out all the chatter from the sidelines.

McClain's agreement to coach the team had stemmed from two strongly felt ideas about sports and their usefulness. The first, simply put, was that participation in athletics, when done right, instills values in boys that will help turn them into productive, successful adults. This concept has been part of basketball's DNA since James Naismith, a robust, thirty-year-old Canadian with a doctorate in theology, invented the game in 1891 at a YMCA in Springfield, Massachusetts.

Naismith was an adherent of "Muscular Christianity"—the idea, roughly, that a healthy body leads to a healthy, Christian mind—a movement that developed in the mid-1800s as industrialization transformed the United States from a rural to an urban country. Instead of working together with their sons on their farms, men were laboring in factories and offices, leaving their boys under the feminizing influences of their mothers and other women. It was thought that boys who spent too much time in female company grew soft, or worse, turned gay. Until then, sports in the United States had been seen as games for kids to play in their free time. The rise of industrialization encouraged a shift toward team sports, where boys could be supervised and guided by coaches. The YMCA network provided the necessary facilities. Luther Gulick, Naismith's boss as the head of the Springfield YMCA and one of the leading proponents of Muscular Christianity, wrote, "Bodily vigor is a moral agent, it enables us to live on higher levels, to keep up to the top of our achievement."

Team sports came to be viewed not only as a proving ground for boys—by the early 1900s, college football games had become vicious bouts with injured players removed from the field—but also as an area to instill "American values" such as discipline and teamwork. In East Coast cities then burgeoning with southern and eastern European immigrants, social reformers saw basketball as a vehicle for teaching these skills, which is why some of the best teams in the early days of the game included the Detroit Pulaskis (Polish), the New York Celtics, and the South Philadelphia Hebrews. African Americans had their own clubs, the most successful during the 1920s being the Harlem Renaissance Big Five, a black-owned team that played its home games on Saturday nights in the ballroom of the Renaissance Casino on West 138th Street, usually as a break during an evening of entertainment by performers such as Louis

Armstrong. These were part of a larger shift in which participation in team sports came to be seen as a quintessentially American activity.

The idea that playing on a sports team can transform a boy's life in a positive way has permeated American thought. The concept has been rehashed in countless sports movies, which tell variations of the same story: A group of undisciplined boys come together under the leadership of a tough but caring coach and learn important lessons about life. Examples run from *Knute Rockne, All American* (the story of the legendary football coach, with Ronald Reagan as star player George Gipp, requesting on his deathbed that his Notre Dame teammates "Win just one for the Gipper!") to *Coach Carter* (with Samuel L. Jackson, playing a variation on his usual role, as the uncompromising, badass basketball coach who whips an inner-city high school basketball team into shape). In these films, the players learn not only how to work together, but how to be men. No matter their limitations when they come in—they may be soft, undisciplined, and spoiled rich kids, or poor, fatherless, and feeling the pull of the streets—the players step outside of their societal surroundings to enter the cocoon of the team. By the end of the movie, they're ready to return, steeled by their experiences together. It's as if the screenplays had been written by the most zealous adherents of Muscular Christianity.

Willie McClain had absorbed this tradition but also adapted it to the needs of his players—African American boys growing up in Seattle in the 1980s, many without fathers in their lives. McClain's own life had taught him that young men need male authority figures—without authority, boys will do whatever they want and make all kinds of wrong choices, just as he had once done. But to guide young men, you need to have structures, and for McClain, organized basketball was an obvious one—boys will turn out because they enjoy playing it, and in the meantime you can use it teach them other skills.

Showing up to practice and supporting your teammates instills responsibility and discipline. Learning to function within the group and to listen to authority—even when you may not agree with it—teaches you the skills you need to succeed in school and work. Learning to trust your teammates—that they will pick up for you on defense if you lose your man; that they will pass to you when you're open—creates fellowship. Committing to the team forms a habit that makes it easier to commit to other things, such as a career, later in life. "The goal is to teach you how to function in society, how to take care of a family," McClain says of the game of basketball. "There are a lot of hidden things. It's more than just running up and down the floor."

If the game could be used to teach those lessons, McClain reasoned, it also could provide a structure for the different sides of this team to find common cause. First, we all loved the game and knew the rules, so that meant we were at least meeting on shared ground. If we could learn to play together as a unit, to trust that our teammates would pass to us no matter our race, McClain thought that a natural bond would start to develop. Friendships would grow from there.

McClain's core motivation, though, was seeing that his son and his teammates got a chance to get into private schools. McClain regarded the situation of his players in simple terms: Society had allocated a certain number of scholarships for young black athletes at private schools. Compared to going to, say, Garfield, private school could be a launching pad out of the Central Area, toward a college education and a good job. He could live with that inequity as long as his guys were on the right side of those numbers. If basketball was a way to get there, and Randy Finley was to be the lever to pry the door open, so be it.

In this, McClain picked up on another American belief with a long lineage—that sports can be an avenue of advancement for African Americans into the mainstream. Edwin Henderson, who became known as the "father of black basketball" after starting the first African-American basketball league in the segregated Washington, D.C., school system in 1906, argued that on the court, where the rules were the same for everybody, whites would have to accept black competitors as equals. Successful black athletes could then serve as role models for other African Americans, playing the same role that W. E. B. Du Bois envisioned for the Talented Tenth. Henderson later said, "I doubt much whether the mere acquisition of hundreds of degrees or academic honors has influenced the mass mind of America as much as the soul appeal made in a thrilling run for a touchdown by a colored athlete." In the 1930s, the boxer Joe Louis and the sprinter Jesse Owens both became national heroes by defeating German opponents during the Nazi era—Louis in a boxing match with Max Schmeling, and Owens with his triumphant four gold medals at the 1936 Berlin Olympics.

The archetype of a black athlete crossing over into white America, though, is Jackie Robinson, who still is cited and celebrated as a black trailblazer. But the commemorations of Robinson's achievements tend to gloss over the conflicts and disillusionment he felt later in his life. The full story reveals a more complex view of the possibilities and limitations of using sports as a vehicle of integration.

Born the son of a Georgia sharecropper in 1919, Robinson soon moved—along with thousands of other blacks at the time—with his mother to Los Angeles. His mom got a job as a domestic servant; he grew up chafing against Jim Crow in Pasadena, but went on to become a football, basketball, track, and baseball star at UCLA. He joined the still-segregated army during World War II. While a lieutenant stationed in Texas, Robinson was court-martialed after refusing to move to the back of a military bus. Though he was acquitted, Robinson knew that if he hadn't enjoyed some celebrity as a former college sports star, the outcome probably would have been different. Upon his discharge, Robinson went to play baseball for the Kansas City Monarchs, a Negro Leagues team.

At the end of World War II, American race relations were primed for change: Thousands of black servicemen had gone overseas, fought for the country, and were in no mood to be treated as inferior when they got back. The war and the jobs it created had pulled another wave of black migrants from the South to cities in the North and the West Coast, and the invention of the mechanical cotton picker meant that many more were soon to make the move. Like the rest of American society, major-league sports were segregated, but it didn't take much to see that there was an amazing talent pool in the Negro Leagues—if a major-league baseball team were to integrate and bring in some of the country's best black players, it would gain a huge competitive advantage. In 1945, Branch Rickey, the president of the Brooklyn Dodgers, took that step and signed Robinson to a minor-league contract. Two years later, on April 15, 1947, Robinson stepped onto the field for his first major-league game.

That season has been recounted in dozens of books and films: how Rickey and Robinson agreed that Robinson would turn the other cheek to provocation; the threats, taunts, and slurs Robinson endured from fans, opposing players, and even his own teammates; Robinson's intensely competitive personality and his excellence on the field, where he helped the Dodgers make it to the World Series; and the overwhelming support of African Americans, who turned out by the thousands to see him play.

Back then, baseball was still the most popular sport in the country and considered the national pastime. Robinson's presence on the field was a step toward visibility for all African Americans. The African-American essayist Gerald Early writes: "Robinson was arguably the person who launched the American era of racial integration after World War II," preceding *Brown v. Board of Education*, Rosa Parks, Martin Luther King Jr., and everything that followed. "Robinson became a public spectacle in a way that no other African American had quite been before, and he subdued Western culture through his sheer will to win."

After Robinson's pioneering season, the segregation of other sports quickly ended. In 1950, twenty-two-year-old Earl Lloyd entered a game for the Washington Capitols, becoming the first African American to play in the National Basketball Association. He preceded an explosion of black talent in the sport during the following decades: Bill Russell, a six-foot-ten shot blocker and rebounder, led the University of San Francisco to college championships in 1955 and 1956 before going on to join the Boston Celtics, who won eleven titles during his thirteen-year career; the seven-foot-tall Wilt Chamberlain in 1962 became the only player ever to score a hundred points in an NBA game; and Elgin Baylor, who could seemingly suspend himself in the air, brought unprecedented athletic virtuosity to the court.

Jackie Robinson's ten seasons in the major leagues are by far the most-told part of his story, though not the end. After his retirement in 1956, Robinson became deeply involved in civil rights, pushing for legal remedies such as voting rights as well as economic power through black business ownership. An outspoken advocate for Black Capitalism, he helped to found and then chaired a black-run savings and loan in Harlem. He took a position as a corporate vice president with the restaurant chain Chock full o' Nuts, and instead of just cashing in on his fame, actively worked to improve conditions for black employees. His belief in business as the way forward for African Americans led him to campaign for Richard Nixon against John F. Kennedy during the 1960 presidential election—a position he later renounced—and become an aide to Nelson Rockefeller, New York's moderate Republican governor. "I was fighting a last-ditch battle to keep the Republicans from becoming completely white," Robinson wrote later.

Robinson, in effect, tried to bridge the early philosophies of Booker T. Washington and W. E. B. Du Bois: He wanted black economic empowerment in tandem with legal victories and advancement toward equality. By the 1960s, though, many African-American leaders thought it would be impossible for blacks to ever gain equality under the capitalist system that had once enslaved them. For example, Du Bois joined the Communist Party later in life; he died in exile in Ghana in 1963 at age ninety-five.

Some African-American athletes also began to question the assumption that achievement in sports would lead to full acceptance in American life. The most prominent was heavyweight boxing champion Cassius Clay, who, with the encouragement of Malcolm X, joined the Nation of Islam in 1964 and changed his name to Muhammad Ali. Ali refused to report when he was drafted into the army in 1966 and shunned the idea of the black athlete as an integrationist role model. Robinson, whose son fought in Vietnam, said at the time, "He's hurting, I think, the morale of a lot of young soldiers over in Vietnam." Ali simply said, "I ain't got no quarrel with them Vietcong."

In essence, Jackie Robinson's integrationist position began to seem passé to many blacks as the 1960s advanced. When he questioned the wisdom of the black separatism of people such as Stokely Carmichael, militants labeled Robinson an "Uncle Tom." In a much-publicized spat, Malcolm X accused Robinson of simply working for his "white boss," Branch Rickey. Malcolm noted that in 1949, Robinson had agreed, if reluctantly, to testify before the House Un-American Activities Committee to refute Paul Robeson's statement that African Americans, because of their treatment in the United States, would not fight the Soviet Union if a war started. "You let yourself be used by whites," Malcolm X told Robinson.

Robinson kept up his fight, starting a construction company to build housing for the working class in New York City and continuing to speak out on the discrimination and poverty faced by blacks. But by the late 1960s he was increasingly disenchanted by what he saw as a lack of progress toward equality and the failure of the country to address it. By 1972, at age fifty-three, Robinson was suffering from diabetes, his hair had gone white, and he was nearly blind. He died of a heart attack that October.

In his autobiography, published the year of his death, Robinson remembered the optimism he felt during the singing of the national anthem at the opening of the 1947 World Series, and said it was long gone.

"Today as I look back on that opening game of my first World Series, I must tell you that it was Mr. Rickey's drama and that I was only a principal actor," he wrote. "I cannot stand and sing the anthem. I cannot salute the flag; I know that I am a black man in a white world." Robinson questioned what his achievements on the baseball diamond had translated to in American society at large. While he had integrated the field of play, he was incensed that the positions of power in baseball were still all white. "It is not terribly difficult for the black man as an individual to enter the white man's world and be partially accepted. However, if that individual black man is, in the eyes of the white world, an 'uppity nigger,' he is in for a very hard time indeed."

Robinson knew he'd been chosen for the major leagues not only for his talents, but also for his ability to control his temper. He recognized that there were many other black players who could have excelled at the highest levels had they gotten the chance. The playwright August Wilson took up this theme in *Fences*, the story of Troy Maxson, a former Negro Leagues power hitter who was too old to play in the major leagues by the time Robinson had integrated them. The play is set in 1957, and Troy is embittered, working as a garbageman in Pittsburgh. When his wife and a friend suggest that Jackie Robinson had changed things for blacks in baseball, that Troy just came along too early, he explodes: "There ought not never have been no time called too early! . . . I done seen a hundred niggers play baseball better than Jackie Robinson. Hell, I know some teams Jackie Robinson couldn't even make! . . . Jackie Robinson wasn't nobody. I'm talking about if you could play ball then they ought to have let you play."

Always aware of his own good fortune, Robinson found that America feted him for his athletic skills but was much less interested in hearing him talk about lack of opportunity, the hundreds of Troy Maxsons who languished behind one Jackie Robinson. "I can't believe that I have it made while so many of my black brothers and sisters are hungry, inadequately housed, insufficiently clothed, denied their dignity, live in slums or barely exist on welfare," he wrote. "There was a time when I deeply believed in America. I have become bitterly disillusioned."

Randy Finley, born in 1942, was a decade older than Willie McClain and had in almost every way grown up on the opposite side of the racial and

cultural divide. As a kid in the late 1940s, he had moved with his family
to Seattle's Capitol Hill neighborhood, into a house that was only a few
blocks from the East Madison neighborhood of the Central Area, which
at the time was swelling with new black migrants from the South. Just as
Willie McClain's mom warned him never to cross the railroad tracks in
Gulfport, Mississippi, Randy's parents told him to stay away from the
Central Area, which, of course, just made it more alluring. "I can remember it being one hundred percent black down there on Twenty-third
and Madison," he says. "Riding my bicycle, I was scared to death, but I
was always very curious."

Finley, like McClain, had roots in the South. His father had grown
up in Asheville, North Carolina, where a black woman had wet-nursed
him. When Finley's father enrolled in college at Duke, she went along to
wash his clothes and take care of him. After the family moved from
Washington, D.C., to Seattle—Finley's mother had grown up in Washington State—Finley's father hired black laborers to work around their
house. "We had some contact," Finley says. "There was a very comfortable relationship."

In 1951, his father, a lawyer, was elected to the Washington State
Supreme Court, and the family moved to Olympia, sixty miles southwest of Seattle. Finley soon discovered a love of sports and joined the
basketball, football, and swim teams in high school. "I loved competition," he says. "I really was a basketball player trapped in a football
player's body. I never could jump very much, but I loved the sport of basketball." Finley struggled in his classes, though, especially with writing.
Outside of school, he tooled around in his '48 hot rod and generally
raised hell. "I was drunk probably five nights a week," he says. "We'd
take hypodermics and squirt vodka into oranges and then eat them at
lunch at school."

He started college in the 1960s, taking eight years to earn a degree
from the University of Washington. In the meantime, he served in the
army reserve, worked as a night guard at the King County Juvenile Detention Center, spent months at a time in Mexico City learning Spanish,
and sold trinkets at rock shows. While Willie McClain was taking to the
streets, Finley was actually living in a house in the Central Area that he'd
rented with a white roommate. "We knew there were dangers, but we
were also very sympathetic," Finley says. "I wanted to contribute to what
we thought was happening. We thought our generation was changing the

world"—Finley laughs at the statement—"and we were just trying to be a small part of it in Seattle. It sounds kind of dreamy, but it was a couple young men interested in being better citizens and helping other people be better citizens."

In 1969, Finley was thinking about going to graduate school when he saw a double feature of François Truffaut's *Jules et Jim* and Ingmar Bergman's *The Seventh Seal*. Afterward, while smoking a joint with his wife and some friends, he had an epiphany—instead of grad school, he was going to get into the film business, deciding, "I'm going to open a theater just like one of those porno, skin-flick theaters on First Avenue. I'm going to build a little small theater and play nothing but films based on literature."

His first place, near the University of Washington, was a cramped room with only ninety-three seats. Finley discovered that the idea of showing only films based on books wasn't realistic, but he soon became known around Seattle for his oversize personality: He wore an army jacket with his name sewn on, had a beard down to his chest, a wild head of hair topped with a Russian Cossack hat, and greeted customers by serving them tea and coffee. He expanded throughout the 1970s and eventually owned sixteen theaters, located in quirky places such as old American Legion halls. In the early 1980s, though, he found he was having a hard time getting the rights to show popular first-run movies. He filed an antitrust suit against several big theater chains, charging them with colluding to block him out. Finley was far from the type to shy away from a fight, but as the lawyers stacked up billable hours, the battle began to burn him out. In 1986 he decided to sell his theaters. He'd already begun to rustle around for somewhere else to invest his considerable energy.

Finley had mixed feelings about sending Maitland to Lakeside. He appreciated the education but found the other students to be "too rich and too spoiled," and worried that Maitland would become a "snob." ("It's amazing they let a few plebeians like us in with their young captains of industry," he says of our families the first time I interview him.) When he spied Willie McClain's team, he saw a chance to open the minds of the Lakeside kids a bit. He wanted us to learn something about black people and perhaps form some friendships. "That was the hope—that as a unit we could all begin to think of each other as just people," he says. "Basketball was a vehicle to do a lot more than just play basketball."

Willie McClain was cautious when Finley approached him—taking his players out of the Central Area to play basketball with a bunch of rich white kids would open him to the charge that he was letting them be exploited. But McClain quickly grasped the possibility in Finley's offer: "What was so attractive when Randy talked about bringing the teams together—and we talked about it a lot—was the idea of these kids going on to private schools, and that really kind of blew up in my head. I said 'Really, do they have an opportunity to do this?' "

• • •

On weekends, we pile into McClain's van. Randy Finley has signed us up to play in the Amateur Athletic Union, a nationwide youth-sports organization. Anyone can form an AAU team, and you can recruit any player you want as long as he is within the age limits. The AAU league is a netherworld of games in dimly lit gyms against players none of us have faced before. McClain and Finley drive us to tournaments around Western Washington—from Bellingham and Mount Vernon up north to Redmond, the suburban home of the Microsoft "campus," just east of Seattle across Lake Washington.

From the stands, players are numbers and statistics. You identify them by their traits: The short kid with the fade cut into his hair can dribble right or left; the big one who sweats a lot is a tough rebounder; that kid who's hustling after the ball has a deadly jump shot. The game's immersive world, the beautiful geometry, the shifting angles, players jostling for position, the ball floating toward the hoop make it possible to forget that anything exists off the court, outside the moment.

From the bench, where I usually sit with Damian, Myran, and JT, I take in every move my teammates make on the court. I know all their tics as players, but almost nothing about their lives away from the court.

For example, I have no idea that JT, who is sitting next to me and cheering on Tyrell, has been observing Tyrell from a distance since they were little kids. Back then, Tyrell and Donnico, his brother, used to go out with their dad on the playground at Garfield. Tyrell and Donnico shot baskets while their dad grabbed the ball and whipped it back to them. Seeing them out there, JT felt envious of how tight they were, how much fun they were having. He wished he could run onto the court and join them, but it wouldn't have seemed right—it was a father-and-son thing. JT didn't want to intrude.

JT cherishes the few moments of paternal-type guidance he's had out on the playground—he's learned his defense and rebounding skills from Dennis Johnson, the starting point guard for the Seattle Super-Sonics when they won the 1979 NBA championship. JT's mom, Sharon, was best friends with Johnson's girlfriend, and the three of them went to games together, young "John-John" sitting on Sharon's lap at courtside. During the week, Sharon was a clerk at Blue Shield. Away from work, she was so fun and pretty that she'd been nicknamed "Hollywood Sharon"—JT found her totally glamorous. Dennis Johnson took a liking to JT and decided to teach him how to play. JT hardly sees his own dad, except at his grandfather's house at holidays. When they do meet, they're polite to each other but nothing more. JT finds substitutes for the father and brothers he is missing through playing on Willie McClain's team. "I loved being able to go over to people's houses to eat dinner, spending the night all the time, doing things with them, like with the McClains," he says. "They had brothers, and a mother and a father, not a single parent, doing family things, and I'm able to be involved. So I think just growing up I was just looking for a family, looking up to Willie McClain."

Myran, like JT, has found a refuge on Willie McClain's team. He was seven the last time he saw his dad. They'd been out in the middle of the street, with Myran hiking a football to his father, who then passed it to him. His dad was a charismatic guy who loved to dress sharp. He also sold drugs. Not long after that game on the street, Myran's father went down to Seattle's Chinatown to play cards in a gambling den and was shot dead. In the years since, Myran's mom has been mired in her own struggles, and Myran has spent most of his childhood with his grandma, who works as a nurse. Myran's predilection toward acting out is a trait Willie McClain keeps a close eye on. Of all the players on the team, McClain knows that Myran is the most likely to say something that might cause a problem, and that he's the least likely to know how to handle himself in a new social situation. But the McClains have often had Myran stay over at their house. If anyone needs to be exposed to an opportunity that might broaden his horizons, it's Myran. So McClain decided to take a chance and put him on the team. "Myran, he was just special to me," he says. "You know things, and you know he needs to be there."

Damian lives with his mom and younger sister, Toya, and is fiercely protective of both. When his sister gets teased, Damian steps in to defend her. "Damian always took up for me," Toya says. "I don't recall him ever losing a fight. He would beat up the biggest of big guys." On the team, Damian, like JT and Myran, finds surrogate father figures in both Willie McClain and Charlie Hampton. Sometimes he goes over to the Hampton house and just studies Charlie—his tone of voice, his bearing, how he interacts with his wife and kids—trying to learn everything he can.

Tyrell, for his part, loves sports. He's brash and seems born for the public eye, shining in the spotlight ever since he began break dancing and pop-locking at church events, which got him showcased on the local cable-access station. With his array of behind-the-back moves, head fakes, and infectious smile, he is the flashiest player on the team.

Willie Jr. both enjoys and feels pressure in his position as the son of the coach. "I had to earn my spot more than anybody else," he says. "God forbid, if I would've had no skills, I would've been in trouble." His role on the court, he realizes, is to help his dad keep order, which means holding his own ego in line. As a point guard, his focus is on distributing the ball and feeding the player with the hot hand. With the integrated team, he feels a responsibility to make sure things go smoothly, that everyone feels part of the group.

Maitland, as the son of the team's organizer, also has a special status. His feelings on that situation are mixed. He has no choice but to play—his dad thinks that sports are a good way for Maitland to make friends and to combat his shyness. But Maitland also feels an innate social awkwardness. He finds it hard to meet the expectations at Lakeside, where it seems like everyone is expected to be perfect. He enjoys being part of the team, but starring on the court means nothing to him. "I'm one of those people who much preferred practice. I don't really have fun in games. I don't thrive on the pressure," he says. "I tended to like not getting playing time because then I didn't have to worry about anything."

Sean's dad, the cigar-chewing stockbroker, had encouraged his son to play sports, even signing him up for boxing when he was in first grade. "I hated it," Sean says. "I remember one of the first boxing practices, we had gloves on and had to pick sparring partners. I picked this dorky kid with big frizzy hair because I thought he'd be easy to fight. He whipped me so bad."

With his height, basketball was the most natural fit for Sean. "I was never very good, just tall. I'd run around in circles, rebound here or there. I was never aggressive. . . . But it was always fun, I always liked the people I played with. And you do sports as a kid, right?"

Dino, along with Chris, gets recruited by Randy Finley midway into the AAU season to add height and talent lacking in some of the other white players, such as myself. Dino's parents are both immigrants from Greece. His dad, whose first job in Seattle was as a cafeteria manager at a waterfront hotel on Elliott Bay, runs a twenty-four-hour diner downtown that he owns with his brothers. Dino's mom ferries him to his practices and games. Though Dino already attends a Christian school, his mom hopes he can gain entrance to Lakeside. Dino, who doesn't know anyone from either side, just jumps in and begins to play.

Chris knows that he's enrolling at Lakeside in the fall—his father is a prominent alum, and his older brother and sister are both already at the school. But coming from a competitive family has its pressures, and Chris has found that he can use athletics as an outlet. "A lot of people play sports because they're fun, but for me the significance was that during seventh grade, over an eighteen-month period, I grew something like eight inches," he says. "I wasn't popular in school. I was kind of fat, and all of a sudden I went to being six-two and skinny. Sports transitioned from being the things that you just did to being my lifeline, my self-esteem."

For Eric, this team, mixing together his Central Area friends and private school classmates, means both sides of his life are finally coming together. Eric has never thought about why he plays sports. It's just natural. He drops his usual reserve when he plays basketball. It's as if he has a different personality that comes out, one that isn't withdrawn or shy. "I was good at basketball," he says. "What boy doesn't want to be good at sports? That's the way you could shine and get people to respect you."

Sports have been inseparable from my family life since birth. In December 1971, my parents went to watch the SuperSonics play basketball against the Portland Trailblazers. The Sonics pulled out a 107–105 victory, courtesy of some last-minute heroics by Lenny Wilkens. A few hours later, a doctor pulled me out, a week before my due date.

By the time I started playing teeball as a five-year-old, I'd noticed that sports could be a useful lubricant in our family machinery. Though my parents seemed to do little else together, both came to my games. My dad coached several of my Little League baseball teams, while my mom sat in the stands and cheered.

Sports are what I do with my dad: skiing and basketball in the winter, baseball in the spring and summer, and football in the fall, when, on weekends, we go to watch the University of Washington Huskies or the Seattle Seahawks. Each game is a flawless gem, and afterward we're able to hold it up to the light and analyze every aspect, from who the coach started at quarterback to the twenty-six-yard run that broke it open in the second half. Everything is easy to dissect; there are no gray areas.

I revel in the feeling of solidarity I get from being on our mixed team, and I hate it when anything intrudes on it. One night after a game, Coach McClain gives me a ride home. My family has just moved into a new house three miles north of the one where I have lived nearly all my life.

The normal chatter in the van dies as I guide McClain through the neighborhood. We ride past a lot of big houses on big lots, built without regard to architectural harmony—mock Tudor next to California stucco next to Rambler. Tyrell, Damian, JT, Myran, and Willie Jr. crowd to stare out the front window. Even Coach McClain seems to be gaping.

We pull up the driveway in front of my house, a large, gray, modernist structure with two gables. It has a basketball hoop and the outline of a key set in front of the three-car garage. Damian asks, "What side do you live on?"

"What do you mean?"

"Do you live on the right side or the left side?"

It takes me a second to catch on.

"It's just one house," I say, clutching my gym bag.

"You mean this is just for your family?"

"Yeah, we're the only ones who live here."

I pull the door open and thank Coach McClain for the ride.

"I'll see you guys at practice," I say and scurry into the house.

I'm embarrassed. All the gawking undermines the feeling fostered by playing on the team—that we are all equals. I worry that my teammates might not like me after seeing the house. The next day at school, Eric tells me that the guys had joked about my reaction on the way back to the Central Area, saying, "He probably didn't invite us in because he was scared we'd steal everything."

I begin to protest but stop. What I can't tell Eric is that I never thought of inviting anyone in because, even though we've just moved in, I've already begun to detest the house. Like Lakeside, it has hit at a division between my parents—for my mom, it's a beautiful home that showcases our prosperity; my dad simply seems ashamed of it. Being part of the team is an escape from that strife. The last thing I want to do is invite my teammates into that.

At our next practice, Damian sidles up to me. In a conspiratorial tone he asks, "So, Doug, you're pretty rich, huh?"

"No, I'm not rich," I say.

"Well, what about your house?"

"I'm not rich," I explain. "It's my dad's money."

"What's the difference?"

"Well, just because my dad has money, it doesn't mean I'm rich. It's not the same thing."

"Yeah, but you're going to get the money someday."

"It's hard to say. What if he spends it all? What if his company goes out of business?"

Damian shakes his head and laughs.

There is nothing I can really say. I have never seen his house and have no idea how he lives. For the whole season, the black side of the team always makes the commute north. We never visit the Central Area.

Welfare Queens, the Huxtables, and Unlikely Champions

We play "21" all the time, a game the black guys taught the rest of us. It pits a single player against everyone else. The idea is to grab a rebound, clear the ball outside the key, and then put it though the hoop for two points. How you do that is up to you—you can try to drop an outside shot, or you can drive the basket through the rest of the team. If you score, you get a free throw. Hit the free throw, you get another point and the ball back.

21 is a mad scramble, full of desperate shots and trash talk. Everyone has a different tactic: Eric cuts, dashes, and zigzags through the defense until he can squeeze off a shot; JT lays back and positions for a rebound; I wait for a wayward shot or loose ball and try to put it back in before too many defenders pile up on me; Tyrell tries some between-the-legs dribbles and other moves that look good but don't necessarily work when you have to get by nine other guys. Sometimes Coach McClain jumps into the fray, dribbling down toward the hoop and using his hefty frame to knock us out of the way like bowling pins.

We are playing in Randy Finley's barn. Finley owns six acres of land out in the country about thirty miles north of Seattle. The family's two-story split-level is surrounded by lawn and overlooks a river valley. Several pigs root around in a corral in the yard. Finley has nailed up a hoop in the barn, and the sunlight cuts through the dust that hangs in the air, mixing with the shouts and laughs of the players.

Right now, Maitland has the ball out on the wing. He's used his butt to slam other players out of the way and grab a rebound. A knot of concentration curls on his forehead and his lips purse as he observes the tangle blocking his path to the basket. He dribbles with his right hand and turns and backs toward the hoop before swiveling to fire off a shot.

The ball travels at a flat trajectory, hitting the backboard and bouncing off the rim toward the other side of the court, where Myran grabs it. In a second, JT and Willie Jr. are both all over him, trying to strip the ball. Myran stagger-steps, dribbles right, and falls back while throwing up his shot. It arcs up and drops down to rattle around the rim before falling through. Myran pumps his fist, straightens up, and walks toward the free-throw line. He puts his right hand up and calls, "Ball!"

• • •

Years later, when my teammates remember the team, the first things that will come to mind are the capping, joking around during the van rides, and the games of 21. The game was something that everyone could play and be a part of, even though the best player almost always won in the end (in our case, Eric took at least half of the games). We each added our own little touches to 21—Myran's outside shot, Tyrell's drives, Maitland's rebounding—so that all of our styles merged into a larger composition. Unlike our real games, where we were subject to the referees and Coach McClain's oversight, you could pull out any crazy move you wanted in 21. Boldness and improvisation were encouraged. All that mattered was getting the ball through the hoop. My outside shot took on the same worth as Tyrell's winding drives to the hoop and Sean's post-up play near the basket. We all had the same goal and our own set of tools for getting there. Everyone was, for the moment, equal to everyone else.

It wasn't that way off the court. This was 1986, and there were plenty of contradictory messages flying around. On TV, many of the regular depictions of African Americans were one step removed from Amos & Andy. Blacks were generally cast as friendly but somewhat buffoonish characters with catchphrases, such as J.J. on *Good Times* ("Dy-no-miite!") and Arnold on *Diff'rent Strokes* ("Whatchoo talkin' 'bout, Willis?"). On Thursday nights, though, there was *The Cosby Show*, watched by nearly every kid I knew, where Dr. Huxtable presided over his family, administering heart-to-heart talks in the kitchen and breaking into an occasional Harry Belafonte lip sync.

Early in 1986, rap finally began to break through on MTV—then supplanting radio as the avenue through which pop music gained national exposure—with the release of *Licensed to Ill* by the Beastie Boys, an album that followed in the American tradition of white artists taking a black form and popularizing it. At the same time, Run DMC and Aerosmith put out their version of "Walk This Way," which both brought credibility back to the washed-up Boston rockers and shot the rappers from Queens into the mainstream. These breached the way for the rest of hip-hop, much of which reflected the music's roots in the housing projects of the Bronx. One day at practice Tyrell spun my head by reciting, "My story is rough, my neighborhood is tough/But I still sport gold, and I'm out to crush." He gave me an incredulous look when I asked who it was. "LL Cool J," he said, wincing as if my ignorance had caused him personal pain.

For the white side of the team there was an undeniable allure in hanging with guys from Central Seattle just as hip-hop was on the rise, and it was impossible not to try to pick up on some of the style. Chris learned to break-dance. Sean picked up a Fat Boys album. Every Sunday I listened to a weekly rap show on AM radio—the only place you could hear the music in Seattle in those days—trying and failing to master lines from songs like UTFO's "Roxanne, Roxanne."

The black players on the team didn't get any street cred from hanging with the white guys, but they did find other things of value. JT quickly adopted Randy Finley as another surrogate father. Damian was fascinated by being around people with wealth. "I'd go home and tell my mom, 'These people have lots of money!'" he says. Willie McClain Jr. viewed the whole thing as if it were an after-school special about integration and opportunity. "We'd seen it on TV," he says. "This was our chance to better ourselves."

Little differences with larger implications were always there. For example, during weekend tournaments, the favorite place to get lunch was McDonald's. Before we left the gym, guys like Damian and JT would ask Randy Finley for lunch money; they noticed that the white guys were never short. On the way over—it was always "Mickey D's," never "McDonald's"—the kids from the Central Area made a huge deal out of the coming meal, vigorously debating the relative merits of the Big Mac and the Quarter Pounder. I had never considered the distinctions between the menu choices, or that going to McDonald's could be a rare treat to be savored.

These small fault lines hinted at a deeper class divide. If you turned your television channel away from Bill Cosby and his perfect family, you might happen upon a news report about the spread of crack cocaine. Or you might see some pundits discussing what to do about the problem of "welfare queens."

The phrase had been popularized by Ronald Reagan, who first used it during his 1976 challenge of Gerald Ford for the Republican presidential nomination. On the stump, Reagan cited a "welfare queen" from the South Side of Chicago who had "eighty names, thirty addresses, twelve Social Security cards and is collecting veterans' benefits on four nonexisting deceased husbands." He added, "Her tax-free cash income alone is over $150,000."

It appears that—instead of there actually being an incredibly industrious and motivated welfare cheat—the real story that inspired Reagan was far less interesting. At the time he first began using the welfare queen trope, a Chicago woman named Linda Taylor had made the news after a state senator investigating welfare fraud made sensational charges against her. In the end, she was convicted with using two aliases to fraudulently collect $8,000 of welfare. Reagan or one of his staff possibly picked up the story from newspaper accounts.

The exaggerated anecdote was too good to correct—it touched a nerve in campaign crowds and remained one of Reagan's recurring themes in the coming years. It worked, in part, because the extraordinary post–World War II American economic expansion, which saw the growth of a vast middle class, had ground to a halt in the 1970s. As inflation and unemployment increased, people became worried about their futures. Welfare queens, depicted as poor black women who had babies in order to sponge off the system, were a useful political wedge.

The sociologist Christopher Jencks calls Reagan's 1980 election "the end of an era in American race relations." He writes, "Between 1964 and 1980 federal officials had argued about the moral legitimacy and practical benefits of helping blacks catch up with whites economically, but few questioned the basic assumption that the government ought to promote this goal one way or another." That changed with Reagan's ascendancy. Policies such as affirmative action, which aimed to increase the number of African Americans in higher education and white-collar jobs, as well as "social safety net" programs such as food stamps, Medicaid, housing subsidies, and welfare, were called into question. Conservative writers such as economist Thomas Sowell and political scientist Charles Murray argued that these programs were not only ineffective, but they actually encouraged the recipients—i.e., poor black people, though, of course, many more whites received these subsidies than blacks—to become lazy, dependent on handouts, and to have babies out of wedlock. The reasonable conclusion, then, was that such assistance should be terminated.

This was a potent theme. My father's side of the family, small-business-owning and Italian American, picked up the welfare queen idea, repeating it at holiday dinners when the conversation inevitably turned to what was "wrong with America." They concluded that whoever wasn't making it was too ready to ask for a handout and just wasn't trying hard enough.

It also dovetailed with our self-image—we were hardworking descendants of immigrants who had pulled ourselves up by our bootstraps. My grandfather had gone from selling newspapers on street corners in downtown Seattle at age seven to opening a service station in the late 1930s. Twenty years later, he bought the coin-operated laundry company that my dad later took over. In 1979, my grandfather was named Washington State Small Businessman of the Year—a newspaper columnist wrote that he was "making the Great American Dream come true not only for himself but also for others." In the early 1980s, he was one of a group of business owners invited to Washington, D.C., by the Small Business Administration. The trip included a tour of the White House, where Ronald Reagan posed with the group for a photo. When he returned, my grandfather was delighted that an Italian from Garlic Gulch had made it all the way to a meeting with the president. I became a huge Ronald Reagan fan. I loved it when he gave speeches on TV, with his helmet of shiny black hair, head cocked a bit to the side, the knowing smile on his face, and the misty look in his eyes.

My family had good reason to be proud—we had staked a place for ourselves here in this country only a few generations after leaving peasantry in rural Italy. Looking back, the shame of the welfare-queen talk is the way it divided an issue such as poverty into simple categories. It included my family within the boundaries of one side of America—that of right-thinking, hardworking people. Anyone taking welfare fell on the other side of the line. The rhetoric obliterated complexity.

I brought the preconceptions and stereotypes that seeped in through the culture to the basketball court. Had Damian informed me that his mom took public assistance, I would have immediately categorized her in my mind as lazy and not trying hard enough. I had no way of knowing or understanding that his family was working on its own story, as American as my own.

At the same time that my grandfather was getting his service station going in downtown Seattle in the 1940s, Damian's Great-Aunt Geneva was tiring of life in Jeanerette, Louisiana, where shotgun-carrying white men on horseback still patrolled the sugarcane fields where the family worked. When she heard about better opportunities in Spokane, Washington, three hundred miles east of Seattle, she decided to move. She got a job as a domestic servant in a white household and sent word back that life was better in the Northwest. Before long, the whole family, including Damian's grandmother and great-grandmother, another great-aunt, and a great-uncle, came out. Damian's mom, Helen, was born in Spokane in 1954.

In the 1950s and 1960s, blacks made up only a few thousand of Spokane's 180,000 people. Most lived in a part of town called East Central, where they were steered by real estate agents. Though the schools were integrated—there weren't enough blacks around to make segregation economically feasible—the city's lodges and private clubs, the heart of its social hierarchy, were "white only." As late as the 1950s, there were no black doctors or dentists, or even elevator operators or auto mechanics. Most black men worked as laborers or in custodial positions, though some found jobs at the Kaiser aluminum plant, the area's primary employer. Black women worked mostly either as household servants or in one of the local hospitals. Helen's mom delivered trays of food to patients at Sacred Heart Hospital for thirty-eight years. Helen's dad worked at a shop that made footwear for construction workers, where he did janitorial work and shined boots. "Whenever I went there, I never saw him making shoes, I just saw him cleaning them, for *years*," Helen says. "He never moved up, my mom never moved up."

When she was still a little girl, Helen's parents split up. Along with her older brother and sister, she went to live with their grandmother. Although her mom, Aunt Geneva, and grandmother all lived on the same block, the siblings were primarily raised according to Grandma's rules, which tended toward the philosophy of "spare the rod, spoil the child." An ardent churchgoer, Grandma delivered "whuppings" for any number of offenses, such as whispering in church, arguing with a sibling, or failing to wash a plate right. Helen's older brother reacted by staying away from home. Her older sister stood up to Grandma. Helen suffered in silence. "There was no love or hugs or encouragement. I had no role models, no ambition," Helen says. "I never once heard the word 'education.'" Only in hindsight did Helen realize how poor the family was— many of their meals were based around surplus cheese, peanut butter, or canned meat provided by the government.

In 1970, when Helen was sixteen, she went to a house party and met Arthur Sullivan, who had come out from Illinois to study for a teaching degree at Eastern Washington University. They started dating, and after about a year, Helen became pregnant. When Damian was born, in December 1972, Arthur was finishing up at Eastern. He told Helen he wanted to do the right thing, get married, and have her move back with him to Illinois. "He said if I didn't marry him he didn't really want anything to do with me," Helen says. "That's basically how it was." Helen didn't want to leave her family, so she declined. Arthur left and effectively disappeared from Damian's life.

Helen finished high school at an alternative school. After graduation there wasn't much to do except learn how to look after Damian. As far as social life, Spokane didn't have a lot going on—kids hung out at a local tavern and at the racetrack. There were house parties, and sometimes the youth center put on a dance. Helen started to date a construction worker named Stanley. They moved in together, and three years after Damian, his sister, Toya, was born. Stanley was a nice guy, but he also could turn mean and speak down to Helen in public. Another man noticed this and concertedly wooed Helen. The new suitor eventually won out. He had a brother in Seattle and convinced Helen that it was time to leave Spokane. So, in 1977, when Damian was almost five, they all packed up and headed to Seattle. "It was a culture shock for me," Helen says of her arrival in the city. "I wasn't used to seeing a lot of black people, I mean that many."

Helen's cousin, who lived in Seattle, invited them to come to her church—the Harvest Time Church of God in Christ, in the Central Area at the intersection of Martin Luther King Jr. and Cherry. To Helen's shock, her boyfriend, who was a bit of a hustler, embraced the idea. The first Sunday they went, Helen was saved during the service. She immediately broke up with her boyfriend. The pastor of the church and his wife invited the family to stay with them. Helen, Damian, and Toya lived there, in a two-story house in South Seattle, for more than a year. It was a revelation for Helen. "They were my mentors, my true mentors," she says. "Every single day she would cook a full-course meal and dessert and we ate off plates and drank out of glasses, and ate with forks and knives, not plastic. I didn't know people did that."

With the support and encouragement of the pastor and his wife, Helen began to develop more confidence. "When I was saved, it helped me to realize that I was somebody," she says. "I didn't like being on welfare because I knew that I had more in me." She landed a string of low-paying jobs, such as working as a cashier at a combination gas station-convenience store-car wash, and the family moved into an apartment in the Central Area. For a while Helen worked at an ice cream plant. She was the only black on her shift, and one of her coworkers, a young white woman, barraged her with racial slurs. "No one had ever treated me like that before," Helen says. "Honestly, had I not been saved and my mind was like it was before I got saved, I probably would have beat her up. That's how I knew I was changed, because I wouldn't have taken that otherwise."

By this time, Damian had started to play basketball on Willie McClain's CAYA team, and his poverty became the subject of mockery. "I was the underclass of that underclass," he says with a laugh. The other guys called him "Goo Goo Cluster" for the caramel, chocolate, and nut ice cream treats his mom brought home from work. His limited wardrobe earned him the nickname "Purple Pants Boy." No one ever came to his house, where he and his sister slept on the floor because the family couldn't afford beds.

Helen kept applying for jobs. In the mid-1980s she landed a position as an office assistant for the Seattle School District, a full-time job that allowed her to finally get off welfare, though she still took public assistance to support her family—Section 8 housing aid, Medicaid, food stamps. She gradually worked her way up in the school system and became a classroom assistant in a special education class for autistic kids.

Helen now lives in a town house in a mixed-income public-housing development in South Seattle. One day, as we sit on the couch in her living room, I ask what she thought of the welfare queen talk of the 1980s. When she asks what I mean, I give her a capsule description of the rhetoric. "I don't remember," she says. "It evidently didn't affect me." I'm shocked for a moment, until it strikes me that the welfare queen idea was more of a political dog whistle aimed only at certain groups.

Helen tells me what really bothers her is that she never had a chance to get a decent education. She tries to put it out of her mind, but she can't help thinking how her life might be different. "When I go and see the white people living in nice homes, I have to tell myself, you know, they worked for that, a lot of them worked for what they got. And so had that been passed on to me, maybe I would have been in a nicer home. And then I also realize that that's not what's important. What's important is that I have love and we have togetherness in our home, and we get along . . . I go back and forth, because sometimes I trip and I say, 'They got everything!'" Helen laughs at the last thought.

Damian dismisses the welfare queen talk as nonsense. His mom, he points out, works as hard as anyone. Welfare was just a way for her to support her family while she was trying to get her life together. "You have to live in somebody's shoes, you have to be close to them and know them before you make those kind of comments," he says. "I don't give that any credence anyways, that's just people's thought process. They don't have a clue what they're talking about."

Damian tells me he didn't pay attention to what people outside his direct sphere might have thought of his family's poverty when he was a kid. What made a lasting impression was the taunting he took from those closest to him, including his teammates on Willie McClain's basketball team. "I was laughed at, talked about, and treated horribly by my own race because of my economic status," he says. He tells me he would rather have had the white side of our team come to his house than his black friends. "It would have been better you than them, because you guys wouldn't have said anything about me not having food," he says. "You would have kept it in your mind: 'All he has is Goo Goo Clusters.'"

He hated being poor. It meant never owning the place where they lived, and that the landlords could stop in for housing inspections or whatever they needed to do. It meant going with his mom to the Department of Health and Human Services office, where they waited to hand over the necessary paperwork for programs such as food stamps. It meant that you never had complete control over your own life; other people always had power over you.

When both sides of our team came together, it might have been a chance to talk on a level deeper than political sound bites. But we simply didn't have the language or the structure to discuss such things. In fact, it probably was best to leave it alone—if I had spoken about some of the assumptions that came up during my extended family's holiday dinners, the black side of the team would have been, at best, insulted. Had we gone to the Central Area to visit our teammates' homes, would we have remembered anything other than the poverty in the area? And if poverty is tied to laziness—via the welfare queen trope—then what would we have taken away? Even years later, the type of interaction we should or could have had remains open to question.

Coach McClain sees the basketball court as a special place where the standard set of rules allowed us to play together as equals, without the baggage we may have had off the court. The idea, he says, was that after learning we could work together on the floor, the cooperation would then move off of it. Sean, also, sees the game as the "great equalizer," an area where we were able to forget the economic differences. "I just remember looking up and admiring these kids that Randy had brought in from the Central Area because of their great talent. They were talented beyond any players that I had ever hooped it up with, and that was very cool."

Damian, perhaps unsurprisingly, has a completely different take. He says that underlying assumptions prevalent throughout the United States meant that the team had to remain a "surface integration." In America, he says, even the black person with the least amount of self-knowledge knows by default something about white America—he simply couldn't survive if he didn't. White people, especially those with money and privilege, can remain ignorant of blacks and other minorities. "You just don't have to know," he says. It would be almost impossible for this not to seep into the formation of the team. "It was all done from the beginning," he says. "I just think the whole attitude from the Caucasian point of view was, 'Let's help these guys and give them experience,' more of a superior-type, 'We're here to help you, you can't help us,' that kind of thing."

· · ·

As Randy and Willie had hoped, basketball is a language we can all speak, though with wildly different levels of fluency. Over the course of the season we win one tournament, up north in Ferndale, near the Canadian border. In others, our play is erratic, a mix of blowing out other teams and then getting blown out by them. Much of that is due to the fact that we've only formed this season while some AAU squads have played together for years. Going into the 1986 Western Washington AAU league championship tournament—which is to be played in Redmond, east of Seattle across Lake Washington—our chances don't look great.

By this point, Coach McClain has narrowed down playing time to the best players. I know I have no chance of getting in the game unless there's an unprecedented rash of injuries. I reluctantly suck up my pride. Instead of playing, I take to manning Randy Finley's video camera on the sidelines. Myran—whose playing time has slid to zero as well—doesn't even show up for the tournament. Maitland plays a few minutes to spell Sean. Tyrell's minutes shrink as well. Chris, Eric, and Dino take the spotlight.

And for a weekend, everything clicks. Rebounds drop right into Chris and Sean's hands. Dino nails his jumpers from twenty feet out. On Tyrell's drives, his arcing shots make it over the outstretched arms of defenders a head taller than he is and glide down through the hoop. Eric dogs the other teams' guards, stripping the ball when they try to drive past him.

We win four games in a row. By the end of the day on Sunday, we've taken the Western Washington championship. Our team runs onto the court to celebrate. The league president presents McClain and Finley with a plaque that has a gold plastic figurine of a player dribbling a basketball attached to it. Eric and Chris grab it and hoist it above their heads. Chris, soaked in sweat, grins widely while a sly smile crosses Eric's face. They pose for a picture, and Tyrell crouches in front of them, his arms spread wide. His smile is the biggest of all.

Left to right: Chris Dickinson, Tyrell Johnson (crouching), and Eric Hampton. To the right is Bryce Kisker, recruited late in the season by Randy Finley to add height to the team.

Part Two

Transitions

Just as white college basketball was patterned and regimented
like the lives awaiting its players, the black schoolyard game
demanded all the flash, guile, and individual reckless bril-
liance each man would need in the world facing him.

—*Kareem Abdul-Jabbar*

Moving On

In the 1986 film *Hoosiers*, now considered a classic of the sports movie genre, Gene Hackman plays Norman Dale, a big-time college basketball coach who is fired after hitting one of his players. Disgraced, he takes a job coaching the high school team in Hickory, a tiny Indiana town obsessed with basketball.

The film, set in the early 1950s, follows the course of one season. Coach Dale slowly earns the respect of the townsfolk, falls in love, and becomes a surrogate father to his star player, Jimmy Chitwood, a quiet kid with a flawless outside shot whose own dad has died. Doubling down on the father-son theme, Dennis Hopper plays the shack-dwelling alcoholic dad of another player, who finds redemption and a connection with his son after Hackman names him the team's assistant coach.

Coach Dale takes his band of scrappy overachievers to the state playoffs. In the locker room before the semifinal game, Hackman tells his players: "Forget about the crowds, the size of the school, their fancy uniforms, and remember what got you here. Focus on the fundamentals that we've gone over time and time again, and most important, don't get caught up in winning or losing this game. If you put your effort and concentration into playing to your potential to be the best that you can be, I don't care what the scoreboard says at the end of the game, in my book, we're gonna be winners. OK?"

Hickory wins and moves on to the state finals, where Jimmy Chitwood sinks a last-second shot to clinch the title, beating a big-city, African-American team in the movie's climax. In the film's final scene, the camera pans from a young boy shooting a basketball in the Hickory gym in the present day up the wall to focus in on a black-and-white photo of the championship team. It zooms in on Coach Dale and his boys, lingers a few seconds, and then fades to black. The last words of the film come in a Hackman voice-over: "I love you guys."

If our season were a film, the final reel would have ended in similar fashion, with Eric and Chris hoisting the championship trophy as Tyrell crouches below, freeze-framed as the credits begin to roll. It would be the climactic moment of a challenging season during which a group of kids from different backgrounds pulled together, overcame their shortcomings, learned something about each other and life, and triumphed against the odds.

The upset victory, though, means that our season isn't actually over—it earns the team an invitation to play in the AAU national championships in Orlando. That's when things really begin to change. For a few days, it seems like we will all get to go down to Florida in the summer, until Randy Finley announces that there will be tryouts for the national team. He begins to recruit more players—all of them white kids—to compete for slots (he'd begun that even before the championship, finding a tall white kid named Bryce to add height in the middle). Finley rounds up some of the best in the area to try out. It dawns on me—even before he calls my parents to tell them so—that I don't have a chance of making the Orlando-bound team.

It turns out to be the end of the original incarnation of the team. Tyrell, Myran, and Damian don't play on the new version either. Myran, like me, isn't good enough to make the traveling squad. Damian is a year younger than everyone else, so he's off. Tyrell, though, is slated to go to Florida. But before the championship game, he'd told Willie McClain that he was upset about his playing time, which had diminished during the season. With Finley's new recruits, it's sure to go down even more. As the team prepares for Florida, Tyrell just vanishes. Coach McClain will never really know what happened. "I remember talking to his dad to try and find him and get him interested," he says. Although McClain will sometimes later run into Tyrell around the Central Area, they never again have a real conversation.

The trip wouldn't have cost Tyrell anything. Sean's dad, the stockbroker, gets his firm to put up some money, and Finley raises some more cash. In Florida, the team goes to Disney World, hangs out around the swimming pool at the hotel, and visits Gatorland, where the players watch as workers throw chicken carcasses into the waiting jaws of hungry alligators. On the court, though, the team kind of resembles the chickens—they get blown out in the three games they play. The other teams, from places including North Carolina and Michigan, are so much bigger and faster that Willie McClain, who has always prided himself on his ability to give pep talks, is simply at a loss for words during one halftime. "We got bombed!" McClain says. "The talent gap was like this"—he holds his hands about two feet apart—"these cats were dunking the ball! Eighth-graders. There was a little five-nine guy, he jumped the highest. There was just no way."

Back in Seattle, Randy Finley starts a tutoring program for the black players, hiring a former Lakeside English teacher to give JT, Damian, and Willie Jr. remedial reading and writing lessons, assigning them books such as Hemingway's *Old Man and the Sea*. Finley and his sister, the host of a talk show on a Seattle television station, take the kids out for dinners at ethnic restaurants to try new types of food. Finley also starts making the rounds to private schools around Seattle, looking to get them to enroll my black teammates. He places JT in a North End Catholic high school and eventually gets Willie Jr. and Damian into Seattle Prep, one of the top private schools in Seattle. When he's in the Central Area, Finley sees Tyrell on the street a few times and stops to talk. Although Tyrell is always polite, he has no interest in Finley's ideas about private school.

Chris Dickinson enrolls at Lakeside as a ninth-grader in September 1986, a few months after our team ends its run (Randy Finley takes up Dino's cause and lobbies for him to get into the school; he starts the next year, as a sophomore). With Chris at power forward and Eric Hampton at guard, our freshman basketball team is the best in Seattle. Our big game that season comes against the Garfield team, on which Tyrell and Willie Jr. are the starting guards and the stars. The game is at Garfield, and Tyrell and Willie's friends all come to check it out. Unfortunately for the two of them, it isn't close. Lakeside controls the game. The defining moment comes when Willie Jr. drives to the hoop for a lay-in and Chris rejects his shot so hard that it smacks off the wall of the gym. A bunch of kids in the stands—friends of Willie and Tyrell's—hide their faces inside their jackets and run outside in mock embarrassment. After the game is over, we all shake hands and joke around on the court for a few minutes. Tyrell and Willie are embarrassed by their loss, but we have three more seasons to play in high school. We figure there'll be more games.

Most sports films end on a note of triumph, or perhaps run text over the final image, a few lines revealing what the players went on to do later. This tiny bit of information reassures the viewer that the lessons learned during the season were applied to life off the court.

There are alternative endings that don't make for feel-good cinema. After championship seasons, teams can fall apart. What worked one year does not work the next. Runaway egos throw the team chemistry out of balance. Key players get injured; others enter inexplicable slumps. Some athletes simply peak one year and never again regain their form. The championship moments are fleeting. The flip side is how fast a career in organized sports can simply come to an end, disappearing before a player even realizes exactly what happened. At that point, the lessons learned playing the game might not apply to life away from it at all.

On the court and the field, a good player is the center of attention, lauded for the skills he's developed since early childhood. The rules are clear, and the team plays for the same goal. The coach, if he's good, makes sure that everyone pulls in a mutual direction. It takes discipline to succeed, but the steps to success—running through drills, lifting weights, learning plays—are simple to grasp. It's a matter of applying yourself and having the necessary talent. The rewards can be quick and tangible.

Life away from the playing field also rewards discipline and hard work, but the rules can be difficult to learn, unevenly applied, and sometimes totally contradictory. As with grasping the nuances of basketball, it can take years to pick up the techniques and tricks necessary to succeed in school or land a decent job. Connections are sometimes more valuable than talent. The simple strictures of the game give way to a bewildering array of choices and options that require careful navigation. This transition out of sports can land on those who aren't prepared for it like a blind-side hit from a blitzing linebacker.

For Tyrell, Myran, and JT, it's all just about over at the time we win the championship. Myran has a little bit of stardom left. Right after our season, he moves up to the suburbs north of the city's boundaries to be with his mom while she stays in a residential drug-treatment program. While he's there, he plays running back on a local football team, the only black kid on the squad. The other players joke that they only need three plays: Myran to the right, Myran up the middle, and Myran to the left. Myran leads them to the league championship and is named MVP. He's so dominant that people who see him play—years later, I happen to run into people who remember Myran on the field—speculate that he'll go on to play college ball, maybe even at the University of Washington. But after his mom gets out of the program and they move back into the city, Myran never lasts long enough in one school to play sports at the high school level, something he will later bitterly regret.

JT is one of the only black kids in his class at the Catholic school where Randy Finley enrolls him. His laid-back demeanor wins him friends, but he struggles academically. At public school, he'd been placed in special classes and had tutors who worked with him on his reading. At his new school, the teachers make students read out loud, which JT dreads. "I knew my turn was coming and I didn't want to mess up and have all the kids looking at me like I was this dummy," he says. "My history teacher, after class we would practice the paragraph I was supposed to read."

JT joins the freshman basketball team and scrapes by in school. Then his mom, who has always been the center of his life, starts to use cocaine, and things quickly go south from there. Often when JT comes home, the shades are drawn and all the lights are off. There's no food in the house. People stop by at all hours, laughing and talking while JT tries to sleep. One guy passes out in the living room with a stack of money piled on his belly. JT stops going to school, runs away from home, and takes to the streets, sleeping in bus shelters when he can't find any other place. He never plays organized basketball again.

Tyrell plays freshman basketball at Garfield, but he does poorly in his classes. He starts to smoke weed every day after school. The plan among the players on Willie McClain's basketball team had always been that they would all go to Garfield and win four state basketball championships in a row. Randy Finley's placement of several guys in private schools nixes that idea. "When Tyrell stayed at Garfield, he had no backbone to lean on," Willie McClain Jr. says. "It was tough for him. And of course he went his way and everybody kind of broke apart from there, but that's how that worked." With abysmal grades and attendance,

Tyrell gets transferred to a last-chance alternative high school. He soon drops out. His basketball days over, he begins to get caught up in what's happening in the streets outside his front door.

Damian and Willie Jr. take the route rejected by Tyrell, enrolling at Seattle Prep after Randy Finley gets them admitted—Damian as a freshman, Will as a sophomore. Will burrows in and becomes a standout on the football, basketball, and baseball teams. "I took it as, I'm going to give them what they need"—athletic performance—"and they're going to give me what I need, and that's education," he says. The social scene is strange—when his black friends have parties, they all gather at a house, have some drinks, put on some music, and dance. It gets a little sweaty. The white kids at Prep, in contrast, like to go to places where they stand outside in the cold, drinking plastic cups of beer from a keg. As it is, Will finds he needs to focus on his classwork and doesn't socialize much. "Prep was tough enough," he says. "I didn't need any help in screwing myself up. Senior year they started talking about college and I was, 'Wow, I do have an opportunity to go to college.'" Fulfilling his dad's hopes when he agreed to coach our team, Will gets recruited by college football coaches and accepts a scholarship to play cornerback at Boise State University.

As the first in his family to go to college, he has high expectations. He is quickly disappointed. First, there's the issue of being a black athlete in Idaho, an overwhelmingly white state. "We never left campus," Will says. Will also finds that school is not expected to be a priority for scholarship athletes. "It's not education first," he says. "It's football first, get your studies in when you can." After he's spent two cold winters in Idaho, the head coach quits and a new one arrives with a slate of players recruited out of community colleges. The coach announces that everyone will have to compete for his position. "We'd busted our butts for two years, getting beat up by varsity, waiting for our turn," Will says. "I couldn't take it. College football is like a job. I just didn't want to do it." He calls his dad and tells him he's coming home. Upon his return, he will drift for several years, searching for direction.

Damian nearly flunks out in his first year at Seattle Prep. He only gets a reprieve after his mom and Randy Finley attend an emergency meeting with the school administration. Damian—who, like Willie Jr., becomes a star on the basketball team—finds the culture at Prep "night and day" from his South Seattle middle school. "You had kids coming to school in drop-top BMWs with heated seats, parents expecting them to take over the business," he says. When he gets his first homework assignment, he simply ignores it. He's amazed the next day to find that he's the only kid who didn't complete it. "You're taught to be on time," he says. "You're taught to be professional."

The years that Damian and Will attend the school are difficult ones for the few African-American kids enrolled there; though the school has started to recruit more black students, many of them simply drop out after a while. One black classmate tells Damian, "I just can't do it." One day, when Damian passes a classmate in the hall, he tries to make a friendly joke about the kid being on the computer all the time. The kid responds by muttering "nigger" under his breath. Damian tries to look past the race difference, but the money gap is persistent. Damian and a few other African-American students begin to steal cash from wallets left in the locker room during sports practices. "We had lookouts and everything, we had it all set up," he says. "That's how we were eating during the week, because there's no free lunch at Seattle Prep. I guess that we felt that their parents had money, so it's not a big deal." Though his performance at school has its ups and downs, his mom—always aware of the limitations she feels due to her own lack of education—steadily encourages him to stick it out. Damian makes it to graduation.

Eric Hampton's fortunes begin to change at Lakeside during his freshman year, when Randy Finley helps to recruit a white kid, another point guard, to the school. The kid plays a textbook game of crisp passes and pretty jump shots. Unlike the laconic Eric, he is vocal, running around the court to pump his teammates up. Lakeside's varsity basketball coach leaves Eric on the freshman team and moves the other kid up to the junior varsity squad, signaling that Eric will be the backup for the next four years.

Football is what finally does it. Junior year, the varsity coach has Eric split time at safety with a kid who is nowhere near as good as he is. Eric figures it's a case of a rich white kid getting preferential treatment, and it gnaws at him. "I lost my confidence," Eric says. "I felt I was treated better at Lakeside than some of the other black students because I was an athlete. That's what everybody knew me as. That's why everybody liked me." After the season he drops out of Lakeside and enrolls at a public school in the South End. He plays basketball his senior year, but he never gets back to the level he'd been at a few years earlier.

After graduation, Eric attends the University of Washington for a few quarters but makes a mistake when he drops a class and falls below the minimum number of credits the university requires to maintain financial aid. He loses his aid package but doesn't want to tell his dad about it. As Eric tries to sort out what to do next, Randy Finley reappears and helps him and Damian get scholarships to play for a community college about thirty minutes up the freeway from Seattle. They commute together every day in Damian's mom's Hyundai. Neither of them is happy with the situation, playing basketball way out the middle of nowhere. Eric soon decides it isn't for him and quits the team. He gets a job driving a shuttle van in Seattle and eventually reenrolls at the University of Washington. Though Eric had showed as much promise as anyone on our team when we were in the eighth grade, his sports career never really blossomed. After he returns to the University of Washington, he focuses on his studies and starts to get on with his life.

Damian doesn't last long at community college, either. One day in the locker room before basketball practice, a white teammate accuses him of using the phone in his apartment to make long-distance calls. Damian tells him he didn't do it—he had no reason to be calling anyone—but the guy keeps on him. Damian snaps. He leaves the locker room, hurries out to the parking lot, and grabs a baseball bat from the trunk of his car. When he returns, the guy sees him and bends over to protect himself. Damian, who is a broad-shouldered, athletic, and powerful man, slams the bat into his back once and then feels the rage dissipate. "After I hit him, I was like, 'Damn, what am I doing?'" he says. Before things can get any worse, their teammates jump in and break it up. Damian gets kicked off the team.

The outburst hints at underlying pressures Damian is feeling. But showing a remarkable ability for pulling opportunity out of what could be disaster, Damian discovers that the academic program he followed at Seattle Prep, a Catholic school, has gained him automatic admission to Seattle University, a Jesuit school on the western edge of the Central Area. Damian enrolls, walks on to the basketball team, becomes the starting shooting guard, and lands a scholarship. He plays for two seasons, but his life, which for several years has bridged a gulf between South Seattle and his attendance at elite schools, begins to unravel. When his grades fall below the eligibility level, the basketball coach cuts him loose. Damian is barely hanging on. Without a drastic change of direction, he's heading toward flunking out.

In *Power at Play*, a book based on interviews with men who had competed in organized sports, sociologist Michael Messner examines what boys get from athletics and how they feel when their careers in competitive team sports end. The book is based on Messner's interviews with white, black, and Latino athletes from a range of income levels. He finds a lot of similarities among the men: They report that as boys they got into sports with the encouragement of older men, such as brothers and uncles, but generally used athletics to forge emotional connections with their dads; many of them say that sports were the only area where their fathers entered their lives with enthusiasm, and playing and being good at sports became a way to keep the bond that had been made when they were little boys.

Across the board, boys who were very involved with sports tended to be shy and socially uncomfortable. The men tell Messner that sports offered them a way to connect, that their teams became "family," places where they could find acceptance. "The most important thing was being out there with the rest of the guys—being friends," one man says. The clearly defined rules and structure of athletics allowed the boys to form attachments with others, but within boundaries that let them retain a bit of distance and separation. Boys who could play sports well found they got attention for it, which drove them harder to excel. Wearing the uniform and being out on the field, where people would watch and talk about them, felt good. But even though the main competition was against other teams, there was always rivalry among teammates to be the best— the men noted that if another teammate beat them out for playing time, the coach would bench them and they'd lose the attention they had worked to gain.

A stark divergence emerges among the men when the time comes to leave organized sports. Messner finds that the men from poor and working-class families tend to describe their sports experiences in the context of the communities in which they lived—lacking equipment at home, they often had grown up playing in public parks, so were known as athletes. That identity gave them a "cloak" to avoid other problems. As long as a kid was identified as a basketball or football player, gangs and other forms of trouble gave him a pass.

The middle-class boys in the study realized much sooner than the poorer ones that their sports careers were going to end. In response, they began to shift their interests to other pursuits. Sports for them was a way to "bolster" their identities, not the main part of their lives. When the time came, they transitioned into other options, such as college and careers. Poor and working-class boys did not. Commenting on the men in his interview study, Messner writes, "A few athletes from lower-class backgrounds . . . do manage to take advantage of the opportunities afforded them through athletic scholarships and get a college degree that moves them into a profession. The majority of athletes from lower-class backgrounds, however, end up with a difficult, sometimes traumatic period of disengagement, which is commonly characterized by identity crises, interpersonal problems and financial instability."

While every player on our team reacts differently to the end of his time in organized sports, Messner's conclusions fit us pretty well. The transition, overall, is much smoother for the players from Lakeside.

Sean goes to college in Washington, D.C., at Georgetown, which is known for the bruising basketball teams under its famous black coach, John Thompson. Even though he's grown to about six-foot-eight, there's no way Sean is going to make the team. "I wasn't fast enough, wasn't strong enough, wasn't good enough. Couldn't shoot, couldn't jump," he says with a laugh. He redirects his energy toward politics, interning first for a congressman from the suburbs of Seattle and later for Republican senator Bob Dole of Kansas. "It was kind of turn you loose and open letters and write mail to constituents and do little research projects here and there," Sean says. "Internships are unglamorous and sort of tedious, but I loved it."

After he gains admission to Lakeside in tenth grade, Dino plays on the basketball team but begins to develop other interests. In the summer, he works downtown at his family's diner. After their shifts end, he and his dad head down to a racetrack south of Seattle, where Dino finds an interest in handicapping the horses and figuring out which one has the edge. At Lakeside he discovers the *Economist* magazine and begins to learn about the global financial system. He scours the stock charts in the newspaper, thinking about how he can handicap individual companies. "I really got excited about understanding different businesses and what makes this world go, what makes the economy go," he says.

Chris Dickinson, already tall and muscular when he joined our team in eighth grade, becomes a star football and basketball player at Lakeside. He enrolls at Princeton, where he joins the football team, playing tight end. During his sophomore season he suffers a string of injuries, including a torn hamstring and several ankle sprains. He also decides to take the next year off and come back to Seattle to think things over.

That year, he takes an internship with the Seattle SuperSonics basketball team, helping with game operations, doing things like making sure the cheerleaders have their pom-poms. "It was an utter waste of time other than helping me understand what I didn't want to do," Chris says. He also begins to seriously rethink the role of athletics and competition in his life. He joins a conversation group for young men called "Heart of the Athlete," founded by a former Olympic track-and-field competitor. "His whole idea was to think about athletics not as an end in itself but a way to investigate together, in the context of athletics, about what it means to be a man," Chris says. "It was about talking about your family and you and your insecurities, it wasn't really about sports." Through that group, Chris meets a man who teaches courses on Native American spirituality—every few weeks, he leads groups into the woods, where they perform sweat-lodge rituals, tie prayer beads, and do vision cries. Chris begins to participate in the retreats. "I think I was just searching on a lot of different levels," he says.

When Chris returns to Princeton the next year, he rejoins the football team. In a big preseason scrimmage, he drops a pass. Normally, he would beat himself up about it. It surprises him when he finds that he just doesn't care. He quits the team the next day. "I just realized I just didn't like it," he says. "To spend five hours a day doing something that you don't even like when you have so much opportunity to engage in other things seemed foolish."

For Maitland, there has always been a gulf between his enjoyment of basketball and his dad's passion for it. "I think it's ridiculous the way you have to focus on playing basketball in high school. I had to play fall league, had to play summer league," he says. "At the time, I didn't like doing all of that stuff, but I wasn't really going to complain about it either." When Maitland is in tenth grade, Randy moves the family to

France for a year to live in a town in the Alps. When they return, Randy gets in a feud—the exact basis of the argument is still unclear—with Lakeside's head basketball coach. The next year, Maitland leaves Lakeside to go to a smaller private school, where the pressure athletically and academically is not so intense. After graduation, Maitland heads to college. Now that he's in charge of his own life, he is finished with organized sports.

Randy Finley, in the meantime, also goes through several changes. After almost twenty years, he sells his theaters in 1986 and finds himself out of the movie business. The following year, he wins the antitrust case he'd filed against several other theater chains that charged them with colluding to secure the rights to lucrative first-run movies. He walks away with a $900,000 settlement.

After helping Damian, Willie Jr., JT, and another kid, named Anthony Simmons, get into private schools, Finley starts to get calls from other African-American parents. "It was one of the biggest shocks of my life," Finley says. "I kept getting approached by parents who said, 'Mr. Finley, we know you helped these kids. I've got a kid. Can you help mine?' "

With so many people asking for his assistance, Finley feels compelled to do something. "I took this on," he says. "I didn't just want to be a rich guy. I had several million dollars at that point. I didn't want to just sit on it and live a life of luxury." Over the next few years he helps seventeen African-American kids—boys and girls, athletes and nonathletes—get into private schools. This makes a big difference in the life of Willie McClain Sr.—he observes Randy Finley in action and essentially learns how to work the system himself. In time, McClain will get his younger sons into private schools, and even coach the basketball team at one of Seattle's most exclusive prep schools.

Randy Finley, in the meantime, begins to realize the enormity of what he has taken on. The toll of driving around and lobbying private school administrators as well as dealing with the suspicions of people in the Central Area who ask why he is taking the good basketball players out of Garfield, adds up. Beyond that, many of the kids he helps get into private schools have severe struggles once they are there. Finley, who had been a poor student himself, had thought that some tutoring would be enough, but he discovers that many of the kids have little foundation for the academic and social challenges posed by private schools. Keeping track of the kids is an all-consuming job. "I remember screwing around with Damian, chasing a fifteen-year-old kid," he says. "I didn't want to do it full time." In 1990, Finley buys a small winery outside of Belling-ham, near the Canadian border, and throws his energies into running it. Over time, the kids he's helped get into private schools stop calling. He sometimes makes the two-hour drive down to attend Seattle University basketball games, hoping to see Damian, but never finds him. "I always looked," he says.

I don't last very long at Lakeside after our team disbands. In the eighth and ninth grades, I start to become more popular, getting invited to parties and asked to dance by the "cool" girls at school dances. But I seem to be getting more arrogant and obnoxious in the process. The book-reading dork who entered the school in fifth grade is getting eclipsed. Halfway into my freshman year I tell my parents I want to take a "year off." They agree to let me go with the stipulation that I'll return for junior year. I never do.

So I enroll at public school in the suburbs north of Seattle and dis-cover its particular quirks: the electronic bell noise that sounds at the end of every period; pledging allegiance to the flag; home economics classes; cheerleaders; acid-washed jeans; auto shop; military recruiters at school; and guys who actually join the army. At times over the next few years, I miss the sense of superiority I derived from attending an elite private school. Mostly, though, I feel relieved.

Despite playing nearly every day and working out in special shoes designed to increase your vertical leap—they have a platform under the ball of the foot that keeps your heel off the ground, which is supposed to strengthen your calf muscles—I am cut from the basketball team in tenth grade. I've had the bad luck of transferring out of Lakeside into a public high school with one of the best basketball programs in the state.

The only sport I have any talent for is football, where pure effort can substitute somewhat for a lack in athletic ability. At five-foot-ten and 185 pounds, I find that I can take down players bigger than myself simply by making them think I'm more unhinged. Our head coach catches on to this trait. In my senior year, he begins to use me in an "inspirational" drill meant to fire up our lackluster team, having me line up against a six-foot-five, 260-pound teammate who will go on to receive a scholar-ship to play defensive line at the University of Georgia.

In the drill, my teammate carries the ball through one of three alleys demarcated by tackling dummies. My job is to stop him. The only way to do it is to lower my head and lunge at his knees. Once, I make the mistake of tackling him high, my helmet meeting his chest. We fall over, my behemoth teammate pushing me backward as he topples. I grab on like one of those stuffed animals with suction cups on its hands and feet that people stick to their car windows. He pancakes me, expelling every last bit of oxygen from my lungs. As I shakily climb to my feet, our coach applauds: "Did you see that, men? Now that's heart!"

I especially seek the approval of Coach Stubbs, our linebacker coach, a squat man, totally bald except for a fringe around his head. In his spare time he's a volunteer firefighter, and he often wears the jacket from his department. He communicates in grunts and seldom gives praise. It's as if he's studied football movies and decided to embody the Platonic ideal of the taciturn, tough coach. The only time he ever compliments me comes at the end of my senior season, when he says, "You really found your manhood this year."

A desire for that kind of approbation leads me to play football at the small college I attend in Los Angeles. It's a terrible mistake. I quickly realize that running around in the sun and smog is not fun. I don't like many of my teammates, either. Midway into the season, a few of them break into the dorm room of a guy who has written an article in the student newspaper mocking macho behavior on campus—it is clearly aimed at certain elements of the football team—and piss on his stereo. In the locker room, they laugh about how they had gotten the "faggot." Another football player has some teammates hide out on his balcony and spy through the sliding glass door while he has sex with his girlfriend. It's like James Naismith's nightmare: The lessons we're learning on the field about aggression and knocking the crap out of people are crossing over into life off of it.

The following spring, Coach Stubbs, who also was the head coach of the baseball team at my high school, hangs himself in the team's equipment shed. He is thirty-five. There is no note or explanation.

The suicide is an utter shock. I become more unsettled when I read the account in the newspaper. Our head coach calls Coach Stubbs a "mystery guy." "I don't know a thing about his family," he says. "I don't know a thing about his personal life." It strikes me that I had relied on these men for guidance, but they knew nothing about each other, much less about me. I realize I've been looking for meaning in an area—and from men—that can't supply it. I know I will never play football again. As when Coach McClain ended his sports career twenty years earlier, it is, for me, the start of a transition will leave me knocking about for a new identity for years to come.

That August, as I'm home after my freshman year in college, I pick up the *Seattle Times* off my parents' doorstep. The news splashed across the top half of the front page tells of the hastening decline of the Soviet Union. My eye scans down. In bottom left corner a headline reads, WHAT WENT WRONG? TYRELL JOHNSON WAS YOUNG, BLACK, MALE—AND MURDERED.

I sit down and try to comprehend what I'm reading: "On a brilliant, hot summer day recently, [Tyrell] Johnson was buried. . . . His body had been found, wrapped in a bedspread, in a wooden ditch in Rainier Valley."

Tyrell had been shot in the back of the head. Both of his legs had been dismembered. They were not found with the body.

The newspaper illustrates the article with a photo of Tyrell in our old yellow uniform. He's down on one knee, the number 24 on his chest, a grin running across his face. The rest of us have been cropped out.

Instead of fading out on a black-and-white photo of the 1952 Indiana state champions, my version of *Hoosiers* ended with Coach Dale swinging from the rafters and Jimmy Chitwood hacked up in a ditch.

· · ·

Just as every individual on our team was going through his own changes, Seattle was transforming in ways that would eventually affect all of us. These shifts began to gain speed in 1986, the same time we were out on the court together.

Toward the end of March that year, one of my Lakeside classmates brags in the locker room after gym class about how his dad had gotten in on the initial public offering of Microsoft stock. On its first day, the shares shot from $21 to nearly $28. "You could only get a good price on it if you had a connection," my always-annoying classmate announces to the rest of us as we change out of our gym clothes. "My dad's broker got him some because he's such a good client. It's too late to buy it now, though," he assures us.

Standing there in my underwear, all I know about Microsoft is that

SOUTH EDITION
Where teen moms will find refuge
Northwest, C1

SEAHAWKS RELEASE JOHNSON, SKANSI
Sports, F1

STEVENS MAKES HIS MARK
1st win in Mile comes aboard Louis Cyphre
Sports, F1

TUTE TICKET PAYS

TRACKING DOWN DIABETES
Scientists search for clues in genes
Discovery, E1

The Seattle Times

WASHINGTON'S LARGEST NEWSPAPER • COPYRIGHT © 1991, SEATTLE TIMES COMPANY

35¢
44 pages

MONDAY
August 26, 1991

18 days adrift in capsized sailboat

2 B.C. men rescued off Vancouver Island

Associated Press

VICTORIA, B.C. — Two boaters said prayer and efficient organization helped them survive 18 days at sea in a capsized sailboat.

"When the ship came along we were reading the Bible. That's the only book we had," said Ian Evans, 20, a pilot from Vancouver.

The pages were all glued together and we had to take a knife and try and scrape them apart. It gave us something to do. It kept our spirits up," he said.

Evans and his 59-year-old companion John Mason, a Nanaimo marine biologist, were rescued Saturday by a Philippine freighter. They were released yesterday from a Nanaimo hospital.

The pair set out Aug. 5 in their 30-foot trysail sailboat Windspeed from the Queen Charlotte Islands, southbound for Nanaimo.

One day out found them in a ferocious storm. For hours the Windspeed rode 40-foot waves, until the vessel's sea anchor gave out and a wave caught the ship broadside, flipping it over.

The boat remained capsized for the entire ordeal — with the men and Evans' 3-year-old terrier Brandy inside. They built a small wooden sleeping platform above the water level.

On the third day they put a hatch in the keel and peered out. They counted their supplies, began rationing their 12 gallons of water.

Then they started making their capsized hull as visible as possible, draping it with flags and a sheet. They even built a makeshift radar deflector out of empty tin cans.

The pair passed the hours reading their lone book and talking.

"We talked about all sorts of things — our life as children, our relationship with parents and relatives, our love lives. We got to know each other very well," Mason said.

The two men joked about the possibility of putting Brandy on the menu if things became rough.

"We were talking about it, and I said, 'Gee John, I hope it doesn't get to that point,'" Evans said, laughing.

Evans said they saw a freighter on the morning of the sixth day "and that's when I found out our flares were no good."

"We didn't see one for about another week," he said. On day 18 they managed to attract the attention of the Philippine vessel.

AFTER THE COUP

Remaking a nation

Gorbachev calls for elections

Times news services

MOSCOW — Soviet President Mikhail Gorbachev called today for early presidential and parliamentary elections and indicated new openness to giving breakaway Soviet republics their freedom.

In a speech before the Supreme Soviet, the nation's governing body, he admitted a share of the blame for last week's coup and said the Union Treaty should be signed as soon as possible.

The treaty will give more autonomy to Soviet republics. Conservatives so feared it would reduce Soviet power in the world that they attempted to overthrow Gorbachev last week one day before the signing was scheduled.

"Straight after signing the Union Treaty we should start the election campaign for all union organs, including the president," he said.

While Gorbachev was elected president last year by the Supreme Soviet — which in turn was chosen by the 2,250-member Congress of People's Deputies — he has been expected that his successor will be elected directly by the people.

Gorbachev said all 15 republics should have a choice on whether they remain in the union.

"One should take the position toward the republics who do not sign the treaty — they should be given the right of independent choice," he said. "After the signing of the Union Treaty we must start at once businesslike negotiations with those who want to leave the union."

Gorbachev dropped his past

Please see SOVIET on A 5

A changing Soviet Union: what it might become

Boris Yeltsin's plan would allow the independence of six republics: the Baltic states of Latvia, Lithuania and Estonia as well as Armenia, Georgia and Moldavia. Byelorussia and the Ukraine, two republics Yeltsin hopes to keep in a union, have also declared independence. But their declarations, as well as that of Moldavia, could be negotiating positions and could be altered or rescinded if the new union is to his liking.

Probable member states of the new union

Probable independent states

Could go either way

Yeltsin's vision of a new union

by Thom Shanker and Howard Witt
Chicago Tribune

MOSCOW — Continuing his grab for power, Russian President Boris Yeltsin has proposed a radical restructuring of the Soviet Union that would minimize the role of Soviet President Mikhail Gorbachev and reduce the nation to a loose confederation of nine republics.

Yeltsin yesterday outlined his vision of a new Soviet Union to replace a Communist nation that is rapidly dissolving along with the party that controlled it for the last 74 years.

Yeltsin's concept accepts the independence of six of the existing 15 republics — Lithuania, Latvia, Estonia, Armenia, Georgia and Moldavia.

His vision might not be possible without the membership of Ukraine, which declared its sovereignty Saturday. Byelorussia declared its sovereignty yesterday.

However, decisions taken by those two republics appear to be negotiating positions that could be altered or rescinded if the terms of union are approved by their populations.

The would confederation would also include Russia, the dominant republic with three-quarters of the nation's territory.

Yeltsin's concept is the charismatic leader's proposal for independence in the Baltics — Lithuania, Latvia and Estonia — will undoubtedly be well received in the West. Although uneasy over the turmoil that might be created by the break-up of the

Please see YELTSIN on A 3

AZERBAIJAN
Population 6.5 million
Area 33,400 sq km miles
Resources Oil, iron ore, cotton
Chief industry Oil, gas, iron and barium ore, synthetic rubber, electrical and chemical equipment

ARMENIA
Population 3.5 million
Area 39,800 square miles
Resources Copper ore, aluminum, molybdenum
Chief industry Machine building

BYELORUSSIA
Population 10.2 million
Area 80,200 square miles
Resources Potash, peat
Chief industry Machinery, vehicles, tools, chemicals, steel, cement, textiles, paper, glass
Main crops Grain, flax, potatoes, sugar beets

ESTONIA
Population 1.6 million
Area 17,400 square miles
Resources Oil shale, phosphorite
Chief industry Textiles, shipbuilding, electrical and machinery equipment

GEORGIA
Population 5.4 million
Area 26,900 square miles
Resources Manganese ore, coal, natural gas, oil
Chief industries Fuel, textiles, iron, steel

KAZAKHSTAN
Population 16.5 million
Area 1,048,300 square miles
Resources Coal, oil, iron ore, copper, bauxite
Chief industry Oil, coal, iron, chrome ore, uranium, lead, zinc
Chief crops Grain

KIRGHIZIA
Population 4.2 million
Area 76,600 square miles
Resources Coal, mercury
Chief industries Cloth and horse bread
Chief crops Cotton, tobacco, sugar beet

LATVIA
Population 2.7 million
Area 24,700 square miles
Resources Peat
Chief industry Main producer of electric railway passenger cars, telephone equipment

LITHUANIA
Population 3.7 million
Area 25,200 square miles
Resources Peat
Chief industry Cutting, textiles, food, electronics equipment

MOLDAVIA
Population 4.3 million
Area 13,100 square miles
Main crops Grains, fruits, vegetables, tobacco
Chief industries Textiles, food, electrical equipment

RUSSIA
Population 148 million
Area 6.6 million square miles
Resources Coal, oil, iron, gold, silver
Chief industry Fish, canning

TADZHIKISTAN
Population 5.1 million
Area 54,000 square miles
Chief industry Farming, cattle breeding, mining, metalworking
Chief crops Cotton, grain, rice, fruits

TURKMENISTAN
Population 3.5 million
Area 188,400 square miles
Resources Oil, natural gas
Chief industry Oil, gas, chemical, textile, food

UKRAINE
Population 51.8 million
Area 233,100 square miles
Resources Coal, iron, manganese, natural gas
Chief industries Metals, machinery, sugar beets
Chief crops Grain, sugar beets

UZBEKISTAN
Population 19.9 million
Area 172,700 square miles
Resources Oil, natural gas, coal, copper
Chief industries Cotton, textiles, silk, hemp, rope, cement
Main crops Cotton, rice, silk, fruit
Resources Coal, sulphur, copper, oil

Few top jobs: Feminist group says old-boy network to blame

Associated Press

WASHINGTON — Less than 3 percent of the top jobs in Fortune 500 companies belonged to women in 1990, and that's partly because of an enduring old-boy network, says the feminist group that released the study.

But Peter Eide, manager of labor law for the U.S. Chamber of Commerce, says it's a "pipeline issue." Women and minorities didn't enter the business world in large numbers until the 1970s, he says, and they now have the experience to be in line for mid-level positions and are being given

higher-level positions all the time.

Of the 6,502 jobs at the vice presidential and higher level in the nation's largest corporations, only 175, or 2.6 percent, were held by women, said the study by the Feminist Majority Foundation. The report was based on 1990 figures compiled by a researcher at the University of Southern California.

"At the current rate of increase in executive women, it will take until the year 2466 — over 450 years — to reach equality with executive men," said Eleanor Smeal, the former president of the National Organization for Women, who now heads the Feminist Majority, a Washington-area research and advocacy organization.

The study found that women hold 40 percent of all management and administrative positions, up 24 percent in 1976. Only five women held the chief executive officer position at Fortune 500 companies last year.

What went wrong?

Tyrell Johnson was young, black, male — and murdered

by Elouise Schumacher
Times staff reporter

Their friendship had all the makings of a clichéd movie script: rich, white suburban kid befriends needy, black inner-city youth.

Only this time there's no happy ending.

It began when John Doces' family in Yarrow Point sponsored a Christmas celebration for Tyrell Johnson and his family in the Central Area through a community program. The boys, then 13, became buddies, then

Now Doces grieves for his friend, wondering if there might have been anything he could have done to alter the path of Johnson's life. Doces' conclusion?

"If Tyrell had had my life, he'd be in the same place I am if not better," says Doces. "I'm positive of that. It's his circumstances and where he grew up that caused his death."

Doces uses the analogy of traveling down a highway to contrast the two lives. For Doces, a doctor's kid, the exits leading to failure are few and far between, with numerous re-en-

WEATHER
Increasing clouds tonight with a chance of showers. Mostly cloudy tomorrow with a chance of showers. Highs, upper 60s; lows, lower 50s.
Details, F 7

Medical insurer stops referring to 3 area hospitals

Qual-Med rejected in attempts to force deep cuts in charges

by Bob Ortega
Times South bureau

RENTON — Qual-Med Inc., which operates one of Washington's largest health-care plans, has stopped referring its members to three of the biggest hospitals in the Seattle area.

All three — Valley Medical Center in Renton, Swedish Hospital Medical Center in Seattle and Overlake Hospital Medical Center in Bellevue — had rejected the company's demand for deep discounts on medical rates.

Qual-Med is engaged in a pitched battle with hospitals throughout Puget Sound over medical charges. It's a battle the company has won in Denver, San Francisco and other cities, where Qual-Med slashes its members to certain hospitals in exchange for special discounts.

But those tactics haven't worked as well here, according to some observers, because Seattle-area Qual-Med's $0,000,000-plus hospitals didn't need the company enough muscle to get its way.

Qual-Med contracts with 25 Washington hospitals, including seven in King County and Stevens Memorial Hospital in Snohomish County. It had contracted with Valley, Swedish and Overlake since 1985.

Insurers often negotiate small discounts from hospitals in exchange for their business, but Qual-

---

What went wrong?

Tyrell Johnson was young, black, male — and murdered

by Elouise Schumacher
Times staff reporter

Their friendship had all the makings of a clichéd movie script: rich, white suburban kid befriends needy, black inner-city youth.

Only this time there's no happy ending.

It began when John Doces' family in Yarrow Point sponsored a Christmas celebration for Tyrell Johnson and his family in the Central Area through a community program. The boys, then 13, became buddies, sharing an attraction to sports, girls and hanging out. Cultural differences seemed to diminish as they spent more time together.

But as the two grew into adulthood, the roads to their futures began to diverge. Doces and his friends at Bellevue High School talked about attending college; Johnson and his friends spoke of gangs and the boredom of the schooling they'd left behind.

This summer, 19-year-old Doces lives in a fraternity house at the University of Washington, waiting to begin his sophomore year of college.

On a brilliant, hot summer day recently, Johnson was buried. His body had been found, wrapped in a bedspread, in a wooded ditch in Rainier Valley on Aug. 10. His killer shot Johnson once in the head, cut off his legs and tried to sever one arm. His legs are still missing.

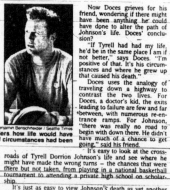

John Doces, right, wonders how life would have been for Tyrell Johnson if circumstances had been different.

Benjamin Benschneider / Seattle Times

Now Doces grieves for his friend, wondering if there might have been anything he could have done to alter the path of Johnson's life. Doces' conclusion?

"If Tyrell had had my life, he'd be in the same place I am if not better," says Doces. "I'm positive of that. It's his circumstances and where he grew up that caused his death."

Doces uses the analogy of traveling down a highway to contrast the two lives. For Doces, a doctor's kid, the exits leading to failure are few and far between, with numerous re-entrance ramps. For Johnson, "there was really no road to begin with down there. He didn't have much of a chance to get going," said his friend.

It's easy to look at the crossroads of Tyrell Dorrion Johnson's life and see where he might have made the wrong turns — the chances that were there but not taken, from playing in a national basketball tournament to attending a private high school on scholarship.

It's just as easy to view Johnson's death as yet another mark on the tally of young African-American men who die violently. The statistics are staggering: Violence is the No. 1 cause of death for black males between the ages of 15 and

Please see TEEN on A 4

the founders had gone to our school and that the company has something to do with computers. Its sudden stock-market success seems like a total fluke—this is Seattle, after all. For decades, the local economy has fluctuated with the fortunes of Boeing, which employs tens of thousands of people, and creates related jobs for tens of thousands more. Everyone knows that when things go bad in the airplane business, the whole region takes a dive.

In the 1970s and 1980s, the city had something of a civic inferiority complex. It seemed like a great place to live—clean, polite, near the water and the mountains—but the national media always treated Seattle like a charming backwater full of loggers and rain-loving eccentrics. Underneath it all, there was a nagging doubt—if we're so great, shouldn't someone else recognize it?

By the end of the 1980s, that begins to change. Unbeknownst to the average person living there, Seattle has developed what a marketing consultant would call an "aesthetic." Microsoft, a software giant that will create thousands of millionaires through its stock options, drives the economic side. The company also draws other tech start-ups to open in its shadow, just as Boeing had once done with firms that manufactured parts for its airplanes.

Other changes are incubating. In 1987, a businessman named Howard Shultz buys a local chain of eleven coffee shops, Starbucks, with the intention of building a national empire of espresso bars. In the late 1980s, REI (Recreational Equipment, Inc.), a Seattle outdoor clothing and equipment store founded in 1938, begins to open several new locations across the country every year, playing up its Northwest roots in its advertising. In 1988, Kurt Cobain, an angst-ridden musician from a logging town a hundred miles southwest of Seattle, forms a new band and soon signs a deal with an independent Seattle record label named Sub Pop. Nirvana will be promoted with several more of the label's bands, which mix and match portions of Black Sabbath, punk rock, alienation, and masculine bravado with Northwest clothing style. All of these things—the coffee, the outdoor fixation, the music scene—simmer for years before springing into national attention in the early 1990s. Suddenly the life of an "average" Seattleite—if you go by the media depictions, a white guy who grabs a cup of Starbucks on the way to hike on Mount Rainier on Saturday morning, and then comes back to drink microbrews and catch a Mudhoney show that night—becomes cool. In

October 1993, Pearl Jam's Eddie Vedder—face distorted in an anguished howl—makes the cover of *Time* magazine with the headline, ALL THE RAGE: ANGRY YOUNG ROCKERS LIKE PEARL JAM GIVE VOICE TO THE PASSIONS AND FEARS OF A GENERATION. That signals the high point of grunge's prominence; Kurt Cobain's suicide the following year marks its end.

The music, though, is only one aspect of a fundamental change. Seattle has long been a city with a large number of college graduates. In the 1990s, though, the percentage of adult Seattle residents holding bachelor's degrees will jump from 38 percent to an astonishing 47 percent, 8 points higher than Washington, D.C., and nearly 11 points higher than Boston (the national average of adults with a bachelor's degree for the country's one hundred largest cities in 2000 was 24 percent). While median household income rises 6.5 percent, to $45,700, rents go up 10 percent and home prices almost 35 percent. This is driven, in large part, by the proliferation of tech work. According to one estimate, the number of technology-related jobs in the Puget Sound area—which includes Seattle and the eastern suburbs that house Microsoft—shoots up between 1995 and 2000 from 93,400 to 146,200.

Seattle's next national cover boy, after Eddie Vedder, turns out to be East Coast journalist Michael Kinsley, who moves west to launch the Internet magazine *Slate* for Microsoft. Kinsley fronts *Newsweek* in May 1996, looking goofy in yellow raingear (Seattle natives never carry umbrellas or wear rain slickers—the proper protection is a brightly colored Gore-Tex jacket). The headline reads, SWIMMING TO SEATTLE: EVERYBODY ELSE IS MOVING THERE. SHOULD YOU?

Newsweek hails Seattle as a leader of the "postindustrial" economy and highlights, among other things, the locals' love of gourmet food such as lavender-fried quail, the breathtaking politeness (drivers actually stop at yellow lights!), the tech jobs, the mountains, and work habits so relaxed that even lawyers take it easy. In *Newsweek*'s description, the city becomes a spiritual Yukon for New Age seekers, drifters, slackers, and fortune hunters, drawing "rootless youths seeking alienation beneath Seattle's brooding skies" and "middle-aged strivers betting that Microsoft can create one more millionaire." According to the magazine, "Even those constrained to spend the 21st century in some less-favored city will inevitably feel the tug of Seattle's gloom."

You could be forgiven for envisioning some kind of a white, upper-middle-class paradise where the only problems were deciding what software company to work for and—as anyone who watches *Frasier*, which debuted in 1993, could tell you—how many shots of espresso you want in your *macchiato*. The magazine notes that Seattle elected a black mayor in 1989—the genial Norm Rice—and that the city "is generally progressive on racial matters."

In 1998, the comedian Dave Chappelle summed up the popular image of race in Seattle on an episode of HBO's *The Larry Sanders Show*, in which Chappelle, playing himself, meets with a writer and some television network executives about a possible show. The writer wants to set it in Seattle. After the comedian objects, the show is relocated to Baltimore. As Chappelle tells the writer, "That whole Seattle thing? I don't think I ever met a brother from Seattle in my life. I don't know if that's the place where we would really, really live."

. . .

After 1990, I observe most of the changes taking place in Seattle from a distance. At about age twelve, I became convinced that the city was incredibly dull and real life was elsewhere. I go to college in Los Angeles, which, at least until I arrive, seems very glamorous.

As graduation nears and my classmates work to line up jobs with consulting firms or slots in law school, I have no idea what I want to do. I end up driving back to Seattle, where I take the same job I had through college—installing washers and dryers in laundry rooms for my dad's company. That summer, my parents begin a separation that eventually leads to divorce. I live with several musicians in a ramshackle house just north of the Central Area and begin to write articles for local newspapers. Mostly, though, I operate at half power, struggling to get out of bed most days. My interest in sports has evaporated—I don't want to watch or play them.

What I do want is to get as far away from the Northwest as I can. Just as the first shoots of dotcom mania are beginning to burst forth in Seattle, I move to Budapest, Hungary. I find that, in post-Communist Eastern Europe, just about any native English-speaker with even the barest modicum of competence can do well. Shortly after arriving in the country, I start to work at the Ministry of Defense, teaching Hungarian military officers conversational English. I soon land a job as an editor at an English-language business newspaper owned by American expatriates when my predecessor goes missing after a booze bender.

The big stories in Hungary, in the years after the end of the Soviet Union, are globalization and privatization. During socialism, each Eastern European country had maintained factories to produce necessities such as steel and iron instead of importing. The system was inefficient, but it guaranteed employment, even if your job was nothing more than sitting around and stamping papers in triplicate. After 1990, the state either shut down or sold off these relics of the old system. Western corporations such as General Electric relocated factories to Hungary, where they could take advantage of lower labor costs. This ushers in an immense social shift. People suited to the new system—the educated, those who speak English—see their standards of living increase enormously. People who are not prepared for these changes lose their jobs and watch as their pensions shrivel. As a naïf arriving with little idea about anything, I'm astonished at how swiftly a political and economic system that had seemed static and insurmountable can wither. Those who are not ready, and not agile, get left behind.

The years I live in Budapest coincide with a triumphalism about the "end of history" and the ascendance of American-style capitalism. Reminders of Seattle are constant, as the stock prices of companies such as Real Networks and Amazon.com march straight up. I hear about high school classmates who have become millionaires through their stock options in Internet start-ups. I have it pretty good, too. I meet my future wife, an Australian who works at her country's embassy in Budapest. We move into a massive apartment with two balconies overlooking a square and a view out to the Buda Castle. I can't believe my fortune after having arrived in the city with a backpack.

But with all the euphoria about the "New Economy," I don't really feel changed at all, just relocated. The memory of Tyrell sometimes creeps back on me. I remember swimming in a lake when I was a kid, treading water, my legs churning beneath the dark surface. Sometimes a tendril of weed would brush my foot, sending a cold shiver through my body.

After three years in Eastern Europe, it feels like time to leave. I return to the United States and begin graduate school in the Bay Area, while my fiancée goes back to Australia to pursue her own studies. The dotcom crash has already darkened the sunny promises of the Internet boom. A month after my arrival, terrorists fly planes into the World Trade Center. History is restarted, an unpredictable force that swirls and eddies and carries us all along at its whim.

I live in the cramped attic of a house in Berkeley. Sitting there at night, my mind often returns to the team, and especially Tyrell. I look up the story published after his death in an online database and read it again. It doesn't give a reason for his murder. The reporter had pieced together a few details—a bust for selling crack and a habit of hanging out at an after-hours gambling club—but no one had any idea why Tyrell had been killed. In the article, people who had known him call Tyrell "likable" and "not rebellious."

Reading the story again, it becomes clear that the reason Tyrell's death was considered worthy of the front page was his involvement in integration programs—there was one where wealthy families from the suburbs "adopted" poorer ones at holiday times; and there was our team. The reporter spoke to Coach McClain, who told her, "We thought it was a good idea to expose these different kids to each other, to combine inner-city kids with rich white kids. And it worked."

I wonder if it had actually "worked" for anyone. Did any of the white kids still think about it? What had happened to my black teammates who'd gotten into private schools through Randy Finley's efforts? It was nearly twenty years since we'd all practiced together in the Lakeside gym. How had my teammates fared? What kind of men were they? Did anyone, like me, miss the camaraderie we got from playing together?

It's only a short flight up to Seattle, so I decide to try to find out. In October 2002, while still in graduate school, I make my first trip back. I don't expect to write a book. I just really want to know what became of these guys.

Tyrell, naturally, is foremost in my thoughts. The other player who has really stuck in my head is Myran. He had always been so outrageous. Since he had such an ability to chatter, I guess that he is probably a salesman. I imagine household items such as vacuum cleaners. I can see Myran loading up on commissions.

I proceed through word of mouth. I get Sean's number through his dad, who still works as a stockbroker. I meet Sean on a Sunday afternoon at a pub in the Madison Park neighborhood, near the shore of Lake Washington. As the Seahawks play on the televisions hung on the walls of the busy tavern, Sean, who is now a prosecutor, laughs when he remembers the team. The first things that come to mind are "playing games in rotten gyms" and riding around in "that brown, piece-of-shit van."

Our conversation is brief because Sean has to return to the office to work. He tells me about the whereabouts of some of the Lakeside players, including Dino, who he says did very well during the dotcom boom. It happens that Dino's parents own an Italian restaurant a few doors down from the pub. We walk to it on our way out. Dino's dad is at the counter. He tries Dino on his cell phone, chats with him a minute, and hands the phone to me.

Some teammates aren't so easy to find. Though both McClains have seen JT around town, they have no idea how to get ahold of him. Willie Sr. has bumped into him at Safeway and had some words. Willie Jr. tells me that JT generally looks pretty run-down. "It's like life's eating away at him," Will says.

I go to the courthouse and pull JT's criminal records. He's pled guilty to two felony charges in King County. I type a letter and mail it to the three addresses I find in the papers. A few days later, JT calls and leaves an excited message on my voice mail. He wants to get together as soon as possible.

We meet at a Starbucks in what, not long ago, was a rough corner of the Central Area. When he sees me, JT, who wears jeans and a Los Angeles Lakers warm-up jacket, walks over and grabs me into a hug. At about six feet and 280 pounds, he dwarfs me. As we sit down, he slumps back as if molding into the chair. He has a thick black beard and soft brown eyes that seem to implore for something as he speaks. His words tumble out in a mixture of manic enthusiasm and wistfulness. "The team was like family to me," he says. "Sometimes you only get one chance in life. That was mine, and I blew it."

I find that Damian has given perhaps the most thought of anyone to our team and what it meant—and what it did not. On one of my first nights in town, I drive twenty miles down the freeway, exiting just south of the airport to a neighborhood that was known as a home to working-class whites when we were kids. Driving west on a busy road, I pass a series of apartment complexes with stately names that don't match the utilitarian nature of the actual developments. Damian Joseph lives in a grouping of town houses called, for no discernible reason, Cedar Estates.

He meets me at the door, wearing black slacks, loafers, and a dark purple sweater. We walk past the couch and TV in the small living room and into the kitchen. Damian's wife, Michelle, comes in to say hello before disappearing into the back. Damian pours us glasses of nuclear-green Kool-Aid from a jug kept in the refrigerator.

A wide-shouldered man at a little under six feet but more than two hundred pounds, he maintains a loose-limbed, coiled athleticism. His hair is shaved close to his head, and the ghost of a mustache haunts his upper lip. When he wants to make a point, his eyes narrow so that a "V" takes shape in the lines of his forehead, pointing down at his nose. If he's just said something that comes out as strange, amusing, or hard to believe, he leans back and exclaims, "Yes, sir!"

As we sit across from one another at his kitchen table, Damian and I fall into an easy banter. We haven't seen each other since high school, but he's as eager to talk about the team as I am. In the intervening years, it has come to seem like a curious anomaly in each of our lives.

Well into the conversation, Damian asks if I recall the old taunt that Lakeside students chanted when one of our sports teams was losing: "It's all right, it's OK, you'll all work for us someday." He tells me that he remembers hearing it during a basketball game against Rainier Beach High School, a mostly poor, mostly black public school in the South End.

I haven't thought about it in a long time, but as soon as Damian mentions it, the memory springs back. I recall sitting in the bleachers, my Lakeside classmates, the upperclassman leading the crowd.

"It was embarrassing," I say.

I ask Damian why, after all this time, he remembers that particular cheer.

"I hate to say it," he says, "but it was probably true."

Part Three

Money, Work, Career

To talk about race is fundamentally to wrestle with what kind of people are we, really? What kind of nation are we, really? Not just how many material toys we have, not just whether the economy's okay for a certain slice of the population, stock markets and budget deals and so forth and so on. What kind of people are we, really?

—*Cornel West*

Strictly for the Money

When Damian was a sophomore at Seattle Prep, the school where Randy Finley had enrolled him, some younger kids who lived on his block asked him why he wasn't dealing drugs—it was a pretty good way to make some cash, they said.

At the time, Damian was already living what he calls a "double life," shuttling between the small house in South Seattle where he lived with his mom and his sister and a private school that was nearly all white and wealthy. He remembers going to a classmate's house and seeing that it was four stories tall and equipped with Ping-Pong and foosball tables, a pinball machine, a swimming pool, and an indoor basketball court. What impressed him most was the giant refrigerator loaded with food; when he went to houses like that, he always made sure to eat as much as he could. He also was tired of the other black guys from our team ragging on him for being poor. When he thought over the idea of dealing, he was receptive to making some fast money. He went in with a friend—they bought a pound of weed, broke it up, and started to sell it to people they knew.

JT and his mom lived near the intersection of Twenty-third Avenue and Union Street, in the heart of the Central Area. By 1986 there were kids out on the corner dealing. JT was already friendly with a group of older guys who lived in a house down the street—they used to call out to him when he walked by in his football uniform on the way to practice—so he stole some cocaine from his mom's stash and brought it to them. "They were like, 'Wow, man, how'd you get this?'" he says. The guys in the house had some friends who knew how to cook it up, and JT had his first supply of crack to sell. "I'd just walk out my door, walk down the street and hit the corner and there's people ready to buy," he says. "I used to watch the older guys and say, 'I'm going to be just like them. One day I'm going to be able to jump in my drop-top Cadillac and get me some rims, and I'm going to be able to roll with them.'"

Tyrell lived with his parents right around the corner from JT and saw the same things. The most trouble he'd gotten into as a kid was shoplifting some Polo shirts from a department store downtown. Now Tyrell, along with his older brother, Donnico, started to see guys they'd known their whole lives—and whose parents had grown up with their parents—with nice clothes and cars, flashing cash. "They were ghetto celebrities to us. Everybody loved them, and they had the jewelry and the money," Donnico says. "What you have to understand is you walk out of your apartment, this is in your face every day. And then your friend is doing this and doing that and wearing these shoes and you're not, so, 'Hey, let me try this.' That's how it really broke down—'Let me try this.' Because we both started off with really four rocks apiece. It went from there."

While the corner at Twenty-third and Union was the center of the world for guys like JT and Tyrell, it was just one of thousands of end points in a global supply chain that started back in the jungles of Colombia. From there, it flowed up through the Caribbean, into Mexico, over the border into the United States, up to the street gangs of Los Angeles, and then north on Interstate 5 to Seattle, where the product finally filtered down to the final link that put it in the hands of consumers. The drug and the money hit with such force that—just as the dotcom explosion would do a decade later with a different part of Seattle—it overturned nearly everything. Suddenly, at age fifteen, you could pocket several thousand dollars on a good day just by going to your neighborhood corner.

"It was easy," Damian says. "Quick money, you didn't have to work. There was high demand. And I didn't have any sense. I was just ignorant, unlearned, and foolish.

"Other people, they have a nice car, they have nice clothes, maybe they have a pretty girlfriend, all these things, and so you're like, OK, you know? Just not having what everybody else had gave you the desire to want to get that. So, OK, what's the quickest way to do this? Well, I can go get a pound of weed and sell that, an ounce of crack, I can sell that and make it quick.

"You know, you go to a club, and everybody else has Jordans on, and you want to step in with some Jordans. If you don't have the power to resist it, you'll get sucked in. And that's not just in the black community, that's all over. I mean look at the people at Enron, they got sucked in to that, they're just on a bigger scale. You get sucked in and it's hard to resist that, it's like, 'I can make some pretty good money here, so let me go ahead and do this.'"

Cocaine, in one form or another, has been getting people high a long time—indigenous South Americans chewed the leaves of coca plants for energy before the arrival of the Spaniards in the 1500s. In 1859, a German chemist figured out how to extract cocaine from coca leaves, which allowed the drug to be incorporated into medicines, anesthetics, and commercial products. Several years later in Atlanta, a former Confederate soldier and chemist began to sell a "health tonic" that included an infusion of the drug; in 1886 he named it "Coca-Cola." At the time, cocaine could be bought legally as powder, in cigarettes, and in a form that could be shot into the veins. It was hailed as a therapy for clogged sinuses and hay fever. By the turn of the century, the drug was available in hundreds of patent medicines that were little more than cocaine and flavored syrup.

In the early 1900s, attitudes toward lightly regulated narcotic drugs such as opium and cocaine began to change. Not only were addiction rates going up, but also the drugs became associated with minority groups. On the West Coast, opium was connected with the Chinese laborers who had come to work on the railroads, and its use became considered "un-American." In the South, it was "feared that Negro cocaine users might become oblivious of their prescribed bounds and attack white society," writes David Musto, a professor of medical history at Yale. Among whites, rumors held that cocaine gave black men superhuman strength and made them crazy for sex with white women. Musto, in his research, has found no evidence at all of high cocaine use among southern blacks. But these weren't the beliefs of just a few rednecks; in 1914, for example, the *New York Times* published an article titled "Negro Cocaine 'Fiends' are a New Southern Menace," claiming that

114 Money, Work, Career

"murder and insanity" were "increasing among lower class blacks" due to cocaine "sniffing." That year, Congress passed the Harrison Act, which allowed the federal government to regulate and tax the import, production, and distribution of narcotics. A black market for cocaine developed, prices shot up, and the drug became, for several decades, a boutique thrill.

It didn't really begin to come back into the mainstream until the 1960s, when drugs of all types began to be more widely smoked, injected, and snorted. In the 1969 movie *Easy Rider*, the two bikers played by Dennis Hopper and Peter Fonda smuggle coke inside their gas tanks, their drug-dealing fueling their travels across the country in pursuit of the American Dream. In the 1970s, the drug helped power the rise of disco and club culture. Cocaine's lofty price tag meant that it was mainly a high for people with plenty of cash. The drug was viewed as fairly innocuous—it pepped you up, increased your sexual prowess, and made you, at least in your own head, a great conversationalist.

As the appetite for cocaine grew, Colombian cartels did exactly what would be expected of commodity suppliers in a global economy: They increased production (the big cocaine cartels operated what were essentially factories in the jungles of Colombia, complete with landing strips, healthcare facilities, and dorms for workers). In the late 1970s, huge quantities of coke began to flow north into the United States. The full-blown arrival of cocaine culture was reflected in the early 1980s in the movie *Scarface*, with the classic over-the-top performance by Al Pacino, and the television show *Miami Vice*, which often climaxed with the pastel-clad detectives Sonny Crockett and Rico Tubbs blowing away a coke dealer and his henchmen.

With more product available, the next logical step was figuring out how to expand the market. Cocaine had been smoked in the form of "freebase" in the 1970s, but the process of making it was tedious and involved combustible chemicals. Sometime in the early 1980s, someone— it's thought the method was invented in the Caribbean, where tons of cocaine transited before being smuggled into the United States—realized that all you had to do to make smokable cocaine was to mix it with baking soda and cook it. The result delivered a short but all-consuming high that some people compare to the intensity of an orgasm.

This new variation of coke could be broken down and sold in $5 "rocks," making what was formerly a luxury product available to the masses. It was especially well received in urban areas, where black unemployment was double the national average or more, and there was both a supply of users seeking escape and a ready-made distribution network of young men looking to make some cash. On the West Coast, cocaine was brought up through Mexico and smuggled over the border, where it was then sold to already established street gangs in Los Angeles. They converted the powder to crack and began to sell it in their territories, with violence often erupting when one set infringed on the turf of another.

With their own markets saturated, the Los Angeles gangs began moving the drug to other cities, which was as simple as loading the trunk and heading up the freeway. A web of family connections dating back to the black diaspora from the South decades earlier provided the backbone of the network. One of Damian's sources, for example, was a relative from the Inglewood section of L.A. who also was a Blood. JT, who had cousins in L.A., hooked up with a Crip who became his supplier.

In early 1986—as we were playing on the court—crack was suddenly everywhere, if not in reality then at least in the media. That year, *Newsweek* and *U.S. News & World Report* compared the drug's spread to that of "medieval plagues"; *Time* called it "the issue of the year"; the *New York Times* ran articles on rock cocaine spreading to the wealthy Connecticut suburbs. In the fall, CBS aired "48 Hours on Crack Street," which featured then-U.S. Attorney Rudy Giuliani going undercover to score on a corner in New York City; the show was the network's highest-rated news program in five years. Three days later, NBC responded with its own report, "Cocaine Country." On *NBC Nightly News*, anchor Tom Brokaw informed viewers that crack was "flooding America." That June, college basketball star Len Bias, the first-round draft pick of the Boston Celtics, died of what was reported as a crack overdose (it later came out that he had been using powder cocaine, which caused cardiac arrhythmia), adding to the sense that crack was everywhere. As *Newsweek* put it in August 1986, the "plague is all but universal."

The first time crack really registered in my consciousness came that March, when a different issue of *Newsweek* landed in our mailbox. The headline KIDS AND COCAINE was splashed on the front. "The new coke goes by many names on the street, but it is usually called 'crack' or 'rock,'" the magazine cautioned breathlessly. "It is smoked, not snorted, and the resulting intoxication is far more intense than that of snorted cocaine—much quicker, much more euphoric and much, much more addictive."

One toke, warned an expert quoted in the article, could lead to "instantaneous addiction." The hyperbole continued: "In New York, eager buyers queue up outside crack houses like movie fans outside a theater—and the lines, according to one drug agent, 'are loaded with kids.' There are white kids, black kids, Hispanic kids—kids from the ghetto and kids from the suburbs."

It's doubtful that this multicultural group of teenage crack enthusiasts ever existed except in the imagination of a *Newsweek* reporter and his source, but the image of crack as a "smoke it once and be forever addicted" drug was prevalent. Crack is certainly addictive, and it hit the hardest in areas where people were looking to escape or were suffering from untreated depression or other mental health problems (you can think of rock cocaine as the poor man's Prozac). In Seattle, the hard drugs of choice for white people have typically been heroin and, more recently, methamphetamine. Crack, though certainly not confined to blacks only, hit the Central Area and the South End like a tsunami.

Nick Metz came on to the Seattle police force as a twenty-year-old in 1983, working the Rainier Valley in South Seattle. He remembers the beat as relatively mellow at the start—in his first two years on the job, he didn't personally respond to a single gunshot call. When there was violence, it was almost always of the domestic or bar-fight variety. Drug dealing remained mostly out of sight, done from taverns, in workplaces, or in private homes. In about 1987, though, it felt as if he woke up one morning and the world had changed. "All of a sudden, we're getting lots of gunshot calls, lots of gunshot victims, getting calls left and right from neighbors, residences, and businesses about people hanging out on street corners and dealing drugs," Metz says. "And then obviously the pressure on the police department began to mount, 'You're not doing enough, you need to do more.'"

The arrival of crack broke the Central Area and South End of Seattle into a number of separate fiefdoms, each populated mainly by teenage kids. You could track them straight down Twenty-third Avenue. The first spot was at the northern end of the Central Area, at the intersection of Twenty-third and Madison, the area where William Grose settled in the 1880s. Running south on Twenty-third for one and a half miles through the Central Area, you came to the intersections with Union Street—where

Tyrell and JT hung out—down to Cherry, past Garfield High School, and on to Jackson. After Jackson Street, Twenty-third Avenue runs another mile south and heads down a hill before it spills into Rainier Avenue South, which soon crosses Martin Luther King Jr. Way, which it parallels through the South End. That area had its own corners, such as Rainier and Othello Street, where Myran sometimes could be found.

The kids who sold drugs on each of these corners generally had grown up there—in many cases, their parents had, too—and they formed what could loosely be thought of as gangs. "You were in a gang because you lived in that neighborhood, period," JT says. Of course, someone like JT, who had lived his whole life in the Central Area and had family all around, knew people at every intersection, so he could go anywhere in the Central Area and hang out. "It wasn't really that rough, not when you know everybody in the neighborhood," JT says.

In about 1988, though, real gangs—the Crips and the Bloods from L.A., and the Black Gangster Disciples from Chicago—began to recruit new members in Seattle with the goal of taking territory and drug sales. Each tried to get a toehold in an area by getting in with the guys who were already there. The Crips, for example, took over Twenty-third and Cherry, just four blocks south of Union. Because the Crips would use violence to protect their turf, this made the area much more dangerous— even local guys like Tyrell and JT had to avoid it. In the meantime, ramping up the potential for conflict, the Black Gangster Disciples began to recruit kids from Twenty-third and Union.

The separation into territories also hit along the old divisions of South Seattle versus the Central Area, a rivalry that ran back to community league sports teams, when CAYA would play Rainier Beach. Donnico Johnson, Tyrell's brother, says that Tyrell wasn't into gang life enough to become a full-fledged member of the Black Gangster Disciples. Nevertheless, several of Tyrell's friends were, and distinctions between hanging out with members of a gang—who, after all, were your childhood buddies—and being in it were fluid. Tyrell's dad, Doug Johnson, remembers driving Tyrell around one day and seeing Tyrell and a kid in another car scowling at each other. Johnson was shocked because the kid, who had played football for Rainier Beach while Tyrell played for CAYA, had only a few years earlier come over to the Johnson house to play. When Doug Johnson asked his son what was going on, Tyrell told him that the kid had joined the Crips.

"For some reason, Seattle, it just opened up like this, and if you stayed here and you ran with this bunch of guys—the guys you had played sports with and grew up with—all of a sudden they were against each other," Doug Johnson says. "I never understood that part, and to this day I don't. Because if you stayed south, you couldn't come over here no more, and if you stayed on this side, you couldn't go south. All of a sudden it was the Bloods, the Crips, and the BGDs."

Random violence began to hit streets of the Central Area and the South End. In 1988, a twenty-six-year-old Crip leader who had moved up from Los Angeles fired out of a car and hit a sixteen-year-old boy walking near Garfield High School. The kid, who was injured but not killed, had been wearing a red jacket, the color of the Bloods. It turned out the victim had no gang affiliation. The shooting turned up the heat on the Seattle police, who heard increasing calls from community groups to do something to make the streets safer.

"Our first instinct when everything started happening was to arrest our way out of it," recalls Seattle police officer Nick Metz. The Seattle cops, to that point, had had no exposure to the type of wide-scale corner dealing that arrived with crack. Metz joined a newly formed street-level narcotics unit that was tasked with arresting as many street-level dealers as it could, mainly by going undercover, buying drugs, and then swooping in to make arrests minutes later. In March 1989, the narcotics unit busted Tyrell at Twenty-third and Union after observing him offering rock cocaine to people walking by. They found he had 1.2 grams of crack and a loaded .32-caliber handgun. Tyrell, who was seventeen, pled guilty and got five days in detention; he also had to agree to be home at his parents' house by ten P.M. every night.

The narcotics cops also began to go into crack houses to make undercover buys. It was hair-raising work. Metz remembers dealers holding guns on him as he made his purchases, not because they thought he was a cop but because they were simply worried about being robbed. Once the narcotics team scored, SWAT units moved in. In 1987, the Seattle police conducted 500 drug raids and seized 282 weapons. These raids were often based on informant tips, and the police went in blind. This led to some tragic results in the Central Area and the South End. In February 1988, two men were killed during such operations. William Tucker, who was forty-four, was shot when a police officer on a raid tripped and fired his gun. The incursion into Tucker's house was the third in a month;

the cops had found drugs and weapons on the previous two. Erdman Bascomb, who was forty-one, was sitting on a couch when the police busted in with a battering ram. As he began to get up, the cops spotted a black object in his hand and shot him to death. He turned out to be holding a remote control. A prior raid on Bascomb's apartment had reportedly turned up small amounts of cocaine and marijuana. No drugs or weapons were found on the night he was killed.

The Seattle police seized 6 kilograms of cocaine in 1986, 24 kilograms in 1988, and 89 kilograms in 1990. But no matter what the police did, Metz says, the influx of drugs didn't stop. "Every time we took three or four guys off the street corner, there were three or four more behind him to resume business." When they did make busts, Metz says, a lot of times all they got were "clucks"—crack addicts who dealers sent out to be middlemen. In exchange for a piece of the product, the cluck would hang around areas known to be drug spots, find customers, and then take the money to the dealer, who was off in a car, a house, or otherwise out of sight. When the cluck brought the cocaine back, the undercovers would arrest him while the dealer remained free.

While the drug economy spread throughout the region, the worst impacts were localized in the black community. The Central Area became a destination for anyone seeking to score in Seattle. Metz remembers seeing BMWs and Mercedes pull up to the corners, running the plates, and finding out they were from the wealthy suburbs of Mercer Island and Bellevue. "They were coming down to the 'hood to get their stuff," he says.

Doug Johnson, Tyrell's dad, observed the whole scene from the window of his apartment. He understood the teenage dealers' desire for money, but he also knew their efforts were futile in the end. "Every time you'd look out you'd see a guy out there, just dealing like they had a license," he says. "I watched a lot of them who had come up this year, they were flat on their ass next year. They had either gone to jail or got killed or shot or something of that nature—it never was good. You could say it was good, it seemed like they were having a little bit for a little while, but it never even lasted."

If you lived in the Central Area or the South End of Seattle in the 1980s, it was impossible to escape the impact of crack cocaine. Crime and violence rates rose. People who had been stable members of the community got hooked and slid down the tubes. "I had known people for years that had used drugs, they were using powder cocaine, but they were never like the people that used crack," Doug Johnson says. "Once they messed with that crack they were a totally different person. It just changed them." The drug also flipped the earning power in the neighborhood, with fifteen-year-old kids suddenly able to make more—by a large multiple—than their parents. The guys from our basketball team who were in the thick of it reacted pretty much in line with their individual personalities.

Tyrell was never really all that ambitious—he just went with the flow. While his brother, Donnico, and other friends began to see themselves as Tony Montana-esque figures—Donnico had a videotape of *Scarface* that he put on the TV every day—Tyrell would dabble just enough to make a few bucks to see him through. He still lived in his parents' apartment near Union Street. He kept his room spotless, with a shelf full of basketball trophies, a giant stuffed Mickey Mouse, and posters of his favorite basketball players, including Marques Johnson—a small forward who Tyrell liked because they shared the same last name—and Andrew Toney, a smooth guard for Philadelphia known for delivering huge games against the Celtics. Everything about Tyrell had to be immaculate. Damian remembers hanging out with him during middle school and Tyrell taking forever to leave the house because he had to starch and iron his jeans so they would have just the right crease.

Tyrell also was friends with a white kid named John Doces, who was later featured in the *Seattle Times* article after Tyrell's murder. Doces was from Bellevue, a suburb east of Lake Washington. He and Tyrrell met when they were both about twelve, after Doces's mom had signed up for an "Adopt-a-Family" program established by the city of Seattle, in which wealthy families brought over food and toys to poorer ones on Thanksgiving and Christmas. The Doces were assigned to the Johnsons, and Tyrell and John found they both loved basketball. The friendship, which lasted several years, centered around the game. Doces either came over to the Central Area to hang out, or picked up Tyrell and brought him over to Bellevue, where they played basketball on shortened "dunk" hoops. Doces remembers Tyrell as quiet, but also with an innate cool that surprised a white kid from the suburbs. One day, Doces and his mom dropped Tyrell off at his apartment. As Tyrell walked away, Doces yelled good-bye. Without looking back, Tyrell raised his arm in a Black Power salute.

During high school, the pair sometimes went to parties together on the east side. Tyrell was always shy until he and Doces drank and smoked a little. It was still the days when rap was just coming into national popularity. As he loosened up, Tyrell would break out his rhymes—same as he did when we played basketball together—impressing all the white kids at the parties. The friendship faded in the later years of high school, especially after Tyrell dropped out and Doces got ready to go on to college at the University of Washington, only a few miles north of the Central Area. It ended in freshman year. "My whole mentality changed," says Doces, who is now a professor of political economy at Bucknell University. He and Tyrell had nothing to talk about anymore.

After he got away from basketball, Tyrell was basically drifting. Donnico, who was less than a year older than Tyrell, remembers a day in eleventh grade when they were both attending an alternative high school. They skipped out and went with a cousin to get tattoos on their shoulders. Donnico had a .45 put on with his name below it (the quality was so poor that people later made fun of it, saying it looked like a cigarette lighter, which it does). Tyrell got a .357 Magnum with the words "T-Baby for the records" written below. When I ask Donnico why the tattoos of guns, he shrugs: "I guess we was thinking we was hard," he says. "Everybody had them."

Tyrell's police record, mostly low-level crimes, grew: the bust for selling crack in March 1989; in August 1990, he was the passenger in a car when the driver pulled over to buy some cocaine; that November, he was caught with a mobile phone that had been stolen out of a car at a Texaco station near the Central Area while its owner was inside paying; in February 1991, Tyrell was the lookout while a friend climbed through a window to burglarize a Central Area apartment; they were caught in the act.

During all this, Tyrell managed to retain the charm and charisma he'd always displayed on the court. "He was such a sweet, decent guy," his public defender, Martin Powell, remembers. Tyrell was immature, he says, and there was still a basic goodness about him. When they had meetings, Tyrell would come to Powell's office—only a few blocks from the

Johnsons' apartment—and they would spend time talking, with Tyrell listening and Powell trying to get him to think about getting away from the streets. "He was the kind of client you would want to spend more time with because you felt like there was some hope," Powell says, "and the truth is you want to spend more time with people that you like."

Powell also remembers going to pretrial hearings at the King County Courthouse and seeing the other defendants greet Tyrell—these guys were all friends, Powell realized, and the shuffle into and out of the courtroom had just become part of life for them. With Tyrell, Powell says, there was a resignation that going to jail was inevitable, which struck Powell as strange in someone so young. "Unfortunately, [with] guys like Tyrell, who are out doing these low-level felonies, you just kind of do the best you can," Powell says. "You get them in and talk to them, and maybe there's some program or something that they can get into. Ultimately, your job's to get them though the system with as little harm and as much protection as you can."

Tyrell's principal motivation, Donnico says, was simply to have fun and keep some cash in hand. "See, Tyrell never saved his money," he says. "He would spend his on sweatsuits and shoes and stuff like that. Looked good, though, you would think he had a pocketful of money. He had on a nice Fila sweatsuit, Fila shoes to match, Fila hat," Donnico says with a laugh.

Tyrell may have been heading toward getting in deeper, but no one can say now. In the meantime, Tyrell—who had never in his life left the state of Washington—was just another guy out and about in the Central Area. In the summer of 1991, he was riding with a friend when they pulled up next to Eric Hampton at an intersection. They honked to get Eric's attention. "He rolled down the window and this smoke and smell came out, the strongest marijuana smell I ever smelled in my life," Eric says, laughing. They chatted for a few minutes, keeping it light. "We may have exchanged numbers, you know how that goes—'I'll look you up'— and he just drove off."

Not long after, on August 10, 1991, a couple out taking their baby and dog for a stroll on a beautiful summer afternoon saw a bundle lying in a ditch along a wooded road in the South End. The man noticed it was about four feet long and wrapped in a blanket. It looked suspicious, so he went to take a closer look, poking at it with his walking stick. Whatever was inside was firm. He thought that maybe someone had disposed of a dead dog. He reached down, pulled the blanket back, and found Tyrell.

"It crushed me," JT says of Tyrell's murder. "It was like losing my best friend, a friend you've been knowing since childhood. And you're hearing about legs and arms and stuff, like a leg was chopped off, they was trying to chop his arm off, wrapped up in carpet."

It was impossible to understand why someone would want to kill Tyrell. If anyone would have been a more likely target at the time, it would have been JT; while Tyrell was going sideways, JT was moving up.

JT's friendly personality and large network proved to be good qualifications for the drug trade—people naturally gravitated toward him. "I was always the guy, if there was a new Starter jacket out—this was back in the break-dancing days—my uncle would give me this fly jacket and they'd be like, 'Wow, where'd you get that one from?'" JT says. "I was always, as a kid, someone who could come up with it, get something that other people couldn't, so they would attach to me, you know?"

At the time, that meant hooking up through a relative with a Crip from L.A., who became JT's connection for cocaine. JT soon moved off the corner and became a supplier. He rented a place out in the North End and simply watched his pager. When someone needed a hookup, he put some in his trunk and delivered it. At any one time, he'd have as much as $100,000 in cash hidden in his basement and in his grandma's house. There wasn't much he could do with it, so he spread it around, spending it on partying and the costs of living. It came so easy he figured he could always make more. You don't really respect drug money, anyways, JT says—it doesn't feel like you've really earned it.

JT took a huge blow in 1989 when his grandfather, who had moved up from Louisiana decades earlier and opened a dental practice, became sick with lung cancer. The plans for family succession in the practice had fallen apart when JT's dad and uncle got hooked on heroin, but JT's grandfather remained his primary male role model. As he was getting sicker, JT's grandfather asked him if he was selling drugs. Since his grandfather had always told JT, "Don't lie, don't ever lie," JT didn't. His grandfather erupted and screamed at him to get out of the house. "That hurt, man, that really hurt," JT says. As his grandfather deteriorated,

JT's aunt smoothed things over and JT returned to his bedside, but his grandfather soon passed away. "I still wish he was here, just so I could ask his advice about things," JT says.

As the calendar rolled into the 1990s, the situation in the Central Area and the South End—as in urban areas throughout the rest of the country—became more violent. Seattle's homicide rate spiked up from an average of about fifty murders a year through the 1980s and early 1990s to nearly seventy in 1993 and 1994. In March 1993, JT was inside a nightclub in downtown Seattle. James Credit, a teammate from Willie McClain's old CAYA team—he didn't make our mixed team but sometimes came to practices and games to hang out—was outside. James had cut up some Ivory soap, which happens to look just like crack, and sold it for $6,400 to a kid named Otagus, whom they had all known from childhood. When Otagus arrived at the club that night and saw James, he pulled out a handgun and fired several shots at him. James died on the way to the hospital.

"My thing was, 'I want to make money.' I wasn't into shooting at people or hurting people," JT says. "This was a way to buy a car, get an apartment, get some clothes." At the same time, he says, some guys couldn't hustle but found they were good at fighting, brandishing guns, and acting tough. They were looking for trouble. Of course, you also had to project at least a certain capacity for violence or you would put yourself in the position of getting ripped off, which is what eventually got JT.

When he got some money, he fulfilled his earlier dream of getting a nice car, and bought a '62 Chevy Impala with Dayton rims and hydraulic shocks to bounce it up and down. Unfortunately, it wasn't all he thought it would be. "That car became a headache because people kept stealing it," JT says. One day in March 1993, it went missing from the house where he was staying, and his friend tracked a trail of hydraulic fluid to the garage of a place nearby. It turned out that an eighteen-year-old kid had stolen it and was removing the stereo and the rims to outfit his own car. JT and several friends went by, grabbed the guy at gunpoint, threw him in a van, and beat him up while driving around Seattle. After threatening his life, they eventually let him go. The kid reported it to the cops, and JT and his friends got picked up on kidnapping charges. JT pled guilty and was sentenced to a year in prison.

As he says now, JT was looking for the same sense of "family" on the streets that he'd once found through playing basketball. Rolling around in his '62 Impala with his pager, he was the center of a social network. Damian, in contrast, approached the drug trade according to his own cautious personality—he was, in his words, a "freelancer." After starting high school at Seattle Prep, Damian hardly ever ran into old teammates like JT and Tyrell, who were doing their thing on Union Street. "Those guys were trying to get rich off of it," he says. "So it was like the rent is dope money, the car, everything. I wasn't trying to be that dirty."

Damian sometimes saw Myran, who also was living in the South End. A few times they both went down to sell in Belltown, a neighborhood just north of the downtown business district that in the early 1990s was home to a number of homeless shelters, artists' lofts, and rock clubs. It also was an open-air market for anyone looking to score crack. In general, though, Damian liked to work on his own, selling to people he knew. "I always slid under the radar, never tried to make myself seen, never tried to be flamboyant. Kept my hair cut, shaven, you wouldn't know," he says. "I got pulled over a couple times, but I was legitimate, had my license, insurance, registration."

After he started at Seattle University in the early 1990s, Damian started to sell $20 bags of marijuana in clubs on weekends, which he discovered was more lucrative—and safer—than dealing crack on the street. He saw it as a side business to make some extra cash—he estimates he was pulling in about $600 a month. "I wasn't doing it because it was fun," Damian says. "I was doing it to take care of things. I didn't enjoy the danger, and I didn't have a conscience about it. I was just doing it strictly to make money."

In the end, his mom, Helen, got him to stop. Although Damian—who was never busted and was still living at home—had kept everything so lowkey that Helen didn't even suspect what he was up to, she had a dream that two men were going to set up her son and kill him. When she told Damian, he had a feeling she was right. He decided to get out. He discovered later, through the grapevine, that two men he'd known had been planning to rob him—and possibly worse—for his drug supply, just as Helen had warned. "I think the only thing that kept me from the penitentiary or being dead was my mother's prayers. I believe that to this day," Damian says. "Those guys could have put me in a ditch and nobody would have known."

In about 1993, at the same time Damian was getting out of drug-selling, something unexpected happened: Crack use in Seattle and around the country began to decline. By 1995, the rise in violence that had come with the introduction of crack cocaine to places such as the Central Area rolled back as suddenly as it had hit.

The reasons for this are still contested. The arrival of crack and its prominence in the media prompted a legislative reaction that imposed severe penalties on crack dealers and users. Before the elections in the fall of 1986, Congress passed the Drug-Free America Act. Two years later, as Michael Dukakis and George H. W. Bush campaigned to succeed Ronald Reagan, each accusing the other of being "soft" on crime—this was the time that the Bush campaign ran the infamous Willie Horton ads—Congress enacted more antidrug legislation. The bills included mandatory sentencing for powder and rock cocaine based on the idea—backed by no scientific evidence—that the smokable version is fifty times more addictive than the kind you snort. Congress doubled that number and came up with sentencing guidelines to reflect a 100 to 1 ratio. For example, getting caught with 500 grams of powder cocaine would get you a five-year sentence, while only 5 grams of crack would do the same. The result was that thousands of low-level crack dealers and users began to get shipped off to prison, and the rate of incarceration in America—especially for African Americans—began a relentless climb that has yet to abate.

Conservative social scientists, such as James Q. Wilson, claim that more vigorous policing and the rise in imprisonment accounted for the decline in violent crime since the mid-1990s. Those on the more liberal side of the debate point to the improving economy during the Clinton years and argue that job creation gave opportunities to people who might otherwise have been on the streets. A group of University of Chicago and Harvard economists take another tack, claiming that the hardening of drug-selling territories—essentially establishing "property rights" to deal drugs in certain areas—meant that violence was no longer as necessary. Steven Levitt, the coauthor of the book *Freakonomics*, advanced the theory—now widely debunked—that the legalization of abortion in 1973 resulted in less "unwanted" children born to families unable to give them guidance, hence less crime when that generation reached its late teens and early twenties.

As far as the decision to get out of crack dealing, JT's experience after his release from prison in 1994 suggests that many factors played a part, but the harsh penalties tied to the drug took a primary role. Upon his return to Seattle, JT went right back to doing what he'd been doing.

By 1995, though, the feds—the DEA and the FBI—were stepping up their infiltration of drug networks. Three of JT's friends got busted, and he became almost certain he was going to be next. His friends each got ten-year-minimum sentences in a federal penitentiary. JT, who still doesn't know how he stayed free, figured he had pushed his luck far enough. "I got out of the game, quit selling it because I was so nervous and scared that they were going to come get me," he says.

At the same time, a social stigma became attached to crack use. The older generation had been the chief users when it hit in the 1980s. Younger people looked on and realized that being a crackhead was not very glamorous. Snoop Dogg and Tupac began to wax poetic about the mellower pleasures of weed and cognac. In fact, as both Damian and JT found, selling weed was a better option than crack—it wasn't really harmful to the user, so you didn't have to feel guilty about it, and the punishment if you got caught was far less severe. Using his skill for making connections, JT hooked up with a white guy who had a line on some powerful and colorful bud that was grown in basements on a commuter island across Puget Sound from Seattle. JT became the only black dealer around with this certain type of coveted weed, so it became his trademark. He was "the purple bud guy."

In 1997, a friend told him that one of his connections, a Crip in Los Angeles, wanted JT to bring the purple bud down to California. He said they could make a lot of money selling it there. JT and his friend put two pounds in the trunk of a car and headed south. When they arrived, though, the guy wanted them to take it to the 'hood and move it themselves. JT thought that stepping on someone else's territory would be a good way to get killed. They told the guy to forget it and began the drive back to Seattle, the cargo of premium marijuana still in the back. As long as they were down there, they thought they might as well do some sightseeing, so they headed up the coast, enjoying the vistas of the Pacific Ocean along Highway 101. They made it to Oregon before they were pulled over. The road trip came to an unhappy end when the cops searched the trunk. "Busted again," JT says. "Back to the penitentiary."

• • •

On a cold, sunny winter day in February 2003, Damian and I drive to Belltown, the neighborhood north of downtown where he came down to deal a few times. It has transformed since the early 1990s. Now, every block seems to house at least one restaurant offering "Northwest fusion" cuisine. New luxury condos, complete with panoramic views of Elliott Bay, have sprouted up. A small park on the corner that used to be a basketball court and a hangout for dealers and the homeless has become a dog park where owners, plastic-lidded cups of coffee in hand, watch their pets frolic off-leash. Somehow, amid all the development, dealers and users—out of habit, tenacity, or just because they don't have many other places to go—still do business in the neighborhood.

Damian pulls his Nissan sedan into a parking lot. We walk over to a busy corner on Second Avenue and stand in front of an office building with tinted-black glass windows. Damian, who has been heavily involved with the church for a decade, wears a black suit and pressed white shirt. As people pass by in their winter jackets, Damian talks about dealing on this corner with Myran a decade earlier.

"It was rough up in here," Damian says. "There were a lot of people looking for drugs all up and down these streets. The police would ride up around this corner on their bikes. Bikers, that's what we called them. I used to case the place to see if it was hot.

"One time, I was out here with Myran and the bikers rode up and had me jacked against this window"—Damian points to the office building—"but I'd left my dope in the car. Myran, he'd hold it in a brown paper bag in his hand. When the cops came, Myran would act like he was dancing, like he was crazy"—Damian twirls around and waves his arms in imitation—"and he'd throw it away. If they catch you with it in your pockets, that's when they have you."

Damian stops and nods at a gaunt, middle-aged woman in a hooded sweatshirt shuffling down the opposite side of the street. "See, she's looking for some dope right now."

We climb back in Damian's car and drive half a block when Damian says something I at first assume is a joke: "I think that's Myran over there on the street."

I crane my head around and catch a glimpse of a man with a shaved head walking down the street in baggy jeans and a dirty yellow parka.

"I'm going to roll on him," Damian says.

We take a right, drive around the block, and pull up next to Myran as he waits for a crossing signal on the corner diagonal to the one we were just on. He stands in front of a mission for the homeless. Psalm 23 is spelled out in plastic letters inserted into the reader board on the front of the building:

> *The Lord is my shepherd*
> *I shall not be in want*

"All right, get up against that wall over there!" Damian barks, imitating a cop.

Myran, who is digging into a Styrofoam container of chow mein with a plastic fork, is startled. He peers into the car, recognizes Damian, and smiles.

"Hey man, what are ya doing?"

"We're just driving around. You remember Doug? He used to play on that basketball team with us, up at Lakeside School."

"Hey," Myran nods at me. His eyes, which look dull and glassy, give no hint of recognition.

Myran shifts his gaze to Damian.

"You lookin' sharp."

"You know what I'm doing."

"Yeah, I heard about that."

Myran fidgets as a man approaches him from behind.

"I'm getting ready to go to work. I gotta go."

"Well, take care," Damian says.

We drive off in silence, both of us looking ahead. Damian is pensive, the "V" etching his forehead as he stares through the windshield. "He's still in the mix," he finally says. "If it was just me, it would have been better. Sometimes I pick him up and give him a ride. He's always running something. He asks me for money and I just say, 'Man, don't run a game on me, because I know how that's played.'"

Boom, Bust

Dino Christofilis's office is a mile down Second Avenue from where Damian and I ran into Myran, on the top floor of a glass-and-steel office building. There is no indication in the lobby of its existence. It takes an alert eye to spot the small sign reading "Archon Capital Management" when you get off the elevator on the fourteenth floor.

At a few minutes after seven on a morning in August 2007, the four analysts who work for Dino hunch over their computers. The fluorescent-lit room is about thirty feet long and fifteen feet wide. As you enter through a door in the middle, the four desks of the analysts are to the right. A framed print of an oil painting of bulls stampeding down Wall Street hangs on the far wall. An oval conference table fills the middle of the room between the analysts' desks. Dino's large, dark cherrywood desk is to the left of the entrance, facing the rest of the room, its surface completely covered with manila file folders and paper printouts of company financial information. File cabinets line the wall behind the desk.

A whiteboard set on a ledge behind Dino's chair is stacked with handwritten admonitions:

BE THE BEST!
FACTS!
INVEST WITH EDGE
LISTEN + ACT
FAMILY

KNOW YOUR COMPANIES
PLAY TO WIN!

The windows along the wall across from the door look out at a taller, matte-black office building that reflects the morning sun. A water cooler stands next to the window near Dino's desk, and a tangle of power, phone, and Internet cables run next to the wall the length of the room.

For more than an hour, the analysts—all young men dressed casually in jeans or khakis, Polo or button-up shirts—barely speak as they flip through papers, read articles on the Internet, and listen to quarterly company conference calls through headphones plugged into their computers. For long stretches of time, the only sound is the clicking of computer mice and the shuffling of papers.

Dino arrives at eight forty, pulling a black roller-bag briefcase bulging with printouts and pink copies of the *Financial Times* that spill out from its unzipped compartments. The energy level immediately notches up. At six feet tall, Dino looks like every bit of spare fat has been sandblasted off his body. He parts his straight black hair in the middle, and his face is thin, so that each feature—black eyebrows, high cheekbones, brown eyes—is individually defined. His chocolate-brown suit, worn over a blue shirt with no tie, hangs off his frame. He nods at me and goes straight to his desk, jettisoning his roller bag as he sits down and begins to look through his side-by-side Bloomberg terminals, which display real-time quotes on the forty or so stocks he holds positions in. After a few minutes he begins a running conversation with seemingly everyone in the room.

To Marc, who is looking into the financials behind the initial public offering of the online travel site Orbitz: "How fast is Expedia growing? How much cash is Orbitz generating?"

To John, who sits in the far corner near the window and is following a company that makes meters for utility companies: "How much revenue do they potentially lose with this contract?"

To Carson, who sits near Dino to his left: "These guys are messing around with the tax returns, too."

To me, as he flips through screens on his computer: "Europe is fading fast."

Dino started his hedge fund in July 2004 with $1.5 million, about half of it his own money. Back then, the whole operation consisted of him sitting at a computer screen, working the phones for information, and trading stocks. In its first three years, the fund grew to more than $100 million in assets and returned 232 percent (in the same period, the Standard & Poor's 500 benchmark index of large companies returned 39.6 percent). That record placed it among the best-performing of the nine thousand or so hedge funds in the country. Dino hired an old fraternity brother from the University of Washington to work as an analyst, moved to a bigger office, and then had to tear out a wall in that office to double its size in order to fit more people. Institutional money managers in New York and Los Angeles who used to ignore his calls began to meet with Dino when he visited town. Despite his success, there's no room for complacency. "You can't sit still because there's guys out there that are going to pass you right by. You have to actively, aggressively look for the next idea, or the next opportunity, or the next data point," he tells me. "You can't let your eye get off the ball. It's the punch that you don't see that gets you. They'll knock you out."

If you were looking to find the single person who has most adroitly ridden the changes in Seattle's economy over the past two decades, Dino could certainly be a finalist. Like a basketball player who always gets to the open spot on the court before his defender does, Dino has examined how things are playing out and hustled to position himself ahead of the money.

As it turned out, our basketball team worked out for Dino perhaps better than anyone. Though he had been rejected by Lakeside twice, Dino got into the school in sophomore year. He credits his admission to his family's persistence, higher visibility from being on our team, and Randy Finley's cajoling of the school administration.

The school changed the course of Dino's life. While he was used to feeling at ease with his Greek family, Lakeside forced Dino—a fierce competitor on the basketball court but fairly shy off of it—to interact in a different way. "They helped you formulate opinions and articulate them, because I was more introverted, I kept things to myself," he says. "It really kind of pushed me on that front." His interest in business and finance grew from reading newspapers and business magazines in the school library, and his first job in the field—working part-time at the brokerage department of a bank during his senior year—was set up by a Lakeside contact.

By the time he graduated, Dino knew that he wanted to manage money for a living. He enrolled at the University of Washington, where he majored in finance. He knew that if he planned on working as a money manager in Seattle, instead of moving to a financial center such as New York or San Francisco, he was going to have to stand out from the crowd. So he upped his hours at the bank to full time and took classes at night, with the thinking that he would finish college with the real-world experience that others would only get in their first jobs after graduation. He had virtually no social life in college, but coming from a family of Greek immigrants from poor, rural backgrounds, he felt he had to grab every opportunity while it was there. When he graduated in 1994, everything seemed to be going according to plan. Dino took a job as an analyst at a Seattle-based financial management company, and his career looked to be off to a promising start. It just happened that the city was about to be turned upside down.

The beginning of the dotcom stock boom is generally pinpointed to August 9, 1995, the day when Netscape, the company that had designed the Internet browser of the same name, first offered its shares on the market. Even though the firm was only a year and a half old and had yet to turn a profit, the stock soared from an initial offering of $28 to $58 a share. Its founders were instantly rich.

Like the crack epidemic, the dotcom craze seemed to come from nowhere and land like a fist. But as with crack, the conditions that prepped the way were a long time in building. Beginning in the 1970s, American corporations had begun a "restructuring" process that involved eliminating jobs through layoffs, increasing productivity through the use of technology, and relocating manufacturing operations to cheaper locations overseas. As corporate profits increased in the 1980s, the stock market, which had been moribund for more than a decade, began to spasm back to life. At the same time, Americans started to funnel money into individual retirement accounts, which were then newly invented. Mutual funds sprouted to guide money into the market just as tens of millions of baby boomers began to save for their golden years. All these factors came together to sluice money into the market. This flow needed a place to be invested just as the Internet, in the mid-1990s, began to come into the public consciousness. No one knew exactly how people were going to use the Internet, but it seemed sure that they would. Companies that figured out how to profit from it would make fortunes. With the Cold War over and American economic dominance seemingly stretching as far into the future as anyone could see, anything seemed possible.

Russell Horowitz, a 1984 Lakeside graduate who had worked as an investment banker in New York, watched Netscape catch fire and realized that people who got in early on the Internet could make a lot of money. He came up with an idea for a dotcom and recruited John Keister, a former Lakeside classmate and soccer teammate, as a cofounder. The company, Go2Net, was a web "portal," a site that offered people a variety of information—stock prices, sports scores, news headlines—all in one place. The idea was to draw traffic and then make money through advertising. Though Horowitz and Keister were six years older, Dino had gotten to know both of them through the annual Lakeside alumni basketball game. After he'd started to work as a financial analyst, Dino kept in touch with Keister, occasionally calling him and passing on stock tips. The pair approached Dino and asked him to join their start-up. He became Go2Net's fourth employee.

Dino was one of those rare people who know from a young age exactly what they want to do—in his case, manage money—and then single-mindedly apply themselves to getting there. The job with Go2Net offered him two pieces that fit with his ultimate goal. The first was the chance to get in and observe how a company actually runs, so he could use the experience in evaluating the management of other businesses as an investor. Second, he was put in charge of the stock market section of Go2Net, including writing a column of investment advice, so he remained in touch with the market. "The whole passion behind it was staying in finance and sharing my knowledge with individual investors, that was the reason why I went there," Dino says. "I didn't know what the Internet was going to be like. It was early." The early days passed quickly. Go2Net went live on the Internet in November 1996. Five months later, the company went public at an initial stock price of a little under $7. Two years later, it had climbed to $199; a $10,000 investment at the public offering would have been worth more than $280,000.

Though it's forgotten today, in the late 1990s Go2Net often appeared next to Amazon.com when business reporters rolled out examples of Seattle start-ups with stratospheric stock prices and world-changing

potential. Articles such as "Young, Rich and Wondering How to Spend"
ran in newspapers, relating tales about people like the Taco Bell manager
from Phoenix who moved to Seattle, joined a dotcom, and became a millionaire before age thirty. Exactly as it had in the days of the Klondike
Gold Rush a century earlier, Seattle swelled with new arrivals looking to
make quick fortunes.

The euphoria created by easy money is hard to relate. Though I
didn't live in Seattle during the dotcom frenzy, every time I visited and
went out with high school friends for drinks, the talk always centered
around who had landed a job at what start-up as well as rampant speculation about how much he might make when he could cash his stock options. The idea that, by age thirty, you could be rich enough not to work
for the rest of your life was intoxicating, leading people to abandon their
plans and desperately seek—with a lust similar to Humphrey Bogart's
cascading mania for gold in *The Treasure of the Sierra Madre*—to get
on with the hottest dotcom. "Greed was driving a lot of new people that
wanted to get into the industry. They weren't there for the right reasons. . . .
It was across the board from the top to the bottom," Dino says. "Once
you get one guy making money, it's like, 'Jesus, that guy made a million
bucks, I'm going to do it, too.' "

As Go2Net rode the wave, Dino took a new job in the company as
head of investor relations and vice president for corporate development
and strategy. By 1999, Go2Net, which had revenues that year of $22 mil-
lion and a net loss of $10 million, was worth more than $1 billion. Then,
on March 11, 2000, the dotcom bubble—which had inflated the value of
hundreds of companies to ridiculous levels—burst. Over the next year,
the tech-heavy NASDAQ stock exchange lost 60 percent of its value.

The plunge trimmed the price of Go2Net's stock, but it shouldn't
have finished off the company, which still had cash in reserve and was
not losing a ton of money. The beginning of the end came in July 2000,
when InfoSpace, another Seattle Internet company, acquired Go2Net for
what was then valued at a $4 billion deal. Naveen Jain, a charismatic
CEO who had formerly worked as a software engineer at Microsoft, had
founded InfoSpace in 1996. It was basically a phone book on the Internet. Jain later announced that the company, for a monthly fee, would
begin to deliver stock prices and other information to consumers through
their cell phones. Wall Street analysts bought into it, the masses bought
the stock, and, at the time of the merger, InfoSpace—which had never

turned a profit—was worth more than $11 billion. Dino, though, didn't agree with the move to join the companies. "I wasn't a part of that whole process. I maybe said, 'Hey, it looks interesting,' but I wasn't really involved in the decision," Dino says. "After that merger I left. It wasn't a pretty time."

Things quickly went sour. In an article published several years later, the *Seattle Times* reported that before the merger, InfoSpace executives had been using "accounting tricks and dubious deals" to boost revenues to keep the company's lofty stock valuation from collapsing. After the companies formally merged in October 2000, Jain and Go2Net's founder, Horowitz—the chairman and the president of the company, respectively— began to bicker as the dotcom bubble continued to deflate. In January 2001, Horowitz left. Jain remained at the helm for two more years, but it was a long way down. In a mirror image of the heady early days of the dotcom boom, $10,000 invested in InfoSpace in March 2000 would have yielded $20.67 by June 2002.

By then, Dino was long gone. He'd decided that he was going to do what he always wanted to do: work for himself and make a living buying and selling stocks.

A hedge fund is basically an investment vehicle for very wealthy people— Dino's, for example, requires a minimum outlay of $500,000—looking for high returns on their capital. Unlike mutual funds, the way the average person invests in the stock market, hedge funds are lightly regulated. That allows managers to both go "long" on stocks—betting that their prices will go up—while also selling "short," which entails taking a position against a stock in the belief that the price will go down. This means that a fund can be "hedged" to perform well no matter what direction the market takes. Hedge funds typically take 20 percent of profits as well as an annual management fee of 2 percent of the money in the fund.

The job of a hedge fund manager is to scour the global markets to find investments that will beat the average return, whether that is investing in a Seattle software company, platinum mines in South Africa, or betting that the value of the Japanese yen will rise against the U.S. dollar. Some hedge funds use computer models to try to predict shifts in the stock market, allowing their managers to place large bets on those movements. Other funds, like Dino's, seek to identify companies whose fortunes are changing—for better or for worse—and buy their stocks or sell them short before other players in the market catch on. In many ways, the job of running a hedge fund is similar to that of a professional athlete. As in sports, performance is easily measured—by points, rebounds, and assists in basketball, and by overall return as a hedge fund manager. Underperformance will end your career. Dino nods when I mention the analogy. "You're as good as your numbers. If you don't do well, guys fall like that," he explains, snapping his fingers.

Until fairly recently, hedge funds were a fairly arcane type of investment, mainly known by Wall Street insiders and the rich. Occasionally, hedge fund managers made the news, such as when Long Term Capital Management, a huge fund, lost $1.9 billion in one month in 1998 and set off a global financial crisis. Hedge funds really began to grow in popularity after the dotcom crash. While the stock market fell 40 percent between 2000 and 2002, the average hedge fund stayed even. That—as well as low interest rates after 9/11 and easy money created by the housing boom—spurred an inflow of money to such funds. In 2000 there were about four thousand hedge funds with $324 billion under management. By 2007, there were an estimated total of nine thousand hedge funds responsible for around $1.5 trillion.

By midmorning on the day I visit Dino's office in August 2007, the market has dropped several hundred points. It is the beginning of the subprime mortgage crisis, in which tens of thousands of people, lured into home loans by low introductory rates, began to default as the teaser rates expired and reset higher. Most of the people classified as "subprime" mortgage lenders either had spotty credit histories or lower-than-average incomes for borrowers. Their loans had been made possible by inventive Wall Street securities that bundled the mortgages and sold them as bonds (in the old days, mortgages were issued by local banks, which had a greater interest in making sure a borrower could make monthly payments). As long as interest rates stayed low and the price of homes kept rising, everyone made out—people with lower incomes got to buy homes, and Wall Street made a killing. Now, with credit drying up and insecurity about what would happen next, markets from New York to London to Shanghai were seizing up.

Several huge hedge funds—many with assets valued well in excess of $1 billion—had already gone bust or lost large percentages of their capital. All had been "quantitative" hedge funds, which had relied on computer models to guide their investments. The risks of the subprime meltdown and resulting credit squeeze had not been factored into their calculations.

"The quants are the ones really getting hit by this. We're doing all right. We have a lot of shorts out," Dino tells me as he looks at his portfolio on the computer screen. A cover ripped from a February 2007 *BusinessWeek* magazine is taped on the wall behind Dino's chair, with the headline IT'S A LOW, LOW, LOW, LOW-RATE WORLD. Dino tells me that he stuck it up there to remind himself, in contrarian fashion, that the days of easy credit were probably just about over. "I knew it was near the end," he says. "It was time to short the debt plays."

The brunt of running the fund involves finding investment ideas through research—basically, what the analysts do full time. When I ask Dino for an example of an investment that went well, he tells me about a brand of expensive designer jeans called True Religion. While Dino was researching, he saw a reference to the company and found out that the jeans were hot in L.A. and New York. Dino and his analysts checked out the firm, calling stores and distributors to try to gauge how the jeans were selling. They spoke with the company's management to see if they had the ability to manage the brand as demand increased. When Dino invested in True Religion, it was trading at $1. Over the next year, as the jeans became a mainstream fad, the stock climbed to $20.

As we sit in his office, Dino calls the CEO of a small company that is one of many trying to capture the market to stream movies over the Internet. Dino chats with the CEO on speakerphone for a few minutes before the CEO launches into an extremely detailed explanation of the company's technology. As he does, Dino mutes the phone and continues to do about five things at once—sending instant messages to his trader, looking at his portfolio on his computer screen, and carrying on discussions with his analysts. At one point Dino picks up his cell phone as it rings and has a brief conversation.

Just as the CEO finishes, Dino takes the phone off mute and fires questions at him: "How much cash do you have? How much debt? What are the players in this space? What's going to take this to the next level? How comfortable are the big studios with you delivering their stuff, given your size and the amount of capital you have behind you?"

As the CEO begins another explanation, Dino puts the phone back on mute and continues multitasking.

Two years later, in the fall of 2009, Dino and I meet on a Saturday morning in New York City. As we walk from his hotel in midtown Manhattan, we pass several groups of runners dressed in brightly colored outfits and carrying cups of coffee. They have just finished an international "friendship run" in advance of the New York City Marathon, set to start on Sunday. Dino, who is married with three kids and one more on the way, has a rare day off. Yesterday he met with current and potential investors in his fund. After meeting with me this morning, he'll do some shopping and then get on a plane for Madrid, where he's been invited to participate in an investors' conference sponsored by Merrill Lynch. From there he'll fly to Athens to visit family and check out a few potential investments.

The past two years have been trying ones for the stock market, which lost more than half of its value between the fall of 2007 and the spring of 2009. Several thousand hedge funds—including many big players—have folded and disappeared. Dino's fund, in the meantime, has continued its run. Between 2004 and 2009, Dino is up 414 percent, a time during which an investment in the S&P 500 would have yielded nothing. Since my visit to his office in 2007, Dino has hired two more analysts and moved the firm onto a high floor in the Rainier Tower, one of Seattle's most prominent skyscrapers.

We settle in at a large and crowded diner—Dino chats with the manager in Greek—to talk. When I ask how he rode out the financial collapse, Dino tells me that his fund went heavily short on the market in the months before it cratered. "You just gotta listen to what's going on day to day," he says over an egg-white omelet, fruit salad, and plate of hash browns. "When the car wash guy is buying a house, that's just a balloon that's inevitably going to pop."

A key to managing money and dealing with the stock market is keeping an even keel, not letting the daily turmoil get to you, Dino tells me. "You can't get emotional, you can't get caught up in what the markets want you to do, because they'll try to stir your emotions," he says. "No, just be steady, live your life, enjoy your family, enjoy the team that's around you, and collaborate and work together and row the boat."

I mention to Dino an article I've recently read that traced the series of booms and busts that have rocked the world economy since the early 1980s, including financial crises in Latin America, Russia, and Asia; the stock market crash of 1987; the savings and loan bust in the United States; the dotcom bubble; and the housing bust and global financial meltdown. The authors, a pair of economists, argue that the cycle of pumping money into the financial system after a bust has become a disastrous pattern sure to generate more booms and busts. They predict that the next bubble and bust will come in emerging markets.

Dino listens and shrugs. "That's how this world is run," he says. "Envy and greed. Those are cycles. Those all show up at certain parts of the cycle. So those are things I'm cognizant of, you just gotta be aware of them. Fear's another one. We see fear, envy, greed."

I tell Dino that while most people experience a financial bust and call for the government or some authority to do something to stop the next one, it sounds like he sees them as an inevitable part of human economic existence, something to be incorporated into his models.

He nods. "It's been going on for centuries, whenever there's countries growing, you're going to have these. When there's money being circulated, it's going to gravitate toward wherever the easiest way to go is—the point of least resistance is where the dollars are going. It's cheap money, and if you can get into emerging markets, it's going to go there. If it's the housing deal, you're giving money there, it's going to be houses. It's boom, bust."

Later in the day, after Dino and I part, I think about the boom-and-bust cycle he laid out. A part of me resists his depiction of relentless surge and contraction, though when I look at the record, I can't disagree with Dino—economic existence in market societies has for centuries followed that pattern. Some people have made fortunes, and others have been broken; in Dino's words, every trade has two sides. There's no reason to think that this cycle is going to stop. Regulation can work for a time, but the historic pattern is that the lessons of a crash are always forgotten. Greed comes to the fore, people find ways around the rules, and the next bubble begins.

Technology has simply sped the process. Two booms in roughly the past century had centers in Seattle. For the Yukon Gold Rush, you generally had to pack up and get yourself physically to Alaska before you found that you'd wasted all your money. This limited the amount of people who could take part, and at least those who did could say they had a costly adventure. For the dotcom boom, one hundred years later, you didn't even need to get out of your underwear. You could sit at your computer anywhere in the world and invest your life's savings in soon-to-be nearly-worthless stocks such as Webvan and InfoSpace—financial devastation from the comfort of your own home. Now, when we can watch our portfolios fluctuate up and down on our cell-phone screens in real time, it makes life seems ever more lashed to the gyrations of the world markets—mercurial beasts that favor or obliterate 401(k) plans as their owners pray for mercy.

Dino seems born for his work. There is no sense he's in the hedge fund business just to get rich, but more that he loves the analysis, the adrenaline, and the decision-making. He also has an astounding gift for understanding financial markets and an ability to look at economic life unemotionally. In the same way, some people have a great aptitude and love for basketball, and others don't. Unfortunately, in our modern economic system, few of us have the skills of a Dino.

· · ·

One morning at seven thirty, I arrive at Terminal 30, about a mile south of downtown Seattle. I turn off the road into a vast, empty parking lot. To the west, four white cranes rise over Elliott Bay. To the north, I see the side-by-side stadiums of the Seattle Mariners and the Seattle Seahawks. A little bit past them, in the heart of the downtown office district, the black surface of the Columbia Center office tower mirrors the morning sun. The Rainier Tower, where Dino works, juts up nearby. It is at least a hundred yards across the parking lot, which abuts a canal where ships dock. At the far end there are nine white, rusty shipping containers stacked three across and three high on the concrete lot. Past the containers, I park in a line of cars.

A few minutes later, JT pulls up in a white Pontiac sedan. There is a blue baseball cap on the ledge above the backseat. On its front, facing out of the back window, are the silver numbers "206"—the Seattle area code.

JT springs out of the car. He wears a gray sweatshirt with SEATTLE SEAHAWKS written on the front, loose blue jeans, a blue knit cap, and chunky work boots. The thick, black beard he usually wears has been shaved down to a goatee—he thinks it makes him look younger, he tells me later. He walks with a jaunty step and almost reaches me before he stops, pivots around, rushes back to his car, and then comes back smiling, holding up for explanation a pair of blue gloves lined with rubber on the palms for grip.

"I just got off the phone with my mom," JT tells me. "She wanted to make sure I made it down here, that there was no problem with traffic or anything. I told her everything was fine. No way I was going to be late for this."

We walk over to a trailer parked on the lot. About twenty-five people stand outside, some talking in low voices, others keeping to themselves. Several hold cardboard cups of coffee and drink through the plastic lids. All are dressed in similar fashion to JT, in jeans, sweatshirts, and boots, and they range in age from about eighteen to fifty. A couple of the younger kids, with their buzzed hair and eager faces, look like they just walked off the high school football field. Some of the men look like they're coming off hard nights. Four men, including JT, are black. One man looks like he might be Native American. Everyone else, including the two women in the group, is white.

This is an important day for JT. For several years, at the urging of an older family friend who works as a longshoreman, he's been trying to get on with the union. There is more demand than work, so positions go by lottery. JT's number recently came up, and he got called to attend an orientation. A few days before today, he'd gone to a doctor, taken a physical, and peed in a cup for a drug test.

A job on the docks starts at $21 an hour, with benefits. For JT, that's way more than he can make anywhere else he can think of. As he sees it, his other options consist of low-paying work such as detailing cars. "I'm thirty-five effing years old," he'd told me a few days earlier. "I really need this."

The door into the trailer swings open, and we file into a narrow room with several rows, four-across, of plastic folding chairs. At the front, there's a TV on a wheeled cart and a whiteboard upon which the word LASHING is written and underlined. This is another test for everyone in the room, to see if they can handle the physical exertion it takes to lock down—"lash"—cargo containers.

After everyone settles into a seat, a white man in his forties, wearing jeans, a golf shirt, and a mustache, comes out and tells us to write our names on the clipboard he's holding. Then we'll watch a training video before going out to practice.

Later, everyone in the group dons orange reflective vests and white hard hats and files outside to stand around a stack of white cargo containers. They need to use a metal pole to pick up and secure each container with a long bolt. They have thirteen minutes to do all nine containers. JT does his in eight, but he is huffing and puffing by the end. Though the men cheer them on, neither of the two women can manage it.

After everyone is released, JT tells me that he was most excited by something the man with the clipboard had said before the test: "This is a way you can support your family."

"That's what I wanted to hear," JT says.

A few days after we meet on the docks, on a Saturday morning, I drive down with JT and his family to a Boys and Girls Club about twenty miles south of Seattle to watch Kiera, the daughter of JT's girlfriend, play in a tournament. As we enter the gym, we're greeted by the sound of basketballs hitting the floor and bouncing off the red walls as the two teams of eighth-grade girls warm up.

I sit to the left of JT on the aluminum bleachers, which are only four rows high. The gym is crowded with the parents and brothers and sisters of the players. Kiera's team is almost all African American, except for a few girls who look like Filipinas and a white girl. The opposing team is all white. JT wears jeans, Nikes, a baggy white T-shirt, and a thick green rubber band, like the Lance Armstrong "Livestrong" bracelets, around his left wrist. When I ask him what it's for, he tells me, "So I don't get pinched!" I had forgotten that it was St. Patrick's Day.

JT's eleven-year-old daughter, Kamari, sits one row below us, next to JT's right leg. She wears jeans and a pink jacket, has her hair braided in cornrows, and listens to Lil Wayne on the pink iPod Mini she holds in her right hand. On the bottom row of the bleachers, JT's girlfriend, a dental assistant, sits and talks with another mother. JT's seven-year-old godson, Dajon, wears the blue-and-green jersey of the Seattle Seahawks running back Shaun Alexander, and hangs on JT's neck.

"God-Dad, do you know where Milwaukee is?" Dajon asks.

"You mean what state?" JT asks. "I don't know."

"Do you know where Kalamazoo is?"

JT shakes his head.

"Do you know where Austin is?"

"No."

"What about Fort Worth?"

"No, I don't know where it is! Tell me!" JT says, laughing.

"Texas!"

"This one's really smart. He does really well in school," JT says to me. "He's really good at basketball, too."

He turns to Dajon. "How many points did you score in your last game? Thirty-two?"

Dajon looks down bashfully. "Thirty-five," he says.

After the game starts, Dajon goes to play on the other side of the club, where there are foosball tables and lots of kids running around. A little while later, I look over and see that Kamari has climbed up and is sitting on the other side of JT. She is leaning over and resting her head on his shoulder.

JT has three daughters in total: Kamari lives in Seattle with her mother; his two other daughters, four and two, live in Pasco in Eastern Washington with their mother, but come over to visit often. "Growing up without a father, you know how it feels, so you're not going to do that to something you love, and something, you know, that's very important in your life," JT has told me. "I wanna be there so they don't let another man abuse them once they get out there on their own. Some guys can be really just ugly with a female, you know?"

In the gym, Kiera's team takes a big lead but eventually falls apart in the fourth quarter and loses. JT, who had been cheering enthusiastically— "That's what I'm talking about!" he shouted when a girl made a good play—falls silent, shaking his head at the implosion.

"I've got to get this longshoreman thing right," he tells me as we sit in the stands. "I've got to support these kids."

The streets, which had seemed exciting when he was fifteen, JT says, have gotten really old. You get tired of seeing the same people doing the same hustles day after day, year after year. The flush times of the crack era, JT tells me, are long gone—now it's nothing but a grind.

As far as the longshoreman job, even though he has passed all the tests, it could be years before he qualifies for a full-time job. Junior members of the union have to work up the ladder, filling in on call when there's a need. Because of that, the friend of JT's mom who hooked him up with the union has recommended he also take a course on how to be a flagger on construction projects—one of the guys who holds signs telling oncoming traffic to stop or slow down.

"When people ask my daughters, 'What does your father do?'" JT says to me, "I want them to be able to say, 'He's a longshoreman,' not, 'He's a drug dealer.'

"This is what I want my future to be. I want to make good money, man, take care of my kids. As long as I can take care of my kids and the woman in my life, if I get blessed with anything after that, cool.

"I'm sitting there looking at my girls and I'm like, man, it's up to you to get them out of the situation that they're growing up in. That *I'm* putting them in. You know what I'm saying? A lot has to with your parents, what position they put you in, they play a big role. If I can't get my kids in a better situation they're going to turn out like me. I look at my girls and I'm like, man, I gotta do something to change the situation or they'll be stuck in it. Just like me, James Credit, Tyrell."

Gentrified

For years, the Reverend Samuel McKinney gave a clear message to the members of his congregation at Mount Zion Baptist Church: Resist selling your homes to the influx of white folks looking to buy into the Central Area. Mount Zion, founded in 1890, had become a venerable institution under the stewardship of McKinney, a Cleveland native who arrived in 1958 to head the church. It was McKinney, a friend of Martin Luther King Jr. from their days at Morehouse College, who had arranged King's only visit to Seattle, in 1961. In the following years, McKinney had been at the front of Seattle's civil rights movement, leading protests for open housing and school integration. As whites began to move into the Central Area in increasing numbers in the 1980s and 1990s, McKinney had been vocal about the need for the neighborhood to retain its African-American character.

So the congregation was astonished when he announced in 2001 that he was selling the home he'd owned for more than forty years and moving to one in the South End, ten miles from the church. Even today, says McKinney, who still keeps a post office box in the Central Area, someone approaches him every week and asks why he left. He tells them, "They made me an offer I couldn't refuse." He bought his Central Area house in 1958 for less than $20,000; he sold it for $500,000. Like much of the congregation, McKinney now commutes in on Sundays.

McKinney's exit was simply the highest profile among thousands of African-American departures from Central Seattle. In 1980, with movement south into the Rainier Valley already under way, the Central Area was about 60 percent black (though some pockets were close to 90 percent black). It's now estimated to be less than 30 percent black and more than 50 percent white. Two-bedroom homes that sold for a few thousand dollars in the 1960s now regularly fetch more than $400,000. Over the past two decades, many older African-American residents of the Central Area, retired and on fixed incomes, found that they couldn't afford the property-tax increases on their homes. They sold, took their profits, and moved south. In the meantime, younger blacks without large incomes were priced out.

The result has been a swelling black population in the suburbs south of Seattle, while the number of African Americans in the city dwindles. In 2008, blacks made up an estimated 107,600 of King County's total population of 1.9 million. Of those, 46,000 African Americans lived in Seattle, while 51,700 were in south King County. (Seattle proper's overall population, in the meantime, climbed from 516,000 in 1990 to an estimated 602,000 in 2009.)

The black players from our team haven't been immune to this movement—all of them spent at least part if not all of their childhoods in the Central Area; all of them now live in the South End. In 1998, Coach McClain sold the home he'd bought for $5,000 in 1976 for nearly $300,000. The change in the Central Area only completely sank in for him a few years later when his church—at Twenty-first and Jefferson, really the center of the Central Area—decided to throw a block party. As they walked around to distribute flyers, McClain was shocked at the number of whites who answered their doorbelling. "We really found the makeup of the community had changed, almost like overnight, because no one had taken notice," he says. "Almost every house, I was like, 'Whoah.' There were very few blacks."

The process of gentrification—in which middle- and upper-class people move into a dilapidated neighborhood and rebuild it, often displacing the poor who were there before them—is a global phenomenon hardly unique to Seattle. In Beijing and Shanghai, it's been led by the government, which has bulldozed many of those city's ramshackle old neighborhoods to make way for high-rises. In Harlem, both white and African-American professionals have bought and remodeled the neighborhood's stately old brownstones. Even Finland has seen poorer residents pushed out of its city centers to make way for wealthier residents.

As cities have seen traditional manufacturing industries decline, those businesses have been succeeded by postindustrial ones such as media, finance, and technology. To be plugged into the world economy, companies locate in cities that are transport and communication hubs. While whites fled the city during the 1960s and 1970s, many have been lured back by new restaurants, cafés, art galleries, boutiques, Whole Foods and Trader Joe's, and the frisson of multiculturalism. Every spike in gas prices and minute spent stuck in traffic makes proximity to work more attractive. Private schools have multiplied to serve the needs of those who don't want to put their kids in the public system. As this process ramped up in Seattle in the late 1980s, the Central Area—ideally situated and with dramatically undervalued property—seemed to be crying out for redevelopment.

No neighborhood goes back farther for black Seattle than the one at the northern end of the Central Area, where Twenty-third Avenue cuts through East Madison Street, about halfway between downtown and Lake Washington. It's the location of the twelve acres that black pioneer William Grose bought in 1882. The house he built there, which is now a private residence, still stands on Twenty-fourth Street. As Grose sold off pieces of the twelve original acres to other African Americans, the neighborhood became the city's first black residential community—the aforementioned "Coon Hollow." Black-owned businesses followed along the commercial strip on Madison, west of Twenty-third, which was home to a succession of black-owned bars, barbershops, a fuel-supply business, beauty salons, grocery stores, nightclubs, and pool halls. When Ray Charles arrived in Seattle in 1948, he rented a room in the neighborhood and gigged at the Savoy Ballroom on Twenty-second and Madison, which was next door to the Mardi Gras, another club. Balancing out the sin, Mount Zion Baptist Church moved to its current location at Nineteenth and Madison in 1920.

As much as any other part of the Central Area, the East Madison neighborhood has rapidly whitened. One night I meet Andrew Taylor in front of his festively red, large Craftsman-style house a few blocks north of Madison Street. Taylor, who is white, moved in with his family in 1983 and has been active in the neighborhood since—first in community groups and now also by maintaining a local blog. For Taylor, a short, trim biochemist who wears chunky glasses and has a head of long, unkempt sandy-gray brown hair, the initial attractions of the area were the lower prices and the fact that he could bike to his workplace at a cancer research center in the nearby Capitol Hill neighborhood. As we walk the blocks toward Madison, Taylor outlines the race and class shifts that have happened over the past twenty-five years.

When his family first arrived, Taylor says, the neighborhood was predominantly black—he remembers African-American kids coming over to use the swing set in his backyard; others played football on the triangular patch of grass in front of his house. The next-door neighbors ran a daycare out of their house. Though low-income, he says, "there was a feeling that things were going to improve." Within a few years, though, rock cocaine arrived. Down the street, a home became a crack house, with people coming and going day and night. After a shooting, the police shut it down, but the drug traffic spilled over to the streets as the East Madison area became one of the city's quick stops for crack. A corner near Taylor's house was soon occupied with teenage kids who hung around the pay phone. "The bushes next to them were overgrown, they were great for hiding in, doing drug deals, exchanging drugs for sex," Taylor says.

In response, the community gathered to discuss what to do. "I went along to the first couple meetings, and if you could have captured that energy, it was just astounding. A cross section of the neighborhood— young, old, black, white—everybody was pissed off at the drug dealers," Taylor says. After a few meetings, a community group was formed and a strange thing happened: "We got organized, did things the 'white' sort of way of having meetings and committees, and the black people went away and we never saw them again." When I ask Taylor why, he says, "I don't know to this day. We would reach out to them, we would tell them we were having meetings, we would leave flyers."

When I speak with Adrienne Bailey, an African American who grew up in the neighborhood after her parents bought a house there in the 1940s, she tells me the reasons for the lack of black interest were simple. For one, she says, there were cultural differences in communication, and older black people at the meetings felt they were not shown respect. Then there was the fact that though everybody saw the drug dealing as a problem, for the white people—many of them newcomers—it came down to an issue of nuisance and property values. The black residents had conflicting feelings—they knew the kids out on the street as cousins, brothers, and sons. When they heard whites speak about them as if they were "animals," Bailey says, it hit a nerve. While the solution to the white people in the neighborhood was generally to involve the police, most blacks were unwilling to see the teenagers sent to jail for what they saw as a problem related directly to a lack of jobs, education, and opportunity.

The community association that did form immediately got to work, eventually getting the pay phone removed and successfully goading the city to trim the trees and bushes. They convinced the Seattle police to park a "mobile control center"—basically a big truck with SEATTLE POLICE DEPARTMENT emblazoned on the side—in the neighborhood. What developed, Taylor tells me, was a zero-sum game with the community association that had started at Twenty-third and Union, the corner six blocks down where JT and Tyrell hung out. "Essentially it was Ping-Pong," he says. "When we complained, we'd get more police emphasis, and the trade moved down to Twenty-third and Union. They'd get more emphasis, it would move back to us."

The changes to the neighborhood accelerated in the mid-1990s as the crack era ended and the tech and property frenzies began. In 1993, Norm Rice, Seattle's African-American mayor, announced his vision for "urban villages." The idea was to encourage "managed" growth and density in Seattle by creating a number of zones within which people would live within easy walking distance of daily needs such as grocery stores. The East Madison area was one designated hub within the grand scheme, with the business strip along Madison Street planned to serve the needs of the "village." As the details were hammered out in community meetings and the city council over the next few years, East Madison was rezoned so that lots with single-family homes could be redeveloped into "denser," multifamily residences. Commercial buildings along Madison, which had been low-slung at one or two stories, were allowed to go up to sixty-five feet—about six stories.

The practical outcome was a revolution in architectural style. As the tech economy heated up, the East Madison area—just ten minutes by bus to downtown and an easy drive over to the eastern suburbs where Microsoft is headquartered—became in demand. Developers realized that they could buy the homes on the block—many owned by older African Americans—for about $300,000, knock them down, and replace them with skinny, four-unit town houses. Each apartment in a town house could then be sold for about the price the developer had paid for the property. Taylor and I view the results as we walk down a block on Twenty-first Street just around the corner from his house. Only a few old bungalows and Craftsman-style homes remain, dwarfed by duplexes and two-story, flat-fronted gray and white town houses. I grab a FOR SALE flyer from a box. It advertises a three-bedroom town house unit with red-oak floors, a granite-faced gas fireplace, and a kitchen that will "entice a chef." The asking price is $470,000.

We continue down until we hit Madison. Across the street, where the Savoy Ballroom used to stand, a mammoth luxury apartment complex fills the whole block, with a full-size Safeway occupying the ground floor. Kitty-corner to that building sits an empty lot dotted with grass and patches of asphalt. For years it was home to a small grocery store and a nightclub called Deano's. At night the bar attracted a younger African-American clientele, including JT, who sometimes stopped by to have a drink. The streets outside were often populated with crack dealers and users—generally only the most desperate, as the Seattle police subjected the area to continuous scrutiny. The local community association—with Andrew Taylor as the most vocal proponent—hounded the city to do something about the drug traffic, which they saw as directly tied to the club. After years of stasis, economics took care of the problem—in 2008, right before the Seattle property market crashed, a local developer bought the land from its African-American owner for $7.5 million. The developer plans to build a $60 million apartment and retail complex at the location. The people who will live there are expected to work in places such as the Amazon.com headquarters being built a few miles away, which is in the heart of an old light-industrial neighborhood that Microsoft cofounder Paul Allen has redeveloped with a vision of filling it with biotech firms.

In the midst of all the redevelopment sits a throwback to an earlier time, the beauty shop owned by DeCharlene Williams, a one-story brick building with yellow trim, fronted by a five-foot-high, gated iron fence. Pots filled with plastic flowers are arranged in front of three large windows, which feature framed photos of black women wearing fashions that would have been in style when our team was on the court in 1986. A poster says CONFIDENCE IS ATTITUDE. An old-fashioned striped barber pole hangs from the corner of the building.

One morning I stop by to speak with Williams, a short, tough, and outspoken woman with a taste for the flamboyant, as evidenced by her blond wig. Born in Texas in the 1940s, Williams moved at age four with her mother to Portland, Oregon, where her mom found a job in a ship-yard. Williams started working in the fields picking beans and straw-berries at age ten, married at age fifteen—she lied about her age—and moved to Seattle with her new husband. She studied business at a voca-tional school and soon was working several jobs—serving cocktails to the city's white elite at the Seattle Tennis Club, assisting in special educa-tion classrooms, and cutting hair. She bought her shop in 1968 and re-members that she got the news that Martin Luther King Jr. had been killed as she was moving in. Staying in business hasn't been easy—it's included running off drug dealers, thieves, and corrupt cops looking for kickbacks. "I didn't let them scare me," Williams tells me. "I got a .38 and a .22 and a derringer, and kept them with me, and I stayed out there and tried to help others. You've got to stand up and let them know."

The gentrification of the Central Area presents a different problem. Many Central Area black-owned businesses have shuttered as their cus-tomer base has left. Those that have remained have adjusted to serve the more affluent newcomers, or, like Williams's, have clients who are will-ing to drive in from the suburbs. The developer who owns the empty lot up the street has approached Williams about buying her out—he tells me he thinks it would be a great place for a restaurant—but she bristles when I ask her if she's considering it. "This is prime property here," she says. "I'll go down with it." But when I ask how she sees the future of the neighborhood, Williams tells me, "In twenty years, it's going to be all high-rise places, I would imagine. And whoever can afford to stay. Race is not what it is anymore. It's called money. And so race is money now. If you got money to stay in a place, you can stay."

The implications of gentrification on what was once a geographically cohesive black community can be glimpsed on Sundays. One day, when I attend Mount Zion Church, the large, gravel parking lot is perhaps a quarter full. Inside, a few hundred people sway to the gospel choir. Samuel McKinney, now pastor emeritus, sits in a pew next to his wife. The congregation, almost all black, is well dressed. The average age looks to be about sixty.

At the same time, twenty miles to the southeast, between the towns of Renton and Kent, the Reverend Leslie Braxton preaches to a younger flock at the New Beginnings Christian Fellowship. In 1999, Braxton, who is African American, had become pastor of Mount Zion after McKinney's retirement. Six years later, members of the church began a drive to have him removed; when they listed their complaints, they objected to everything from his sermons to his leadership style. Braxton left and founded New Beginnings, taking several hundred of Mount Zion's members with him. Striking out in a different direction, Braxton has embraced the racial mix of the new suburbs, hiring a white executive pastor—the person who runs the church's daily operations—and making a special effort to reach out to mixed-race couples as well as the area's growing Hispanic and Asian populations. The church, as he sees it, has to embrace the new reality—it can no longer afford to be an exclusively black institution in what is becoming an increasingly jumbled culture.

The two churches straddle a generational fault line: on one side, an older black population that commutes back to the Central Area to maintain its tradition; on the other, a younger one moving on to a future in the suburbs that now surround a wealthier, more exclusive city. Looking at it over the course of decades, the move to Seattle's southern suburbs is another step in the still-unfinished black migration from the South, with the grandchildren of African Americans who came up in the 1950s and 1960s exiting the city, pushed by economic factors as their elders once were from places such as Louisiana and Mississippi.

When white people talk about the gentrification of the Central Area, a common refrain is, "It's not race, it's economics." "People wanted to sell and move to the 'burbs," the developer seeking to buy DeCharlene Williams's property tells me. If anything, he says, Williams just "hates" that white people are moving in. "A lot of black people think there's a conspiracy to freeze people out," he says. "That might have been the case thirty years ago. If anything, it's the opposite now."

Of course, for many black people, thirty years is not that long ago. They remember when the Central Area was left to fester—black homeowners were unable to get loans, their children had to attend substandard schools, and racial discrimination in employment was open and obvious. Those factors created the depressed real estate prices in the Central Area that developers, now that the neighborhood is seen as a desirable place to live, have capitalized on. Given this, it's easy to see why a woman like DeCharlene Williams, who has fought her whole life to make a place for herself, isn't going to easily roll over and sell out.

If there's a tragedy to it, it's that African Americans happened to be sitting on an inadvertently created gold mine—the Central Area—that will now only increase in value. In essence, individual African Americans took one-time payouts to sell their property and moved out. The real value went to the people who bought the land, knocked down the old houses, and built town houses and luxury apartments in their stead. If anything, the people who suffered discrimination for so long should have had a way to pool their resources and somehow profit from the redevelopment. When taxes and the other costs of moving to the southern suburbs are figured in, the reality is that, for the people who sold, very little lasting wealth was created.

Instead, the black community now maintains a mostly emotional connection to the Central Area. When I ask the Reverend Samuel McKinney what the dispersal from the neighborhood means for African-American identity, he responds with a query of his own: "The question is, can we have community without proximity?"

This comes home to me one day when JT and I head to a Starbucks at Twenty-third and Jackson, the area that was the epicenter of the city's rowdy jazz and speakeasy scene from the 1920s to the 1950s, a past alluded to by black-and-white photos hung on the walls. JT's mom grew up nearby in the Yesler Terrace housing projects after her family came up from Louisiana, and JT spent his first few years there as well. The coffee shop, at the southern end of the Central Area, remains a gathering place for African Americans—many drive up from the South End to meet friends there or just to hang out. During the twenty minutes we sit at a table, a number of black people—ranging from teenage to elderly—either wave to JT or come up and say hello. Of course, the African Americans who make it up to Starbucks represent a small percentage of those who either maintain a toehold in the Central Area, or have cars and the time to drive up.

JT tells me that many more people he knows now live in the suburbs south of Seattle, places such as Renton, Kent, Des Moines, and Federal Way, all the way to Tacoma, thirty miles down Interstate 5, working in service jobs such as clerking at Wal-Mart and loading luggage at the airport, if they have work at all. They are not coming up to the Starbucks. When JT thinks about the loss of the Central Area he grew up in, he says, he hurts. "Your family, friends, everyone used to be right around the corner. Now you don't see anyone anymore," he says. "Your roots are gone, you know? It feels like you've lost your life."

Saved

Damian Joseph's church, the Greater Glory Church of God in Christ, is in South Seattle, on Martin Luther King Jr. Way. Arriving from the north, you pass a car-repair shop, some Vietnamese and Cambodian restaurants and grocery stores, and a McDonald's. The recent opening of a light-rail line along MLK has helped to kick-start gentrification—one of the newest additions to the neighborhood is a drive-through Starbucks. The church's beige steeple rises over a U-Haul lot. A cyclone fence topped with razor wire separates the church's property from the trucks and trailers next door.

Sunday services start at eleven thirty. As you enter through the glass doors, a male usher in a black suit hands you a program. Two rows of electric chandeliers cast a bright, almost harsh light. About 150 people are spaced out in fifteen rows of blue-upholstered pews divided by four isles. Most people wear black or navy suits or dresses. A few are in jeans, and one woman has on a black satin jacket with the words GOODWRENCH SERVICE PLUS embroidered on the back. Mothers hold their babies, and kids wander in the aisles. Everyone is black.

The music starts within a few minutes. Up on the low platform behind the wood-trimmed glass altar, the two men and three women in the choir begin a call and response.

"Woke up this morning with my mind," the choir sings. "STAYED ON JESUS," responds the congregation.

"Singin' and prayin' with my mind" . . . "STAYED ON JESUS."

"Hallelu . . . Hallelu . . . HalleluYAH!" shout the chorus and the congregation together.

The choir sings into microphones amplified through speakers hung on the walls. A drummer and an organist accompany the singers. In the pews, people clap, stomp their feet, and sing. A woman shakes a tambourine. The noise reverberates and seems to rattle the building at its foundations.

Damian, a minister in the church, stands on the stage, in front of the choir, in a black suit, white shirt, and red bow tie. He holds his arms above his head, his hands splayed, mouth open in song. Occasionally he fires off a volley of claps that sound like crisp rifle shots and then raises his fists, pumping them in the air.

Before long, Pastor Sam Townsend enters. A trim man in his late fifties, with high-and-tight hair and a brushy mustache, he wears black vestments with gold trim and has a white towel draped over his left shoulder. Townsend paces the floor in front of the congregation, shooting phrases into the wireless microphone in his right hand.

"Do you *feel* God's *presence?*" he asks.

A burst of organ. The drummer brushes his crash cymbal.

"Can you *feel* God's *presence?*"

The music begins to pick up again.

People sway from side to side, their hands held up in the air.

"*Thank you Jesus, thank you Jesus, thank you Jesus,*" a woman chants.

A large man in a blue suit begins dancing, drops to the ground, shakes for a moment, and then springs up with his hands in the air.

A young woman falls to her knees, crying, and presses her forehead to the floor. A female usher rushes over and holds a sheet around her for privacy.

Townsend begins to preach. "I remember when you were hurting, when you were struggling, when your homes were torn apart. Come on, people! You still have an enemy! We still need God, more than we did before. The world is coming to an end. Prophesies are being fulfilled. The only thing that's going to help you today is this altar," he says, striking the pulpit with the palm of his hand. "Do you know who's going to survive the terrorist attacks? It's going to be the black people. We were born where they put us, down at the bottom. We're used to sifting rat droppings out of our food."

As Townsend speaks, Damian crosses his arms and cradles his chin in his right hand, a look of deep concentration on his face. The service ebbs and flows for three and a half hours, hitting emotional peaks, settling down, and then rising back up. Finally Townsend calls forward everyone who feels down, sick, weary, tired, ready for a change. The organ hums. Young and old trickle from the pews until there are ten people in front of the altar, kneeling, heads down, tears flowing as Townsend lays his hands on each one and leads the congregation in prayer that God will give them the strength to find a new path.

The roots of Damian's strand of Christianity go back just one century, but in those hundred years, the Pentecostal faith has grown at a staggering speed. The most influential early proponent of the religion, William Joseph Seymour, was born in 1870 in Centreville, Louisiana, the son of former slaves. In his twenties, Seymour lived in Indianapolis, where he worked as a waiter, moving later to Cincinnati. During that time, he was "saved" by a revival group that believed Christ was soon to return to Earth and that believers should abandon their old churches to form a new, racially inclusive one to be ready for God's kingdom.

Seymour moved on to Houston, where, during a service in a black church, he saw something that amazed him: a woman entered a trance and began speaking in phrases he could not understand. Seymour was touched by what he thought was a depth of spiritual feeling he could not attain. He had never seen anyone speak in tongues before, but he knew it to be a sign of the Apocalypse.

The phenomenon appears in the Bible in Acts, book 2, which tells of Christians gathering to celebrate the Pentecost, fifty days after Passover. Suddenly, a sound "like a mighty wind" comes from heaven, and each feels the Holy Spirit rush in. They begin to speak with "tongues as of fire." Though they are from different nations, they suddenly understand each other, as if the curse of Babel has been lifted. When people passing by think they're drunk, the Apostle Peter stands and announces that it's the fulfillment of prophesy. The Holy Spirit is pouring out into the world, heralding the coming of the Last Days and the return of Christ.

Almost two thousand years later, in Houston, Seymour questioned the woman about her gift. She introduced him to her former employer, Charles Fox Parham, a white preacher who ran a Bible school. Seymour asked to study in the school, but Parham, being a Ku Klux Klan sympathizer, wouldn't let him in. The two agreed that Seymour could sit outside by an open window and listen.

While Seymour prayed to be granted the gift of tongues, he also preached to black congregations in Houston. A woman visiting the city was taken by his sermonizing and invited him to preach at her church in Los Angeles. Seymour borrowed the train fare from Parham and set off, arriving on the West Coast in 1906. When he got there, he found that the congregation was turned off by his message, so he began to preach in living rooms. His first congregants, all black, were domestic servants and laundry women.

Los Angeles was fertile ground for a new religious movement. The city—hyped by boosters and developers hoping to make a buck by luring more people west—was promoted as a kind of utopia, a land of milk and honey offering opportunity and the chance of riches. In a strange twist, the city, settled by blacks, Indians, and Spanish, was sold as a place of racial purity, where Anglo-Saxons could escape the immigrant hordes of the East Coast. In reality, Los Angeles was then—as it is now—a diverse place, with large racial and class divides. Many people on the bottom were primed for a new religious message. As word of Seymour's powerful preaching spread, pilgrims, black and white, sought him out. On April 9, 1906, a number of congregants were stricken and began speaking in tongues. The crowds grew, and the congregation rented a vacant building at 312 Azusa Street—which had last been used as a stable—and began a movement that quickly radiated out.

The Azusa Street Revival ran for five years, with thousands making the pilgrimage from across the nation. Services were held three times a day, with up to eight hundred people inside and several hundred more overflowing outside. Seymour offered a way to directly encounter God without the interference of church dogma. Mixed in with apocalyptic feelings—an earthquake leveled San Francisco a few days after the revival began—and entrenched social inequality, the movement attracted mostly working-class and poor people of all races. "The baptism of the spirit did not just change their religious affiliation or their way of worship," writes religion professor Harvey Cox in his history of the Pentecostal movement, *Fire from Heaven*. "It changed everything. They literally saw the world in a whole new light." Pentecostalism was an equalizer, a religion not dependent on textual interpretations or centuries of doctrine. Anyone—rich or poor, black or white, educated or not—could experience the gift of tongues and a connection with God. All you needed was a Bible and belief. "The New Jerusalem was coming," writes Cox. "Now the rich and the proud would get their just deserts. The destitute, the overlooked, and the forgotten would come into their own. Even more central for Seymour, in a segregated America, God was now assembling a new and racially inclusive people to glorify his name and to save a Jim Crow nation lost in sin."

Seymour saw the interracial quality of the Pentecostal movement as a sign that it represented a coming together of tribes as described in the Bible. But as revivals sprouted around the country, the movement splintered. One of the main drivers was racial, as white preachers broke away to form their own congregations. But Pentecostalism was well on its way to becoming the fastest-growing religious movement of the past century; there are now an estimated 400 million Pentecostals around the world, and the religion has been particularly embraced in poor countries. In June 1907, Charles Harrison Mason, a black southerner, visited Azusa Street. When he returned to Jackson, Mississippi, he began to preach the Pentecostal faith. His church, the Church of God in Christ, now headquartered in Memphis, is the country's biggest predominantly black Pentecostal church, with more than five million members in congregations spread from Alaska to West Africa. Damian's is one of them.

"Most of the individuals in our church, almost everybody in our church, came to me with nothing. Zero. From the streets. Prostitutes, homosexuals, lesbians, thieves, murderers—now, they all did their time!—but they all came to me that way," Sam Townsend tells me early on a Sunday morning before services. "And all of them, probably eighty-five percent of them, have good jobs now. Homes. Families. They didn't have to resort back to street life, drug-selling, those things, to get ahead."

We meet in his office. Townsend sits behind his large desk in a padded leather chair, in front of a bookcase built into the wall. With his tailored black suit and easy smile, he is a charismatic man—you could imagine him preaching on one of the religious stations on cable on a Friday night—and he is quick to make a personal connection. He peppers the several conversations we have with references to my profession and the old basketball team. His speech is sprinkled with both biblical references and jokes.

Born in 1948, Townsend grew up in Grand Rapids, Michigan, where his dad worked for General Motors, and came to Seattle after a stint in the army brought him to Fort Lewis, near Tacoma. After his discharge, he joined the Seattle Police Department. "I was about twenty years old when I came on the police department," he says, "straight out of the military and into Seattle and involved in all kinds of behavior—drugs, you name it, I lived the life." In 1973, Townsend wandered into a Central Area Pentecostal church, where he knelt at the altar and was saved. In 1980 he founded his church in the basement rec room of a Central Area rental house with a $1,000 loan from his father. The congregation grew from its original six members and, in the late 1980s, Townsend bought the current location (Damian's mom, Helen, joined the congregation at that time). Besides its religious services, the church runs a daycare center and an adoption agency for African-American children.

Money is always tight. The church is funded by tithes collected from the congregation of three hundred, at least those members who can afford to pay. Townsend receives no salary. His wife has taken a part-time job with H&R Block to help make ends meet. Though Townsend wears sharp suits that look quite expensive to my eye, he tells me he shops at secondhand stores. The secret, he says, is to have a good tailor. He pulls up the sleeve of his suit to show me a monogram on his white dress shirt. "This shirt looks pretty good," he says, "but it's not my initials on the bottom of it. I don't know who that guy is!"

"Nothing's in my name," Townsend says when I ask who owns the church. "Everything belongs to the parishioners. If I die today, this belongs to the people. It doesn't go to my wife, my kids, or anybody. Again, you're looking at a guy who came off the street, a guy who preaches the basic tenets of the Bible—nothing coming out of the sky, I don't see angels, I don't see nobody—but I read, and I follow the directions of the Scripture."

Townsend often preaches about the divide between the spiritual and secular worlds. Life here on Earth is fleeting, he says, but eternity lasts forever, so you should keep that primary in your mind. Still, he tells his congregation, you've got to get by while you're here. For many of the church's members, Townsend acts as a middleman between them and Seattle's mainstream institutions, helping them to navigate banks, social service agencies, landlords, and prospective employers. Sometimes he also jibes the congregation for what he sees as its desires to partake in the upper-middle-class good life. At one service I attend, he brings up the automated checkout registers that some local supermarkets have installed. A lot of people just view them as signs of technological progress and speed, he says, but he looks at them and sees members of the church losing their jobs.

Townsend rejects the "prosperity gospel," an idea popular in many churches both black and white, which holds that living a holy life will lead to material rewards. "It's not a biblical teaching. It would be unfair for us to take a Scripture and to say, 'God wants us to prosper and be in health even as our soul prospers,' and then you see the difference in economic levels of people in the church," he says. "We're not coming to God to get anything other than some stability in our life. And we say that if we get some stability in our life, then we can accomplish things, then we can go to college, then we can do whatever, but it's not necessarily a divine principle that if you come to God you're going to get off welfare, if you come to God you're going to get a new car, you're going to get big money, something's going to fall out of the sky."

Instead of thinking about getting rich, Townsend says, you've just got to live your life and not let yourself get too upset or blown off course when things are tough. You've got to keep your head, which means surviving within the dominant culture. "We teach that doors can be open for us that no man can shut. So I don't go into the workplace as an African American feeling that someone is going to discriminate against me, even though it does happen. But there's a power greater than those on Earth that's going to open doors greater than no man can shut, so then when I'm presenting myself, or when the young African-American men here present themselves to white America, so to speak, it's not with a hostile attitude," he says. "It's with a spirit of expectation, that this is my job, I'm gonna get it, and if I get the job, I'm gonna do a good job, because what I'm doing is under God and that is unto man, and I don't feel oppressed and I don't feel angry about what happened four hundred years ago, I'm a new creature, all men are brothers, and so let's go for it."

When someone comes into the church, no matter what their situation, Townsend tries to help. If a new arrival needs a place to stay, a member of the congregation will put him up. If he's broke, people will buy him food. If he just got an apartment but has no furniture, people will donate to him. When the person is ready, Townsend has a variety of contacts he can call to set people up with jobs. The main thing, he says, is to provide an example, give people hope, and show them that there is a way to leave behind some of the turmoil in their lives. "I believe the black man has been suffering for four hundred years, and if it takes God another four hundred years for our deliverance, so be it," he says. "But I'm not going to take matters into my own hands and then have inno- cent, well-intentioned African Americans die at the hands of the oppres- sor just because I'm anxious about getting free. I don't think that's necessary anymore. I don't think it's necessary for dogs to bite us and hoses to be sprayed on our people anymore, because you're dealing with a differ- ent generation.

"These young men that we're talking about now—and I know you know because it's your generation—they're hostile brothers, man. You thought my generation, in the 1960s and 1970s, was hostile, no, no, we'd march and then we'd run, but these guys will die. So the last thing they need is a hostile leader. They need a passive leader, to say, 'No, brother, calm down, I know what you want, let me show you how to get it.'

"So when the little hustlers come into church, they've got money. First of all, I don't allow them to give me anything—Brother Damian will bear witness—I don't allow them to give me anything like the Mafia did the Catholic Church. But what I do is I sit them down and help them put together a business plan. 'OK, you're through with the game, you want to get your life together, you need to get some education, even if it's no more than a GED. Then what kind of skills do you have?' 'Well, I wash cars.' 'Then let's do a detail shop. Let's put together a business plan and do something constructive.' If you can show this kid—especially if he wants out, some of them don't want out, I'm only dealing with those that want out—if you can show this guy where he can make an honest buck and be respected by the rest of the folk in society, he'll do it. He'll do it. But you've got to have some examples. You've got to have a Sam Townsend. You've got to have a Damian."

At twenty-one, Damian had been kicked off the Seattle University bas- ketball team and was on the verge of completely flunking out. He was clubbing, drinking, smoking weed, and generally unhappy. In his turmoil, he checked out the Nation of Islam but was turned off by the "black man/white man stuff." He went to the library and read about different religions—Buddhism, Islam, Hinduism, Christianity. One night, when he was hanging out smoking pot with a friend, he kept thinking that his life was headed for a dead end. Not long after, he was at home at his mom's, on the couch. He started to think about God and said to himself, *Lord Jesus, come into my heart, save me. I believe that you died on the cross, I believe you rose from the dead.*

The transformation was instantaneous. "I just became a new person immediately, like stepping out of this glass and looking inside and seeing life totally different," Damian says. "I was no longer dead." His desires—to drink and smoke, to watch rap videos, to use profanity—were gone. His craving for things such as Air Jordans vanished. He distanced himself from his old friends, got his grades up enough to stay in college, and began a new life. "It's like this, Doug," he tells me. "Living in the same city, you still see the same people. But I'm a new person. All they're seeing is what they're doing. I'm seeing in a totally different way."

It would be impossible to understate how much getting saved changed Damian; his faith and the church became the center of his life. Damian met his wife, Michelle, there shortly after his conversion. Besides Sunday services and Bible study on Tuesday and Friday nights, Damian mentors other members and collects tithes. One Saturday a month, he drives down to Tacoma to the Church of God in Christ's Washington headquarters—a cavernous building in a strip mall—where the leaders of the state's nearly eighty congregations meet.

The church also allowed him to separate himself from the street economy in which so many of friends had gotten caught up. "It's just choices you make," Damian says frequently, expressing his belief that everyone has control over his own actions, no matter how much external pressure there is. Obstacles such as racism, while they exist, are not an excuse, Damian insists. One day, when we are driving near his house in the South End, a black man wearing baggy jeans and a huge white T-shirt crosses the road in front of Damian's car. The man, who looks to be in his early twenties, glares at us. "He's blaming the white man for all his problems. That's what they do," Damian remarks, surprising me with the level of scorn I hear in his voice.

"You can be free in the world but bound in your mind and the things that you do," he says. "That's where a lot of my friends—James [Credit] and all—they were bound, and it ended up sucking them to the end. They weren't free from those things, and I'm free now, to the point where I don't have to be bound to those things that held me captive.

"My happiness and joy come from the inside now and not the outside, so I don't have to have those things. Back then, I just had to be on top, I just had to be seen. It's the pride of life, that's how you get caught up in those things. But now, none of those things mean anything. I'm saved, I'm satisfied. . . . I love it, man, it's the best life I can have."

· · ·

Of all the members of our team, Damian is by far the most grounded in the church. With most of the others, religion and spirituality rarely arise in the course of our conversations. Dino mentions in passing that his kids go to Sunday school at the Greek Orthodox Church. Chris attends weekly meditation classes and practices in the mornings.

In 2007, Coach McClain started his own church. He shares space with an older, more established Central Area congregation and preaches to a dedicated flock of about seventy-five people on Sunday afternoons. Every Wednesday evening, he and his wife, Diane, host Bible study at their house. At one session I attend, McClain sits at his kitchen table and leads a group of ten people, including men, women, and teenagers, through a reading of the book of Colossians. For the McClains, the church is a natural extension of what they've done for decades— open their lives to people in the community who need help, guidance, and love.

Willie Jr. occasionally goes to his dad's services. One day, when we go to lunch at a Mongolian barbecue place in the South End, I ask Will if he's religious. "I know all about church, but I don't lead the life of a Christian," he says. Will is big, boisterous, and quick with a joke. He still loves sports, and tells me he enjoys entering darts competitions at taverns, where he often wins money. "I still drink, go out," he says. "They say you can't live Christ's life when you do that."

With Damian, his faith and the church have shifted his life's trajectory, removing him from one path and putting him on another. Though Maitland did not undergo a religious conversion like Damian, he, too, has put a lot of thought into the direction of his life. He's made major adjustments since we were kids.

If Maitland is surprised when I first reach him on the phone, he doesn't show it. I am so taken aback by the lack of inflection in his voice that I ask if his dad, who had given me his number, had told him I was going to call. "No," he answers, and lets it drop. I wonder if somehow Mait's been expecting an old Lakeside classmate to phone out of nowhere and ask him about basketball.

We chat a few minutes, catching up. Maitland is working at a winery in the Willamette Valley, south of Portland. We set a time for the coming weekend to talk further. When I call on Saturday, he doesn't pick up. I leave a message but don't hear back.

It takes two more years of intermittent phone calls before, one day, Mait calls while I'm in Seattle. I'd left him a few messages letting him know I was planning to drive down to California the next week and would like to see him on the way. When his number comes up on my caller ID, I'm so shocked I do a double take.

We plan to meet the next weekend. When I ask him his address, Maitland says, "An address won't do you much good."

On the way down, I pass through Portland and continue another thirty miles south. I exit and head west, crawling through what seems to be an unending succession of little towns lined with strip malls and regulated by poorly coordinated traffic lights. Past the town of Newberg, it all thins out as I head toward Yamhill, which has a population of roughly eight hundred people.

The two-lane road is empty of traffic as I speed past a series of wheat, barley, and hops fields. Yamhill itself has one blinking traffic light on the main street. Maitland lives eight miles out of town. The driveway to his place starts where the road turns from pavement to dirt. As Mait has instructed, I turn left when I see a dead oak tree. My car bounces up and down as I drive up a hill along a rutted path toward a white one-bedroom house—almost a shack. I pull up under the sheltering branches of a massive cottonwood tree and look out over the valley below, the yellow leaves of grapevines shimmering on the hill opposite. Stepping out of my car, I see beer- and wine-brewing materials—five-gallon glass jugs, various measures and funnels—arranged under the awning by the door.

Maitland comes out to greet me, followed by his small, mixed-breed dog, Sangi. Mait is big—at more than six feet tall, he has packed some weight onto his frame. He wears black sweatpants and a black sweatshirt, has dark blond hair, and a long, dark beard. My first thought, as he ambles toward the car, is that it looks like I'm the first visitor who's been out here in a while.

"Quite honestly, I really loved basketball, but I could have cared less about games," Maitland tells me. "I could have taken or left playing basketball on the high school team. It didn't really bother me whether I got playing time or not."

We're sitting across a table in brewpub in McMinnville, about fifteen miles from Maitland's house. He's been working twelve- to sixteen-hour days over the past few weeks, and he hasn't been able to get out much.

It's the fall wine harvest, the busiest time of the year for winemakers. There are literally tons of grapes to pick, sort, crush, and shift into fermenting vats. The work has left Maitland's hands stained a dark purple, the color deepening to black on the creases around his knuckles and the lines on his palm. While his hands look like those of an old crone who has cooked up too many potions, Maitland's face appears almost totally untouched by time, as if he hadn't aged a day since I'd last seen him. His eyes are soft and blue.

We've come into town so Maitland can wash his clothes, with me following in my car to allow Sangi to ride shotgun in his red pickup. Mc-Minnville, home of about thirty thousand people, is a rough-and-ready rural Oregon town leavened with bed-and-breakfasts and other businesses catering to the tourists who come to sample the area's famous pinot noir. At the laundromat, Maitland—who has shaved and changed into jeans and a flannel shirt—throws a small bundle of clothes into a front loader while kids run around us, shrieking and joking in Spanish.

Maitland first learned to make wine in France, where he worked at a few vineyards after graduating from Western Washington University with a degree in French and chemistry. When he came back to the United States, Mait went to work at his dad's small winery near the Canadian border. In 1999 he moved down to Oregon to start work at a much-lauded boutique winery. He's just gotten a new job as an assistant wine-maker at a much larger winery. The work has been demanding—getting up at five in the morning to make the commute in, arriving home at nine or ten—and the weariness shows on his face as we sip on dark beers and talk about basketball.

"I can't speak to my father's motivations," Maitland says when I ask him about the team. "I have wondered at various times, you know, why did this all really happen? What was going on?"

Maitland had, for me, been an object of envy and sympathy. Randy Finley was a big and charismatic man, and his energy was uplifting and contagious. But he sometimes seemed so dedicated to his own visions that they clouded his perception. One of those things he couldn't quite see clearly was perhaps his own son. Randy, it was obvious, really wanted Maitland to succeed in basketball. To an outsider, it was clear that Mait, while having the size, ability, and temperament to make a decent role player, did not have the athleticism or desire to do more.

"I was probably just as much into sports as other people, but sports have not really remained an integral part of my life in terms of what I do," Maitland says. "I've heard my dad say many times that 'I wanted you to experience sports,' that basketball is a great team sport and skiing is a great individual sport. It's all fine and good and it's hard to say what the correct or incorrect thing is. But I was pushed or borderline bullied into doing that stuff.

"As I've gotten older it's more just that masculine, kind of testosterone-driven thing, you know, I'm not into that, I'm not into winners and losers and proving I'm better than somebody else," Maitland says. "That's the way I try to live my life these days. I try not to feel the need to try to prove to someone that I'm right and they're wrong, and I'm better and you're worse. As long as it stays within the realms of the game, the sport, I'm fine with that. I just don't personally get a kick out of it."

Whenever Maitland came up in a conversation with any of my other teammates, the reaction was similar. Mait was a rock—stoic and solid, a good guy. Maitland, perhaps through his silence more than anything, seemed to have things pretty together. Willie Jr., especially, remembers him with fondness, recalling things they did together as the sons of the team's organizers, such as the time when Will, his dad, and Damian took a trip with Maitland and Randy to a cabin the Finleys owned on the Oregon coast, where Randy took everybody out in a boat to go crabbing.

"I got real close to Mait," Will says. "I remember I used to call him on the phone when I was at Prep and he'd talk me through my homework."

Maitland looks shocked when I relay Will's words to him. "I don't remember helping Willie out all that much," he says. "I have good memories of him, definitely. But at that point in time, I was a pretty quiet, shy guy. It took a lot to get me to open up."

The pressure at Lakeside to excel academically, socially, and in sports, Maitland says, made it difficult to tell anyone he was struggling. "It was hard to admit any problems period, because people are expected to be very good if not perfect," he says. "I never felt like things worked very well for me at Lakeside; I think I would have been better off probably elsewhere."

Maitland tells me he remembers feeling anxious, not wanting to talk to anyone, being on the outside and observing. "That social anxiety and depression made it hard for me to follow any friendship," he says. "A lot of people mistook me for being even-keel, and just slightly aloof and unemotional. That was just the way that I dealt with my problems. It was better to shut down, turn around, and not deal with things—be unemotional."

In the years since school, Maitland has tracked his own path as much as anyone from our basketball team—moving away from Seattle, living a rural life, rethinking the lessons about masculinity we learned as kids. He also has dealt with depression, for which he has found that medication has helped. "I think most of my problem is just a chemical imbalance, because it's just like a switch off or on," Maitland says.

Over the years, he says, he's worked on coming to terms with his dad's very large shadow. "He's a very intense guy. It took a long time to learn how to deal with him and be myself and not just acquiesce," he says. "There's enough that we butted heads about, but by and large we both have our mutual respect at this point."

That evening, we return to Maitland's home. From inside, looking out the windows into the dark, it feels a long way from anywhere. The night seems to have coated the shack like a layer of syrup.

There is only one chair in the small living room—a padded armchair upholstered with black vinyl. I sit in it and Maitland on a beanbag. Sangi—named for Sangiovese, the Italian grape—runs inside and leaps onto my lap, leaving mud all over my jeans. Maitland lightly scolds the dog, grabs it, and cleans its paws with a wad of paper towels.

A chess set sits on a folding stand in a corner. The TV is piled with instructional yoga videotapes, and a bookshelf holds works on wine, yoga, and chemistry. Jugs of homemade beer sit under a table near the door.

Maitland tells me he was surprised to run into Chris a few years ago. Chris, at least in his hard-core playing style, was about the opposite of Maitland—during practices in high school at Lakeside, Maitland was given the punishing job of defending him. "He's turned into a pretty interesting person, not what you might necessarily have expected," Maitland says. "I think a lot of what you saw was just a product of where he came from and his family."

Maitland says that the long days making wine are tiring. "Part of getting into the wine industry for a lot of people is an issue of quality of life and the romance of winemaking and all of that, but for a lot of us, it doesn't end up being that way at all. It's just a lot of hard work. You're doing things that you like and love, but I'd like to be able to find just a slightly more sustainable work position."

He tells me he likes the variety of the job and the way it involves coming up with practical solutions. "You got all sorts of things you gotta do. There's problem-solving: How do we move this wine from here to there? Driving a forklift is kind of the same situation, a geometric puzzle: How do I get to this pallet, dig this out? It's not the same thing day in, day out. There's variety. You solve a problem and there's a tangible result. It's good, physical, hands-on labor and troubleshooting.

"And in the end you're hopeful you have helped to make something that people will enjoy. Whether it's the greatest wine in the world doesn't matter, just as long as someone somewhere appreciates it."

When we wake up the next morning at five, the house is completely fogged in. Maitland turns on NPR, and the sedate voices of *Morning Edition* tell of new bombings in Iraq. I pack up my sleeping bag, and Maitland brews some coffee.

The night was cold. I stumble out to warm up the engine of my car and flip on the parking lights, which glow in the mist. Maitland rounds up Sangi, who has been frolicking in the dark. I follow the taillights of his pickup down the hill. We turn right at the dead oak and drive through the deserted roads on the way to the winery. Maitland drives slow, at twenty-five miles an hour, to avoid hitting any deer that might wander into our path.

I can't see any farther than the cab of his truck. Inside, I make out the back of Maitland's head. Next to him, Sangi pokes hers out the window as we silently cut a line through the fog and the fields.

The System

The evening of January 21, 2006, was a festive Saturday night in Seattle. The next day the Seahawks were scheduled to play the Carolina Panthers in the NFC Championship game. If the Seahawks won, the team would reach the Super Bowl for the first time in its thirty-year history. The clubs downtown were crowded with people getting a start on the next day's merriment.

The parking lot next to Déjà Vu, a strip club near the entrance to the Pike Place Market, one of Seattle's top tourist attractions, was packed with cars and people. At eleven P.M., Myran Barnes was wandering among them. He had on a black baseball hat, a black jacket, and black jeans. Two undercover cops standing in front of the strip joint—a garish, brightly lit place with a pink-and-black color scheme and a logo of two crossed female legs in fishnet stockings on the wall next to the door—saw Myran talking to a man sitting in an SUV.

As Myran walked away from the vehicle, one of the cops approached him.

"Anything going on?" he asked Myran.

"What are you looking for?"

"Forty."

"Who you with?"

The cop pointed at his partner.

Myran asked who had the money. The cop said his friend did.

"I'll take you to it, but one of you has to wait here," Myran said. The cop said he would stay behind, and Myran walked off with his partner.

The pair headed two blocks east on Pike Street. When they got to Third Avenue, Myran told the cop to hold on. He walked over to a man standing near a bus stop, who called over a girl who was waiting inside the shelter. The three conferred, and the girl walked back to the bus shelter. When she returned, she handed a bag of crack cocaine to Myran. Myran returned to the officer, handed him the drugs, and accepted $40.

The man and the girl who had given Myran the drugs headed north up Third Avenue before a team of cops sprang on them, putting them facedown on the sidewalk and handcuffing them. Myran, who had walked in the other direction, turned around, saw them, and took off running. A bus happened to stop, and Myran climbed on. For a moment he thought he was in the clear, until he saw that several police officers had boarded behind him. Myran took the two $20 bills out of his pocket and held them out. "Here's your marked money," he said.

This was far from Myran's first arrest. A little more than a year earlier, he'd been busted in similar circumstances. An undercover female officer had approached Myran and asked him for some "cream." Myran told her he had to make a phone call. He then gave the officer his driver's license and a $5 bill to hold while he went off. When he came back several minutes later, he handed the officer 0.1 gram of crack cocaine. The officer gave him a marked $20 bill. The arrest team moved in a few minutes later.

It was a little different this time. The girl who had supplied the crack was searched and found to be carrying 11 grams of cocaine. She was only sixteen years old. The cops booked Myran for violation of the Uniform Controlled Substances Act and for using a minor as a drug courier. The girl's involvement, whether Myran knew her or not, raised the seriousness of the alleged crime to a level III drug offense, the highest in the state of Washington. As the cops booked him into the King County jail that night, Myran was facing the prospect of a decade in prison.

As you drive through downtown Seattle on Interstate 5, the King County Correctional Facility is just west of the freeway. A twelve-story concrete building coated with beige paint, it could be easily mistaken for a parking garage. At any one time, there are about 1,350 prisoners inside. The main entrance is on Fifth Avenue. When prisoners need to appear in King County Court, they walk through a windowless sky bridge that spans from the jail, over the top of the King County administration building across the street, and into the courthouse, which takes up the block between Third and Fourth avenues.

After the day when Damian and I ran into Myran on the street, it had seemed just a matter of time before he was picked up. The areas where he tended to hang out—downtown near the Pike Place Market and a little bit north, up in Belltown—are the targets of constant stings by the narcotics police. For someone involved in the lowest level of the cocaine trade, they are the most obvious places to go to turn a quick deal. If you sell drugs in those areas, it is almost guaranteed you will be caught before too long.

The first time I visit Myran in jail, on a Saturday morning, the bored-looking King County deputy at the entrance halfheartedly inspects my bag while I pass through a metal detector. I learn over the course of several visits, through comments made by some of the guards and short conversations with the families of other prisoners—something about waiting around in a jail seems to make people talkative—that everyone assumes I'm a lawyer.

To get to the visitors' waiting area, you walk up one flight of stairs from the entrance. To the right, as you enter the room, is a Formica shelf stacked with pink forms. You take a golf-pencil and fill in your name, your address, the name of the prisoner you want to visit, and your relationship to the prisoner. The first time I go to see Myran, I puzzle for a minute over what to put down. I consider "basketball teammate" but then decide against it, wondering how I would explain it if the guard asked me. "Acquaintance" doesn't seem to capture it, either. Finally, I write "friend."

After you've finished the form, you walk up to the guard's booth, which runs across one side of the room but is sealed off with bulletproof glass. The guards in the visitors' area wear forest-green uniforms with gold trim that look very much like the outfits worn by National Park rangers. You speak through a small, round stainless steel grille set in the glass and slide your form and driver's license through a slot at the bottom. The guard verifies the name on your license against what you have written on the slip, checks to make sure the prisoner you want to see has visiting hours, and then puts the form in a pneumatic tube and sends it up to the floor where your prisoner is being held. Then you wait on one of a line of bolted-together green plastic chairs. The people in the room are mostly women—mothers with young children who laugh and crash around the waiting area, women in skirts and cleavage-baring tops, old ladies who sit quietly with hands folded in their laps.

A few minutes before ten thirty in the morning, the guard motions to everyone in the waiting room that it's OK to get on the elevator and go up to our designated floors. I exit on the tenth into a small, gray-carpeted, triangular-shaped area. Directly in front of the elevators is a line of booths, painted—for some reason—aquamarine. Thick glass divides the prisoners' area from where the visitors sit. Each side has a heavy black plastic phone connected to the wall by a cord wrapped in a flexible stainless-steel sheath. A small window to the far right lets in light. To the far left of the elevator, you can walk up to a window and peer into the jail. Directly in front is a circular control room, shielded from the rest of the jail by bulletproof glass, at which a guard sits at monitors. He presses a button and his amplified voice, crackly and a bit distorted, sounds through a speaker in the waiting area: "They'll be out in a minute, folks."

Most visitors take a spot in one of the booths to wait. I hang back, standing near the wall. Before long, three prisoners—a black guy with cornrows, a young white guy who speaks in Russian with an older man I assume is his father, and a Latino man in his twenties—show up. They wear red jail outfits that look like pajamas and flip-flops. The guard punches another button and the door between the jail and their side of the visiting area slides open. They walk in and take their places in the booths across from their visitors. A minute later, another black man arrives and goes into a booth.

I am beginning to wonder if Myran is coming when he walks in front of the control room. He's a bit under six feet tall, thin, light-skinned, and his head is shaved bald. He wears small, rimless, rectangular glasses. When he sees me, he breaks into a smile and begins to energetically wave with his right hand. In his left hand he carries an extremely large Bible, about five inches thick and bound in soft black leather.

He points to a booth and we sit down across from each other. The first thing I notice is that the bloat that was in his face when Damian and

I saw him on the street is gone. His eyes look sharp. He is smiling. He looks just about the same as he did as a kid.

We both pick up the phone. "Hey, it's good to see you," he says.

It soon becomes clear that Myran is in a desperate situation. He had been placed in a work release program after his prior drug arrest, but, after ten days, he went AWOL, which resulted in a charge of second-degree escape. The age of the girl involved in the latest drug transaction as well as his prior record means that the prosecutor is seeking a sentence of 120 months. Myran tells me that the prosecutor has offered his public defender a plea bargain for ninety months, which Myran has refused. "If I go away for ninety months, I'm going to be with murderers, rapists, house robbers, people who just don't care what happens to them," he says. "And I'll come out as a repeat offender, which means if I make one mistake, they'll send me right back."

It's hard to sort out all the charges in Myran's record. "The defendant has been booked 28 times since 1990 and has 38 warrants," reads one court document. Looking at the charges, almost all are misdemeanors, including—by my count—fourteen separate charges of driving without a license or driving with a suspended license. Others are for failures to appear in court. The oldest case is a juvenile-court drug charge from 1989. There are two felonies prior to his recent arrests. In 1998 Myran walked up to a woman from rural Washington who had parked at a gas station in the Central Area, near Garfield High School, to ask for directions. Myran ripped the necklace from her neck and ran away. He pled guilty to first-degree theft and got fifteen days in jail. In 1999 he pled guilty to being the middleman in a $40 crack deal, this one also set up by the narcotics cops. He was sentenced to twenty months in prison.

Myran's grandmother and I are the only two people who visit him in jail. Myran tells me that he is sure that my getting back in touch with him is an answer to his prayers for a change in his life. I can see how he would welcome any attention from outside. He has spoken on the phone with a private attorney, who has told him she could get the current charge of dealing with a minor dropped, but the lawyer wants $5,000 for the case, including $2,500 up front, an amount that neither Myran nor his grandmother can muster.

Without money, he doesn't have much leverage. Myran is essentially engaged in a game of chicken with the legal system. He refuses to take the deal the public defender suggests he accept, figuring that the state will eventually come up with a better offer if he holds out, simply to save the expense and effort of going to trial. If not, and his case does end up before a jury, Myran tells me he will explain things himself. He is convinced that the jury will hear how he was set up by the police, realize that it was unfair, and let him off.

Everything is speculation on Myran's part. He asks my advice, but I tell him that I'm not the person to offer opinions on his legal situation. His court-assigned lawyer keeps telling him to take the deal. I phone his public defender several times and leave messages asking if he will talk with me to clarify the charges against Myran, but the lawyer never returns my calls. He also fails to call back Myran's grandmother, cementing Myran's belief that his public defender is just processing him through the system without even looking at the details of his case.

"He told me that I shouldn't be out on Third Avenue if I don't want to go to prison," Myran says to me one day. "I told him, 'I know that. What do you want me to say? I relapsed.'"

Myran tells me that since he was about ten years old, he's had mood swings. For a few days, he'll feel fine, and then a switch will flip and he'll get angry. "A lot had to do with what was going on at home. My family, when there was a problem, would just close the curtains to the outside world," he says. "There were no male figures. It was all women, so I walked all over them."

At school, he would get in fights for no real reason. One day, he lists several elementary, middle, and high schools he attended (in the South End as well as the North End, when his mom was in residential drug rehab). "I got kicked out of all of them," he says. After that, he started spending time on the streets. "I just went down and hung out," he says.

Since he's been in jail, he's been on antidepressants and mood stabilizers. One morning he tells me, "I just took a pill, so I'm on my 'A' game. At about two, I'll start to get tired until I take another one." Without the drugs, he says, things get fuzzy. "My mind starts to close, like this," he says. He holds up his right hand with his fingers formed in a circle, and, in a motion like the shutting of an aperture on a camera, closes the circle down to a fist. "You can be talking to me, but I just don't take anything in." When I ask if he remembers the day that Damian and I pulled up next to him on Second Avenue, he shakes his head. "You guys talked to me? Really? See, that's what I mean. I don't remember that at all."

Myran's moods swing widely from visit to visit. One day, he's upbeat and almost jovial, sure that he is about to get out and everything is looking up. The next time, he begins to cry when talking about his case, tears running out of his eyes before he snaps back and tries to act cheerful again. Some days everything he says seems totally rational, and at other times he rambles from one topic to the next, going into lengthy digressions on the Bible.

Myran says that, on the outside, he has been able to get things together for short spells. A few years earlier, he says, he had a good job at a local hospital. Although he'd never been taught how to use a computer, he got on the one at his grandmother's house and made a résumé full of fake experience, dressed up for the interview, and landed the job. He worked in the storeroom in the basement, ferrying parts like IV pumps around the hospital when a doctor or nurse called down. He tells me he got paid $14 an hour and even had a pager so he could be on call. "That was a really good job. I really liked that," he says. When I ask him what happened, he shakes his head. "I stopped going." His ups and downs have also made it hard to maintain relationships, including those with his girlfriend and children.

When other players on our team talked about what they remembered from playing together, everyone brought up, in one form or another, Myran "acting crazy." Usually that just meant Myran talking, capping on other guys, and running his mouth off, most of the time making everyone laugh through the sheer outrageousness of what he had to say. Some days, Myran seemed totally good-natured; on others, there was an edge. But someone, like Will, Tyrell, or Coach McClain, always kept him under control. I linked Myran in my mind to Richard Pryor—I had a tape of *Live on the Sunset Strip* I listened to repeatedly—whom Myran resembled in his ability to do imitations and say things no one else would.

In jail, Myran often makes me laugh in spite of the serious trouble he faces. Most of his jokes are at the expense of his defense lawyer. He tells me how one day the lawyer came in to talk to him and Myran, who says he spends most of his time in jail studying the Bible, asked, "Do you believe Jesus Christ manifested himself in the flesh?"

Myran takes on the persona of a middle-aged white lawyer, pursing his lips and furrowing his brow. "'I'm not going to discuss my religious beliefs with you!'" Myran says in a nasal voice.

Myran obviously enjoys performing, seeming happy if he can get a reaction. Just like when we were kids, his stories are so out there it's hard not to laugh.

One day he makes a whole routine out of a recent court appearance, playing the roles of the judge, the prosecutor, his defense lawyer, and the guards. In his effort to have his lawyer removed from his case, Myran told the judge that the attorney was making sexual advances at him. Myran mimics his lawyer looking angry and the judge shaking his head and asking, "What do you mean? He's obviously completely hetero."

In his reenactment, Myran gestures around the courtroom. "Oh, I see how it is. You, you, and you"—he points at the judge, the prosecutor, and the defense lawyer—"are all in this together!" He tells me he looked back at the guards, who were rolling their eyes and looking at him like he was crazy. Next, Myran imitates his lawyer talking with him after the session in court: "'You better apologize to me for that little stunt you just pulled or I'm not going to do anything for your little ass!'"

Myran laughs when he tells the story and, though I try to stop myself, I can't help a chuckle. Of course, it doesn't seem like a good idea to antagonize the people who will decide his fate. I only later realize that, in Myran's situation, messing with the system might make some sense. He has no money, no power, and hardly any information about his legal situation besides what the defense lawyer chooses to tell him. He doesn't really have control of his fate, or much to lose.

One day, when we are speaking through the phones, Myran becomes wistful. He tells me that our conversations have gotten him to thinking about the old days. "I was just remembering team picture day, you know, just hanging out and having your picture taken, things like that," he says. "Back when we were kids, there were angels watching over us. When you get older, it's not like that anymore."

I know that Myran is talking, literally, about angels, but when he says it, I have different associations. My mind goes to people like Willie McClain and Randy Finley, men who were there as a backstop in the days we played sports. Behind them, of course, if you were lucky, there were parents, relatives, teachers, and other adults who kept an eye out to make sure you were headed in the right direction. They were practical angels—forces in the background helping you stay on track. You took them for granted. Sitting across from Myran, I begin to think about what it would be like if you were on your own.

In at least one sense, Myran has a lot of company. In 1980, some 500,000 people were incarcerated in prisons and jails in the United States. That number has grown to 2.3 million. Of those, 40 percent are black and 20 percent are Hispanic. The United States leads the world in imprisonment, with 762 out of every 100,000 people behind bars (second-place Russia lags behind with 635). The rise in incarceration has been largely fueled by laws imposing "mandatory minimums" for drug offenses, many of which were enacted in the heat of the "war on drugs" in the 1980s; about 1 in 4 inmates is now in on drug charges, compared to 1 in 10 in 1983. Although African Americans and whites use illegal drugs at about the same rates, blacks make up some 53 percent of people going to prison for drug crimes despite making up only 12 percent of the overall population. Much of this comes from a focus on busting street-level drug sales while dealing done in private residences and off the streets is pursued much less aggressively. Another way of putting it is that one out of every 131 Americans is locked up, but, unless you are poor and black, there's a good chance you don't know any of them.

The increase in the number of prisoners has resulted in what some call the "prison-industrial complex," an economy worth tens of billions of dollars a year. There is a lot of money to be made from jailing people—someone has to provide the bulletproof glass, blastproof doors, closed-circuit TV systems, handcuffs, uniforms, telecom services, and thousands of other products specially designed for jails and prisons. The Corrections Corporation of America, one of several private companies operating prisons for profit, runs sixty-four correctional facilities and detention centers across the country and employs seventeen thousand people. In rural America, where prisons are now almost always located, the facilities offer badly needed sources of employment. The other side of the equation is made up of prisoners like Myran, a vast army of people with little education; possible mental health issues; negligible job skills; and, after their incarcerations, felony criminal records.

Though there are various proposals for the decriminalization or legalization of drugs floating around in policy circles—former Seattle police chief Norm Stamper is one of the most vocal national advocates of legalization—it would take a massive change in policy and a redirection of public spending to shift the priority from jailing people like Myran toward treating them. The system of mass incarceration that has developed over the past three decades has its own logic: When you put people in prison, you know exactly what you are getting. Treatment is hard—people backslide and otherwise screw up, and no politician wants to be accused of funneling money to the "undeserving" and "irresponsible." Imprisonment takes of a whole class of people who, even if they were clean, would then have substantial problems finding work that provided a living wage, and places them out of sight. The people who suffer the most under the current system are those with the least ability to press for change.

· · ·

"Oh, that's really sad," Sean O'Donnell says when I tell him that Myran is locked up on drug charges. "It's a bad rut, once you're in the system. For some people the system—I mean by 'system' prison or jail—actually gives them some stability, gives them some predictability. But too many folks like Myran turn up in the system and you see them all the time."

As a King County prosecutor, Sean occupies the opposite end of the system as Myran, sometimes literally—he tells me that he's occasionally gone out with undercover cops to observe "buy-bust" operations in exactly the same area where Myran was arrested. "It helps you to know what's going on," he says. "You see these guys down on Second or Third Avenue and you sit up on a roof with binoculars looking down, you're listening to communication from the undercover officers doing the buying. It's sort of pathetic—twenty dollars' worth of rock cocaine. It's pathetic but at the same time it's its own little structure, its own little business model. You got the guy with the drugs, you got the buyer, you got the cluck in the middle who facilitates the transaction."

We are speaking in Sean's office, only two blocks from where Myran is locked up. It's a Sunday afternoon, and Sean is doing some last-minute preparation for a trial—the police have broken up a prostitution ring run by a gang based out of southwest Seattle. Five of the accused pimps have already taken an offer and pled guilty. The sixth, a nineteen-year-old who goes by the nickname "Cash Money," decided to go to trial. It starts in the morning.

A long desk runs along one wall of Sean's office. It holds two computers—a desktop and a laptop—and a bobblehead of Washington State's former Republican U.S. senator Slade Gorton, for whom Sean worked after graduating from Georgetown. A framed poster of Winston Churchill in a pinstripe suit, clenching a cigar in his mouth and brandishing a tommy gun, hangs on the wall facing the entrance. Next to the door is a bulletin board with snippets of jokey e-mail exchanges and pictures of Sean's wife and two young sons. File folders full of documents pertaining to the upcoming trial are spread on the floor.

Sean roots through a stack of papers and pulls out some photos that detectives pulled off the Internet. One is of Cash Money and several friends posing for a picture while throwing gang signs. Another features Cash Money and a buddy posing in front of a black sedan while the lower part of a woman's leg, her foot in high heels, extends from the open door of the car. Another is simply of a coffee table with a red bandanna and a fan of $20 bills across the top.

"They called their gang the 'West Side Mobb,' with two *b*'s," Sean says. "Take a guess what 'Mobb' stands for." When I come up blank, Sean tells me, in a voice conveying both amusement and disgust, "Money Over Broke Bitches."

At six-foot-eight, Sean has stayed trim. His light brown hair, cut short, has receded. He answers my questions carefully, considering each one, answering directly and then stopping, as one would expect of an experienced lawyer. When he makes a point that he wants to drive home, he widens his eyes and smiles.

After a few years of working for Slade Gorton in Washington, D.C., Sean came back to Seattle to take a job as a spokesman for Boeing. He went to law school at night, and an internship in the prosecutor's office led to a job upon graduation. Sean is one of 170 prosecutors in the office. Together, they process a combined twenty-five thousand misdemeanor, felony, and juvenile cases every year. King County, which includes all of Seattle as well as large portions of the city's eastern and southern suburbs, is the country's thirteenth-most-populous county, with nearly 2 million people. The office has an annual budget of $56 million.

Only a few months after he started on the job, in the spring of 2002, Sean was assigned to the prosecution team working on the case of Gary

Ridgway, otherwise known as the Green River Killer, one of the most prolific serial murderers in American history. "It was the most important case my office has ever prosecuted and probably ever will," Sean says. "It was the chance of a lifetime, doing what I do as a prosecutor. But it's probably all downhill from here."

Beginning in 1982, Ridgway, then in his early thirties, murdered dozens of women—forty-eight of his killings have been confirmed, though he's claimed more than sixty. Most were teenagers, and almost all were street prostitutes Ridgway had picked up for "dates." He strangled his victims, either in his home or in the covered bed of his red pickup truck. He then dumped them in and around the Green River, south of Seattle. He was only arrested in November 2001. For thirty years he had worked painting Kenworth semitrucks in the suburbs south of Seattle.

In April 2003, Ridgway agreed to a plea bargain: In exchange for life imprisonment instead of the death penalty, he would tell the prosecutors and the cops everything he could remember about the murders. The investigative team set up an office just south of downtown Seattle. What they didn't share with the public was that Ridgway himself was going to live there—he occupied a converted supply closet, which had the door removed and two police officers with automatic rifles posted outside around the clock. When prosecutors arrived at the office, Ridgway, in a chipper voice, would call out and greet them.

"You see him every day at work, he knows your name, he shares your bathroom, he's walking around with a SWAT team, he's got belly chains on, his little red jumper," says Sean, who—in contrast to his normal cool—can become visibly agitated when speaking about Ridgway. "He is confessing to the most horrible acts imaginable, and so not only do you have this that you're absorbing, but you can't share it with anyone for nine months or so. We were in complete secrecy. Complete radio silence. I couldn't tell my parents, friends in the office, no one else what I knew, that he was down living in a supply closet in my office, confessing to horrible acts of murder and desecration.

"I'm still exhausted," Sean says. "Just talking about it, I'm exhausted. Talking to us for ten hours a day. To listen to that asshole's whiny, discombobulated voice."

For several months, the prosecutors and police investigators drove Ridgway around south King County, revisiting the sites where the killer had dumped the bodies and then sometimes returned to have sex with the corpses. The teams left the office at five in the morning, to limit the possibility of the media finding out that they were taking Ridgway out on "field trips." Those excursions consisted of prosecutors accompanying forensic investigators as they combed over twenty-year-old crime scenes, Sean says, "sifting through buckets and buckets of mud and gravel looking for a human tooth."

Prostitutes were easy targets. Ridgway could pick them up in his truck, and he knew that since most drifted from place to place—and many had lost touch with their families after running away from abusive homes—police would not put as much effort into looking for them if they disappeared. His victims were white, black, and Asian. "I'd rather have white, but black was fine," Ridgway told the investigators. "It's just . . . just garbage. Somethin' to screw and kill her and dump her."

One day, when I was speaking to Tyrell's father, Doug Johnson, he began talking about the crack era in the 1980s and then brought up the Green River Killer. "Those were bad times," he said. "You couldn't even turn on the news without seeing a girl you knew from the neighborhood turning up dead. You didn't know who it was going to be next."

"It doesn't surprise me at all to hear Tyrell's dad say he knew a lot of those girls," Sean says when I tell him about Doug Johnson's comment. "Ridgway targeted young girls, fifteen, sixteen years old, low income, a lot of them black. He'd cruise areas like the Central District, Rainier Avenue South. He preyed on them because society didn't give a shit. What's society? Well, unfortunately, it is their parents, it is their schools, it is law enforcement, it's social services. That may be hard saying that they didn't give a shit—I'm sure that there were people who cared and parents who cared—but not in a meaningful way that helped those girls make choices that could have saved their lives. Hooking was an easy way to make money. And their pimps would put them out on the streets. It's a business model. And Ridgway exploited that with great effectiveness. He isn't particularly bright. In fact, he's a moron in many senses of the word. But he was quite good at taking advantage of a disadvantage, and he did that with, in his mind, great success."

After the Ridgway case ended at the close of 2003, Sean went back into the regular rotation—prosecutors generally work for about two years in one of the office's divisions, such as juvenile, drug crimes, domestic violence, and violent crimes. In court, Sean, in a navy suit, with his height and up-right posture, cuts an imposing figure. In one assault trial I watched, he towered over the defense lawyer, a man in his early thirties who was per-haps five-foot-eight and wore a rumpled suit. When presenting in court, Sean tends toward formality, always addressing the judge as "Your Honor" and standing to speak. "It's a privilege for me to be there," he says. "I am acting as a representative of the state of Washington and so I need to ap-pear to the court, the opposing counsel, and any member of the public who may be there as they would expect a representative of the state of Washington to act."

Sean transferred a few years ago to the sex crimes division, where it looks like he will remain. The work—which includes prosecuting pimps, rapists, and child molesters—suits him. "This job gives me a great sense of purpose, and I'm always entertained, it's always interesting," he says. "I can get up in the morning and be excited about what I do, because a successful prosecution means there's one less jerk out there hurting someone."

When I ask how he sees his role, Sean says, "I guess I sort of extract justice from the process for someone who has been wronged—the focus of course is on the defendants, but you don't have defendants unless we have victims. Their recourse, other than some sort of civil reward, is see-ing the offender punished. A lot of people deserve to be punished, and this is the system through which that occurs."

Of course, many cases don't end the way Sean would like them to. One or two jurors may hold out against the rest, resulting in a hung jury. Judges sometimes make rulings that Sean finds incomprehensible. He tells me that perhaps one in ten cases results in an outcome where "the victim of the case comes to you and they can say that they have felt that they've been heard, they walk away from this hard and cold process feel-ing that some bit of justice has been done."

As we speak in his office, he tells me that one case in particular comes to mind—a woman who worked as a stripper and prostitute was kidnapped and raped by her boyfriend and a friend after she refused to continue prostituting. The trial went to court three times—the first two resulted in hung juries of eleven to one—before Sean got a conviction. Each time, the witness had to take the stand and testify for hours about what was done to her.

As he tells me the details, Sean searches through the files on his computer to find a letter that the victim wrote after the case was done. In it, she singles out the victims' advocate of the sex crimes unit, the detective who worked the case, and Sean. Without their support, she writes, *I would have never made it through this hard time in one piece, and I would genuinely like to thank each of them for helping save my life.*

Sean skips down and continues reading the letter to me: *Thank you to those twelve individuals in the jury who saw my side of the story, felt my side of the story, and for some instant lived my side of the story as I told it to you from the witness stand. Your act of consolation, compassion, and understanding for me is greatly appreciated and will never be forgotten for you are the people who helped me move on with my life.*

"That paragraph is the coolest paragraph," Sean says, "because when you present a case, that's what you want the jury to see. You want the jury to live in her shoes just for a moment, so they can see what she went through."

Sean's assignment to the Ridgway case enabled him to skip the drug crimes rotation, which is generally reserved for junior prosecutors. Drug cases such as Myran's take up a lot of manpower—of the average 2,600 prisoners in the King County jail system, 460 are in for drug charges, more than for any other crime. That compares to 304 for assault, 126 for drunk driving, 125 for sex crimes, and 110 for robbery.

"They're a huge resource suck," Sean says of the drug cases. Though he has never worked in the division, as a senior attorney in the office he has been involved in negotiating plea bargains on drug cases—junior prosecutors generally do the gruntwork and then must kick cases up to higher levels for talks with defense attorneys. In those cases, Sean picks up the paperwork and has a look before sitting down to deal.

The options open to the prosecutor include asking for a straight jail term, recommending a reduced sentence that includes drug treatment, or kicking the case over to drug court, a separate system in which the prosecution is suspended and the defendant is released, as long as he successfully completes a monitored drug-treatment program. "There's so many different factors that can go into it," Sean says about how prosecutors decide what route to take. "On a drug case, you'd want to know how many times in the past they'd been arrested, how much drugs were involved, whether there's an addiction problem, whether there's any crimes of violence, whether children are involved, what the defendant has done since his arrest to make amends. Is he going to Narcotics Anonymous? Is he trying to find treatment? Is he trying to keep his job? If they demonstrate genuine remorse and are taking steps to get better, we would consider that."

I ask what would happen in the case of someone like Myran, who has been arrested repeatedly for misdemeanor drug charges, generally for acting as the "cluck" in a transaction. "If there are a lot of misdemeanors, cases that have been negotiated in the past and reduced, there's probably not a lot you're going to be able to do for them," Sean says. "When you think of, 'Hey, where are we going to spend the limited money that we have to help someone?' are you going to spend it on a guy who has made no effort to improve himself over the last fifteen or twenty years, or are you going to try and take the money and maybe you get a kid who's nineteen years old, his first offense, he's scared shitless, and doing those things that on their face look positive. In terms of triaging your resources, you're probably going to go with the young kid, see if he has a chance, but the other guy would have demonstrated, 'I'm not interested in turning things around.'"

• • •

One day, Myran's grandmother and I both show up at his visiting hours but are told he has been taken across the sky bridge for an appearance before a judge. We walk the two blocks to the court and find the right courtroom, where an omnibus hearing is in session. The purpose of these hearings is to keep things moving through the system, setting court dates for defendants, and taking care of other procedural issues.

Myran's grandmother and I sit on a bench in the gallery and wait. There are nearly ten lawyers up front, bunched around two adjoining tables. The lawyers—defense attorneys and prosecutors—are all white. Since the omnibus hearing is informal, very few wear ties. One guy walks in wearing a bike helmet and a yellow waterproof backpack. It's Friday, and there's a bit of relief in the air. The lawyers joke and laugh while they shuffle their papers and await their turns before the judge.

Defendants who are not being held in jail arrive and sit on the benches near us. Defense lawyers approach and ask them their names: "Are you Mr. Davis?" At one point, a female lawyer approaches Mrs. Barnes and me with a puzzled look. "Do you need to sign in?" she asks. "We're just here for support," Mrs. Barnes answers. Other defendants are brought in from the jail one at a time. As they enter the courtroom, one of the guards escorting them takes a key and releases their handcuffs. Whatever they did on the outside, inside the court, in their red jailhouse outfits, in front of the judge, they all look like they have shrunk. All of the defendants brought in from the jail while we wait are either black, Latino, or Asian.

Mrs. Barnes and I talk as we pass the time. A petite woman in a long denim skirt and white blouse, she tells me about her nursing jobs after she moved out to Seattle from St. Louis, and how Myran, as a kid, used to come down after school to the retirement home where she worked evenings to hang out until the end of her shift. "Myran used to stay up, help the old folks eat, play cards with them, give them rides in their wheelchairs, talk with them," Mrs. Barnes says. "They all remembered Myran. When he didn't come, they would ask where he was. They had Alzheimer's—they couldn't remember their own families, but they remembered Myran."

We watch for Myran's attorney, but there is no sign of him. Mrs. Barnes tells me about the work-release program that Myran had left. "It was terrible," she says. "There were lots of drugs available." People in the program paid $400 a month for room and board, she says. You were expected to find your own job—the program did not set you up—and for many it was hard to come up with even $400. "There was just not enough support," she says. "The system is set up so they fail. The government is behind it. How many poor blacks, poor whites, and Latinos are importing the drugs? It's a business. They could stop it if they wanted to."

She continues, "I'm not saying that they haven't done anything wrong, but these are people with drug problems. You don't send them to prison for that."

After about an hour of waiting, Mrs. Barnes goes out into the hallway to call her doctor's office, where she has an appointment. I walk to the front of the court and ask the clerk if she knows what time Myran is going to appear. She looks at a list in front of her and then tells me that his appearance has been canceled—his lawyer couldn't make it today.

After five months in jail, it appears that Myran's stalling strategy might be working. When I visit him, he tells me that the prosecutor has reduced the plea from ninety months in prison to sixty-eight. By my reading of the law, sixty-eight months is the bottom of the sentencing range for the level III drug crime for which Myran has been charged. Myran tells me that after thinking about it, he has decided to still push for trial—he says that since he did not know the girl involved in the drug deal, he shouldn't be punished for her involvement as a minor. I don't offer an opinion, but privately I wonder if it's a good idea: If he is found guilty now, he could be up for all of the 120 months. At the moment, the process is tied up in knots—Myran has requested a psychological review, which is taking months for the court to organize.

I ask Myran if he knows what he's going to do when he gets out, and if he thinks he'll get pulled back to the streets. He shakes his head. "I'm done. I've learned my lesson. My mind is clear, I won't go back again," he says.

"I'd like to learn about twelve languages," he continues. "I'd like to be able to interact with people, be able to really talk with them, to talk with all kinds of people from all over the world.

"I'm going to hook back up with Damian and hook back up with you. Raise the status of my friends. There's a school in Kirkland, a religious school, what do you call those?"

"A seminary?" I ask.

"Yeah, a seminary. I've been thinking about going to that. I'd like to do that. I just spend so much time idle. That's not good, all that idle time."

A few minutes later, the guard in the control room breaks in over the phone line: "Wrap it up."

Myran says good-bye, stands, and lines up with the five prisoners who have been speaking in the other booths. They wait silently. When the door back into the jail slides open, they walk single-file past the visiting room's thick glass window. A young guy who has been speaking with his girlfriend in Russian blows her a kiss and mouths something to her. Myran, who walks behind him, smiles and waves. Then the prisoners begin to exit the visiting room's field of vision. One by one, each fades from view.

Part Four

Schools

Lakeside School fosters the development of citizens capable of and committed to interacting compassionately, ethically, and successfully with diverse peoples and cultures to create a more humane, sustainable global society. This focus transforms our learning and our work together.

—*Complete text of the Lakeside School Mission Focus*

Our Kids Are Not Getting
What They Need

One afternoon in the spring of 2006, I stop into Damian's classroom at Zion Preparatory Academy. Damian stands at the chalkboard, a solid man in black slacks and a black sweater. The fifteen third-graders in the class—all of them African American—wear maroon and gray school uniforms and sit at three rows of desks. The walls are decorated with pictures of the three black astronauts who have been on the space shuttle; posters of LeBron James and Seahawks running back Shaun Alexander; a picture of Maurice Ashley, the first black chess grandmaster; a poster listing the Ten Commandments; and another of Martin Luther King Jr. with the words "I have a dream" written below. On his desk, Damian keeps a tattered copy of the Bible and a small boom box that he uses to play gospel music.

Damian is leading the kids through a logic problem. He reads aloud from a workbook as the students follow along. Five people are going to a market to pick up fruit and vegetables. The question revolves around what each one is going to buy. There are clues related to each of the five people in the problem—for example, James buys twice as many bananas as Karen. The kids are supposed to figure out the exact purchases of each shopper.

"The trick to this is that you need to make a chart to keep track of everything," Damian says, drawing a grid on the board with a line for each character and empty boxes for the produce they get. Damian calls on individual kids to read clues and then has them decide which box to place the resulting information in.

The school day ends before the class arrives at a solution. The kids hop up, stuff their papers and books into backpacks, and grab their coats to go either to the bus or to the school's daycare. A couple of boys get out the game Connect 4, a vertical version of tic-tac-toe in which you stack up chips and try to get four in a row. A kid named Michael challenges me to a game, and we sit opposite each other at a tiny desk to play as the other students gather around. Michael quickly beats me—I lose focus and make a fatal error—to the delight of the kids.

"Brother Damian, you ready?" Michael asks. Damian makes a show of thinking about whether he wants to play, and then consents. "Watch out, I don't want to beat you too bad," Damian says as he sits down in the kid-size chair.

As they begin the game, Damian tells me about what he has just been teaching—test prep for the Washington Assessment of Student Learning, better known as the WASL (pronounced "Wassel"), a statewide achievement test all fourth-, seventh-, and tenth-graders must take. He pauses every once in a while to talk trash to Michael: "Is that what you want to do? Are you sure? You better check yourself. Oh man, I'm shutting you *down*!" Michael reacts by putting his hands over his face and looking out between his fingers, eyeing the game up and down while the other kids laugh and tell him what move he should make next. "I don't think you should listen to the peanut gallery here, Michael," Damian says. "Doesn't sound like good advice to me."

The two play almost to a tie, with the chips stacking up near the top of the plastic structure, until Michael drops one in a slot that allows Damian to get a diagonal four in a row. "Brother Damian got you!" another boy shouts to Michael, who slaps his forehead and leans back. "That wasn't bad. You almost had a draw. You lost your concentration at the end," Damian says as he stands up. "All right, you all need to get your stuff and get ready to go."

Damian and I keep talking as the kids file out. The WASL is Washington State's response to the No Child Left Behind Act, a set of educational reforms passed by Congress in December 2001. One of the main goals of the bill was to eliminate the "achievement gap" between black and Latino students and whites—the "soft bigotry of low expectations" was George W. Bush's sound bite on the subject. The most tangible real-world result of the bill is a mandated series of standardized tests that children must take throughout elementary, middle, and high school. Students and schools must show "adequate yearly progress." In Washington State, students who can't pass after several tries are not allowed to graduate from high school.

As Damian sees it, the WASL test is just another in a line of hurdles that his students need to clear to avoid low-wage futures. "It's a sorting system," he says. "They're weeding out certain people. Not everyone's going to pass the WASL. Not everyone's going to go to college. Some people are not going to have those good jobs. There are kids who will study and study for this test and they're still not going to pass. That's just the way it is." His job, he says, is to make sure that the fifteen kids in front of him every day are in a position to do as well as they possibly can.

Zion Preparatory Academy occupies three squat buildings arranged around a horseshoe-shaped driveway in South Seattle, one block off Martin Luther King Jr. Way. The school was founded in 1982, out of necessity, when Eugene Drayton, the pastor of Zion United House of Prayer in the Central Area, became distressed that several kids in his church's Bible study class had a hard time reading. He also knew that black kids were getting kicked out of the Seattle public schools at an alarmingly high rate for discipline problems. When black leaders went to speak about the problem with school district administrators, the district maintained that kids who misbehaved would be suspended or expelled. But Drayton saw that these same kids behaved perfectly well on Sundays. Maybe the school district just didn't understand how to relate to them. He thought the church could do better educating its children on its own.

Doug Wheeler, then a thirty-five-year-old member of the congregation, took on the job of heading the new school. Wheeler grew up in the Central Area, his father a state probation officer and his mother a police matron who worked security in clubs (his parents also took in foster kids, two of whom were Jimi Hendrix and his brother Leon). The few police officers on the Seattle force in the 1950s and 1960s hung out at his parents' house, and Wheeler always wanted to be a cop. He joined the force after graduating from Seattle University and worked his way up to become assistant director of the Victim's Assistance Unit. Off hours, though, he was wild. But on the morning of August 9, 1980, he heard a voice that told him, "Go walk down the street." He did, entered into the Zion United House of Prayer, and was saved. The chance to head the new school was another opportunity to take his life in a new direction.

Zion Prep began its first year in a two-bedroom house next to the church, with eight students and an initial budget of $13.64. "We went down to the Seattle public-school distribution center," Wheeler says, "climbed into the Dumpsters and got spiral notebooks half-used, computer paper that we could use the back of, and books that were thrown away because the bindings were broken."

Zion Prep took the opposite tack from the Seattle public schools, focusing first on building trust with the kids by bombarding them with love and attention. "The concept was: family, clear structure, building your character and your value of who you are, and then educate you," says Wheeler. "The first three came first. Education was second to us. We were ridiculed by education professionals because we were quote-unquote 'wasting time' in classrooms on noneducational issues. That means our kids are not getting what they need. We said, 'No, we're spending time up front to get the product we want in the end.' . . . Well, our success, as far as the kids and the type of kids we were transforming, became known, and Zion grew."

Zion Prep became known among African Americans in Seattle for turning around children who had been deemed "unteachable" by the public schools. Wheeler calls it a "public school that privately funds itself," meaning that there are no tests to get in and no one is turned away unless a class is already full. Enrollment surged to eighty-three in the second year, and by the end of the 1980s reached four hundred.

As Zion Prep grew, it became tightly linked to some parts of our basketball team. Willie McClain hired on in 1984 as playground supervisor and bus driver; Wheeler promoted McClain to vice principal in 1989, a position he held for more than fifteen years. Damian and Willie Jr. took jobs at the school in the 1990s. The school gave all of them a chance to work at an institution headed by African Americans, deeply embedded in and committed to Seattle's black community.

Randy Finley also became involved with Zion Prep in the 1980s, after he started his mission to help black kids get into elite private schools. He worked with Willie McClain to identify Zion students who could make the transition. Finley, of course, did it with some panache. One of his efforts was to get the chocolate-chip cookie mogul Wally "Famous" Amos to come to the school to give a motivational speech (Amos also was the manager of Finley's sister, Pat, an actress and local television personality). As Finley remembers it, Amos told a school assembly a story about waking up that morning in a fancy hotel room. Amos said he looked around, took in his luxurious surroundings, and made his way to the bathroom. When he got there, Amos told the students, he leaned over the sink to wash his face. When he looked up into the mirror, he told the kids, he got a shock. "I said: 'Lord, I'm black!'" The whole school burst into applause and cheers.

For Finley, the institutional structure and support of Zion were vital—they made his efforts more than just a white guy lobbying for some black kids. "The way you have to do this is working at Zion," he says. "They can build from the inside themselves." But Finley recalls that it was "really tough" getting the kids from Zion into private schools. It was even harder to make sure they received the attention and guidance they needed. The few kids he helped gain admission to Lakeside struggled. "I could never get Lakeside to mentor or stay with the kids," he says. "Lakeside just wanted athletes. They didn't want just ordinary kids."

Finley had more luck with the Bush School, another elite private school, where he found some teachers who seemed interested in working with the kids. The administration also was open to increasing its black enrollment. Finley got about six kids into Bush, but he still found that progress was slow. "I was forced to reevaluate constantly," he says. "I thought I could take these kids, work with them for six or eight months, and then turn them loose, that they could make it." The gap between Zion and the elite, mostly white and wealthy private schools of Seattle, Finley found, was larger and more complex than he had imagined.

A major difference between Zion Prep and many other private schools in Seattle is that Zion is always short of money. Tuition is officially $7,000 a year. All families are asked to contribute something, but those that can't afford the whole thing might pay only $100 a month. Doug Wheeler has to raise up to half of the annual budget of $3.5 million to make up for the shortfall after tuition and regular donations.

"You don't sleep at night, you really don't, because sometimes you don't know if you have enough money to cover all the payroll and wonder where it's coming from. It just gets that tight sometimes," Wheeler says one day when we speak in his office. A tall man with a shaved head and a salt-and-pepper beard, Wheeler wears all black—shoes, slacks, shirt and jacket—and speaks in a soft voice, gently articulating each word. A framed photo of Wheeler with Starbucks CEO Howard Schultz and Magic Johnson hangs on his wall, as well as a plaque Wheeler received from the accounting firm Ernst & Young for being the company's 2003 Pacific Northwest Entrepreneur of the Year in education/nonprofit work.

Wheeler tells me that most of the school's deficit is made up by donations from the CEOs of locally based corporations with whom Wheeler has built relationships, such as Schultz and Jim Sinegal of Costco. "It was amazing to me, literally, to watch some of the wealthiest men in the world walk into this school and sit down at this table and say, 'What can I do? Help me figure out what I can do to help. Just tell me what you want,'" Wheeler says. "They love these kids, honestly they do—they will do whatever they can for these kids, and they have. It humbles you."

The school's results line one hallway, called the Zion Prep Hall of Fame, which is decorated with about twenty posters of former students. Text underneath their pictures describes what they are doing today—one got a degree in engineering; one teaches preschool; one started his own line of clothing; another is the produce manager at a Safeway. "The education here prepared me for the outside world," reads one quotation.

The school follows in a tradition—Booker T. Washington's Tuskegee Institute being the archetypal example—of black institutions looking to develop and prepare African Americans for survival and success in mainstream America. Just as Wheeler has developed relationships with the corporate titans of our day, Washington received much of his funding from those of his, including Andrew Carnegie and John D. Rockefeller. Wheeler says his desire is to provide "a Lakeside education on a Wal-Mart budget."

In the world of Seattle private schools, Zion is a feeder—for those students chosen to make the transition—into elite white institutions. Wheeler tells me that Bush still maintains a relationship with Zion, more than twenty years after Randy Finley first forged the connection. Wheeler has a deal with the school so that the parents of Zion students who get in will still get charged the same tuition they pay at Zion (high school tuition at Bush runs more than $23,000 a year). Bush, for its part, is able to enroll some of Zion's best-performing students. In an era when "diversity" is a priority for elite schools, the arrangement between Zion and Bush is beneficial for both sides. "They want our kids," Wheeler says.

Zion Prep is just one of dozens of Seattle private schools, the vast majority aimed at the middle and upper-middle classes and the rich. Besides

Lakeside, Seattle Prep, and Bush, other elite schools include Seattle Country Day, Villa Academy, University Prep, and the Northwest School. These schools, in turn, are just specks in the shadow of the Seattle public school system, a behemoth that for decades has been mired in a seemingly constant state of crisis. The welfare of minority students, especially, has been a continual issue. "We're not educating our kids," Wheeler says of the Seattle schools and black children. "Ten years, fifteen years, twenty years, it's been the same song. And everyone says, 'This is what we're going to do to improve it,' but it hasn't improved yet."

Overall, Seattle's experience with race, integration, and education has paralleled that of most other big-city districts around the country. In the early 1970s, with recent U.S. Supreme Court decisions mandating that public schools make efforts to desegregate, Seattle came up with its busing plan. The city—and the country—began to back off desegregation after the 1980 election of Ronald Reagan, when the Justice Department made a U-turn in its policy toward desegregation and stopped litigating such cases. The death knell for court oversight of school integration came in 1991 with *Oklahoma City v. Dowell*, in which the Supreme Court ruled that attempts to desegregate a school district could end if it could be shown that "feasible efforts" had been made to do so, even if they were not successful. In effect, as long as a school district did not do anything that could be found to be intentionally discriminatory, it was free to do what it wanted.

Seattle ended race-based busing in the fall of 1997 in favor of "neighborhood schools." After two decades of integration efforts in the city, there had been one clear outcome: In 1973, whites made up 74 percent of the students in the system; today they are 41 percent of the 46,000 students in the system, even though the city is about 70 percent white (an estimated 30 percent of students in Seattle attend a private school).

In 2007, the Supreme Court put the last nail in the coffin of school integration in a decision involving the Seattle schools. After it ended busing, the district had adopted a policy to let students apply to any school they wished. It used several factors to determine admission. The major one was simply if you lived nearby. One of the "tiebreakers" was whether letting in a certain student would help the school achieve racial balance.

A group of parents led by a white mother sued the district, charging that using race in school admissions was discriminatory and violated the equal protection clause of the Fourteenth Amendment. The Supreme

Court agreed in a five-to-four decision. Coming five decades after *Brown v. Board of Education*, the ruling meant that even the smallest measures to increase school integration were dead letters. Chief Justice John Roberts, writing for the majority, delivered something of a Zen koan: "The way to stop discrimination on the basis of race is to stop discriminating on the basis of race."

In terms of racial makeup, many Seattle public schools now look pretty much like they did in the early 1970s, before forced integration. In the South End, some schools are now almost 100 percent minority; North End schools are primarily white. Race and class fissures run deep. Black students are still more than twice as likely as white students to be suspended or expelled—this issue of "disproportionality" has been a hot-button issue for decades—and the "achievement gap" in test scores and graduation rates seems to be as persistent as Seattle rain. Seven out of ten African-American students receive school-lunch subsidies. Parent associations throughout the city make up for budget shortfalls by raising money to fund extra programs and teachers; in wealthy parts of the North End, this extra funding in some schools has topped $300,000 a year. Over the course of several years, the district rolled out multiple plans to shutter a number of schools to save money. The closures—which generally targeted schools that were primarily minority—met with resistance so fierce that in 2006 the superintendent announced his resignation after one particularly heated school board meeting. In 2009, the district's new superintendent—an African-American woman—finally pushed through a closure plan.

Garfield High School, over the past two decades, became a symbol of both the district's academic successes and its racial woes. To help balance the school racially, the district made it a magnet school. Kids in the school system's most advanced academic program were funneled to Garfield, which offered an accelerated track of course work and a comprehensive range of Advanced Placement courses. Garfield now often boasts the most National Merit Scholars in the city, beating out even Lakeside. But white and Asian students far outnumber black students in the AP classes, creating what came to be known as the "two Garfields." African-American parents claim that the school has directed more resources toward the advanced programs than the rest of the school and that counselors steer their kids away from the more challenging courses on the basis of their race. "Our students are not getting these classes. They're getting commercial foods, they're getting gym, they're getting beginning math. Never before has Garfield discouraged so many black kids as they're doing now," one parent told a local reporter.

Taken as a whole, the Seattle schools comprise a ponderous, complex system. The district serves a city that includes the highest number of adults who hold advanced degrees in the country, and one that also includes thousands of recent immigrants—the district website includes translations in Amharic and Oromo (both spoken in Ethiopia), Spanish, Russian, Tagalog (the Philippines), Somali, Lao, Mandarin Chinese, Tigrigna (Eritrea), Vietnamese, and Khmer (Cambodia)—as well as special-needs kids and plain old "regular" students. The district (annual budget: $730 million) also is tasked with educating students for future positions in the global economy, though there is no agreement in Seattle or the country about how best to do this. To try to please the most people possible—and to increase diversity without mandating it—the district went to an "open enrollment" model, which means that families can apply to any school in the district (though people who live near a school get preference, and, after the 2007 Supreme Court decision, race can't be considered). It also has invested heavily in schools with poor reputations, such as Rainier Beach High School in the South End, a majority-black school that in 2008 got a $100 million renovation that included a new performing arts center (the result has been an estimated enrollment increase of thirty kids).

Within this system, it is perfectly possible to get a good education. Slots in the district's advanced programs are especially coveted, an admission that for many parents means saving about $20,000 a year in private-school fees. A reporter who covered the district for several years told me that the people who can manage the system best are those who have the savvy and knowledge of bureaucracy and institutions to get what they want. The children whose parents don't know how to do this, don't have the time, or just don't care end up at the whim of the district.

In 1996, after he graduated from Seattle University, Damian approached Doug Wheeler to ask about work at Zion Prep. Wheeler wasn't overly impressed. "Damian was a wimpy little kid," he says. "He came in and had just finished college, didn't have a certification, didn't know what he wanted to do, wanted to know if there were any jobs."

It turned out that Wheeler had been a running partner of Sam Townsend, Damian's pastor, back when were both on the force in the 1970s, before either of them were saved. "We were ruthless," Wheeler says with a laugh. "I won't go into it, but we were ruthless." When Wheeler called Townsend to ask about Damian, his friend assured him that the kid would be a good hire. "He didn't impress me that way," Wheeler says, "but Sam has never been close to being wrong."

Damian started as the coteacher in Zion's kindergarten class and went to school at night to get his teaching degree. After a few years he moved up to the elementary grade level. Over time he established himself as what Wheeler calls one of Zion Prep's "cornerstones." "If you walk though the school he has the biggest class because parents want their kid with Damian," Wheeler says. "They want Damian. If I put him in whatever grade, that grade will be full because people know if Damian's there—cool."

Over the course of several years, I stop in and observe Damian's classes at least a dozen times. His approach to the kids is both friendly and strict—he will tell jokes but doesn't shy from letting a kid know when he feels the student has failed to lived up to his potential. When I ask Damian to sum up his teaching philosophy, he says, "No excuses." Damian jokes that members of his family, when they hear his ideas, sometimes accuse him of being a Republican. But his philosophy, as I find over time, is much more complicated and not easily pegged as being of the left or the right.

"I grew up poor, OK?" he says. "That was my environment. I teach the kids you can't allow your environment to determine who you are. I only have them for ten months, but I will try to ingrain that in them for that ten months that I have them. What they do after that, I have no control over. But at least I tried to do what I could while I was with them. While you're in my class, you're going to learn something."

Much of Damian's worldview certainly comes in part from growing up poor. But Damian also spent large parts of his childhood—more than any other black member of our team, besides Eric—interacting with the wealthier, whiter parts of Seattle. In elementary school he was bused to the North End. Then there was our team, and the four years he spent at Seattle Prep after Randy Finley got him in. "I was educated for the most influential part of my years at an elite school, so that almost becomes a part of you," Damian says. "They teach you that you don't stop learning here. You learn as you leave, so you're always reading books, it just becomes ingrained. They teach, 'You need to be on time.' When I was late, they made me go and clean out the garbage cans. Now I know why they did it. You have to have expectations if you want individuals to be successful and maximize their potential."

Low expectations for black students, Damian says, come in part from stereotypes that are hard to escape in America—even the "postracial" country that some people now hail. "I would say if you have something in the back of your subconscious—and I think white teachers, most of them, I think they have a good, genuine desire to teach, whoever it is that they're teaching—but when the dominant culture says that and you're raised where black people are just a little less than you, maybe they don't work as hard as you or may not be as smart, then you can easily lower the expectations. And when you lower the expectations then of course African-American children are not going to be as successful," Damian says.

The other side of the equation, Damian says, is that the view of blacks as less able hasn't crept into the heads of just school administrators and teachers, but also into a large segment of the black community itself. One Saturday, I go with Damian and his eight-year-old nephew, David, to see one of David's friends play Peewee League football. The game is at Rainier Beach High School, the predominantly black school in South Seattle. The Rainier Beach community league is playing another league from the South End, and the games are lined up back-to-back for the whole day. Several hundred people fill the stands. Nearly everyone is black. There is a concession stand selling barbecued burgers and hot dogs and strawberry shortcake. Many people wear orange and blue T-shirts—the Rainier Beach colors—with the words WE BE FAMILY written on the back in cursive. The atmosphere is festive. Over the few hours we're there, a constant stream of people—former students and their parents, people from church, and people he grew up with—stop and talk with Damian.

Later, after we drop David off, Damian tells me the whole scene frustrated him. "I want to get out there and get on the bullhorn and say, 'Stop! Stop! Send everybody home! Quit joking around! Stop!'" Damian tells me. "Get the organizational leaders out there and say, 'Parents, just like you support your kids out here on the football field, I want you in your schools on a daily basis supporting your kid's academics and making sure that the school is teaching your child what needs to be taught. Don't hide behind a sport.'"

He continues, "Their priorities are mixed up. They want their child to be the greatest athlete since Barry Sanders, but then academics are put on the back burner, whereas out north academics is first because they know their child has to go to college to get a decent job."

This message about raising expectations in the black community is not new, of course. But in the past few years it has increasingly moved from one conducted behind closed doors among blacks to one with more public visibility, thanks in large part to Bill Cosby, who has traveled the country giving speeches conveying the Booker T. Washington-like message that no matter what the impact of white racism has been and still is, black people need to focus on themselves. "Bill Cosby tried to bring this home and people got mad. And he was absolutely right!" Damian says.

Seattle's class order and social hierarchy are apparent everywhere you look, Damian points out, though this reality is often downplayed. That's the meaning, he says, of Lakeside students chanting, back when we were in high school, "It's all right, it's OK, you'll all work for us someday" at Rainier Beach students during a basketball game. "In the big picture, people send their children to Lakeside strictly for a reason, so that they can maybe take over the parents' business, so they need to have the proper education, or to put them in situations where they can network and have people who will hire them," Damian says, talking about the chant. "It's almost like, 'Yeah, you can play basketball good, but you can't do anything else good.'" Damian laughs. "That's basically what it is—'You can run, jump, dunk, but you're dumb.'"

Even though Willie McClain and Randy Finley tried to bridge race and class divides with our team, Damian says it is almost impossible to do that in reality, simply because society is structured so that people with more money feel superior to those with less. "When you feel you have reached a certain status, it's 'I'm always better than you.' Although you may not say it with your words, the actions demonstrate that. I don't think that that will change because that's human nature."

This analysis of his own experience forms the foundation for Damian's teaching philosophy and works in with a larger observation about the shifting roles of African Americans within the United States as well as the role of America in the world economy. First, the influx of immigrants from East Africa, Latin America, and Asia to South Seattle has made African Americans just one minority among many scrambling to make it. "Things are changing," Damian says. "As you see more and more Asians being successful, Vietnamese, Ethiopians, Africans coming here, I'm hearing it in the community, 'If they can come here and be successful . . . ?' So you're hearing it, but we got a long way to go." In the bigger picture, the United States is also losing its economic hegemony. Before long, Damian tells me, the day will come when large numbers of middle-class white Americans will be shocked when they find themselves answering to Chinese or Indian bosses. "Oh man, it's going to blow some people away," he says. "They're not going to be able to understand it."

For the kids Damian teaches, the future is inside this highly competitive world where the old economic structures—even the one that kept blacks as a group subordinate to whites—have crumbled. For a lot of Americans, Damian believes, the result is going to be lower wages and a lower standard of living. People who don't keep up will just fall off the edge. "That's why they're building the prisons, because they know a certain number of people are going to have to commit crimes in order to survive," he says. The election of Barack Obama helps to demonstrate all of this, he says—it shows that a black person can rise to the highest position in this country, yet the situation of poor blacks remains absolutely unchanged. Obama, Damian says, isn't going to alter the underlying global economic structure.

Several months after the day I watched Damian teach test prep for the WASL, the scores for that year come out. The reaction reinforces many of Damian's points. Of the seventy-eight thousand tenth-graders in Washington State, half had failed the math portion of the exam. Under state law, they would not be allowed to graduate if they could not pass. There was a flurry of activity as parents and politicians contemplated the prospect of half of the state's high school students falling short of a diploma. The government introduced legislation to delay implementation of the requirement and added a $197 million plan for better math education. Newspapers around the state ran editorials about what to do next.

When I speak with Damian about it, he finds some grim humor. "My point is, with the WASL, it is no different than any other systematic way of eliminating certain groups of people; that's what it does," he tells me. "Now that it's starting to affect white people, now, 'Oh,' all of a sudden the state gets an epiphany—'Now we may need to change how we do this because not enough people are passing the math, now we need to change it.' But if it kept on affecting just black people, 'Let's keep it right there.'"

Damian laughs as he tells me this. When I ask why it doesn't seem to upset him more, he says, "Because, man, that's just the way things are."

. . .

In the fall of 2009, Doug Wheeler laughs in disgust when I mention the WASL. After years of problems with the test—mainly too many kids failing the math portion—the new state superintendent of schools has announced plans to scrap it for some other form of testing regime. The WASL—and the whole system of standardized testing as required by the No Child Left Behind Act—was starting to seem like another educational fad that hadn't achieved its goals. "The WASL was supposed to help identify how to close the achievement gap, based on the scores, but it was nothing like that," Wheeler tells me in his office. "It was a bunch of craziness that teachers were afraid to give and get the scores back, and kids were afraid to take, and it still didn't tell you anything. No, the WASL was stupid, but we took it because we wanted to be measured with our donors."

As we speak, Wheeler seems far less optimistic than when I had interviewed him a few years earlier, and it turns out that the financial crisis has hit Zion hard. Before the property crash, Wheeler had lined up a deal to sell the school's current building and seven acres of land—which is only a block from Seattle's new light-rail line, making it valuable space for developers looking to build condos—for $23 million. The plan was to move into another, much cheaper location not far away, and add the remaining money to the endowment to try to gain some financial stability. Not only did the crash kill the deal, but it also pretty much wiped out Zion's existing $3 million endowment, Wheeler tells me.

In addition, many Zion parents felt the effects of the collapse particularly hard—bank tellers at the now-disappeared Washington Mutual; people who worked for real estate companies, insurance firms, and escrow companies; support workers at hotels and convention centers that have seen business vanish. "That means that the single mom who was making $3,000 a month before taxes but sacrificed $250 or $300 because this is a great place for her child now is trying to see how she handles unemployment," Wheeler says. As a result, the school's tuition payments and enrollment shrank. Wheeler, who had to take dramatic action to save the school, eliminated grades six through eight.

There also are problems with the school's positioning within the wider network of Seattle schools. Wheeler tells me that Zion has been hurt because it hasn't been able to offer state-of-the-art computer or sports facilities. While the school's philosophy of instilling discipline and motivation was fine in the 1980s and 1990s, Wheeler says, families are increasingly worried about their children's preparation for the future economy. With Zion unable to afford the necessary equipment, parents have pulled their children and put them back in the public schools.

In addition, while Zion's Afrocentric focus garnered the attention and contributions of donors in its first few decades, the educational trend has recently moved toward globalism and "multiculturalism." Zion, in the increasingly diverse South End, would seem to be in a position to take a leading role in this shift. But when I ask Wheeler whether the school has moved to embrace the ethnic mix of the area, he expresses regret. "We didn't step up to the plate," he says. "Sometimes you're so busy keeping things going that you don't stop long enough to see where things are going. So when the Ethiopian community came in, and the Hispanic community exploded, when the African community exploded in this community, we did not embrace the transition of those cultures into our community." Wheeler tells me the school has recently begun a concerted effort to reach out to Ethiopian families and has enrolled a few Ethiopian students as a result. "We are now beginning to do something we should have been doing a while back, which would have helped Zion greatly if we would have opened our eyes sooner."

Another change in education has been a focus on innovating methods to teach inner-city children. Much of this has sprung from the advent of charter schools, which are publicly funded schools run outside the public school system by nonprofit groups. Students pay no tuition. Charter schools, which now operate in forty states, have allowed for some experimentation with new pedagogical methods. For example, the charter schools of the Knowledge Is Power Program—also known as "KIPP"—have reported dramatically improving test results by teaching a curriculum based around drilling in fundamentals and maintaining high expectations. Donors such as the Bill & Melinda Gates Foundation like the way these programs can deliver measurable results in the form of test scores and a system that can be duplicated in other schools. (Despite the strong results of schools such as KIPP, a Stanford University study found that only about a fifth of charter schools offer a better education than comparable public schools, and that many are worse—the performance of charter schools varies hugely depending on the rigorousness of the academic program and individual management.)

Zion, with its small, family feel and looser structure, feels like a throwback to an earlier time when motivated individuals like Doug Wheeler and Randy Finley stepped in and tried to achieve things on a case-by-case basis through the sheer strength of their personalities. While that type of work brought positive results in some individual situations, it was by nature ad hoc—it did nothing for the vast majority of kids. Ironically, the core philosophy of schools such as KIPP is not very much different from what Zion has been doing for nearly thirty years; it comes down to discipline, care, and expectations. KIPP has institutionalized and packaged it in a technocratic, scalable manner.

Wheeler is well aware of the advances that have been made as far as teaching inner-city kids. He tells me that Lorraine Moore, known for her legendary results as head of Harlem's Frederick Douglass Academy—a highly regarded, public middle and high school that partners with businesses—is coming to the school to speak to the staff. Still, he says, there just hasn't been much chance to innovate at Zion. The financial situation means the focus has been on "survival, not revival." The bottom line, Wheeler says, is that Zion, for all the good it does for its students, can serve only a small number of families. While there probably always will be some demand for an African-American Christian education for children in Seattle, the greater need in the community dwarfs Zion.

Wheeler tells me he has agonized as the performance of black children in Seattle public schools remains far below that of their white and Asian peers. He was incensed after a local newspaper ran an article that purported to profile a student likely to drop out of high school. The answer was an African-American male from a single-parent household. Wheeler steams at labeling a whole group of people as potential failures. More than ever, he is convinced that drastic action needs to be taken on behalf of low-income black children.

The only solution, Wheeler has concluded, is for Washington State to finally introduce charter schools; state voters have three times rejected referenda that would have introduced such schools. The staunchest opponent has been the teachers' union. Wheeler, along with conservative and Christian groups, has been a vocal proponent. He envisions a string of charter schools in the Seattle area, running south all the way to Tacoma. When I ask Wheeler if he imagines programs such as KIPP moving in, he says, "I see professionals who know what they're doing, who have been in the hardest areas, and have proven themselves." If Zion is eclipsed in the process, he says, so be it.

Wheeler is organizing a coalition of conservatives and pastors—he also heads his own church in the Central Area that focuses on helping the down and out—that will work to get the charter issue back on the ballot. Though these efforts have been led in the past by white conservatives, Wheeler tells me that this time he plans to step up and take a high-visibility role. "I can't watch this generation continue going as it's going," he says. "I'm not going to allow you to lock them up anymore, not going to allow you to kick them out of schools anymore.

"I'm sixty-two years old, I got a few more years, maybe twenty. I want to use those now to bring into this community the educational opportunities that we've never had," he says. "We've been talking about the achievement gap ever since I can remember breathing, and we're still talking about it—we did three more studies this year. The new superintendent is talking about what the old superintendent was talking about, which the superintendent before them talked about, which the superintendent before them talked about. I don't want to talk anymore. I'm done."

Between Two Worlds

When Eric Hampton and his wife attend social functions, Eric hates the question *So what do you do?* It is, he thinks, a lazy way to categorize people to decide if someone's worth talking to. He laughs when the inquiry comes to his wife, who teaches sociology at the University of Washington—he finds that people can't conceal their wonderment. "She's young, she's attractive, and she's black, so people love to talk to her once they find out what she does," Eric says. "And there's a natural curiosity because, well, 'How did she become a Ph.D.?' Because it's not the norm."

Eric and I speak at his house, a little before noon on a Saturday. Eric sits on a gray couch in the living room and wears black sweatpants and a black polar fleece jacket zipped over a white T-shirt. He speaks with the same quiet, slightly gravelly voice and thoughtful manner he had as a kid. He has a black goatee and a full head of hair, though he tells me that he's starting to notice some strands of gray. A gold watch hangs loosely around his left wrist, matching his gold wedding band. His sentences are often punctuated with wry laughter.

"Everybody has a perception of what certain people are supposed to be or what they are," Eric says. "It's like, if there's something really bad that happens, the first thing I think about is, 'I hope it's not a black person.' Because then it's going to be, 'See, that's how those black people are.' Whereas if it's a white person, it's, 'That's how that individual is. He's a bad guy but he's not reflective of all of us.'"

A black coffee table sits in front of us, bare except for a copy of *Time* magazine and two white candles in maroon holders. The beige-carpeted living room is spotless. A line of six paper grocery bags sit against the far wall, full of clothes and toys for the baby girl Eric and his wife are expecting in four months. A large window offers a view out over the street. It's a quiet neighborhood—the road dead-ends a bit past Eric's house—in South Seattle. The houses are large and well tended, and Lake Washington is only a few blocks away.

Eric continues, "That happens with all minority groups. Even with the terrorist stuff that's going on, everybody that's Middle Eastern is a terrorist now. I mean that's just what happens. It's unfortunate, but people get lumped into these groups.

"If you get out of those boxes, then people are always looking at you funny. So you almost get forced into these boxes to act in a certain way," Eric says. "If you don't fit into the box, you become invisible. . . . What you see on TV constantly, or what you see on the rap videos or what scares you, you're going to see that. But the black guy in the suit, downtown, he's unthreatening and just doing his thing, you kinda don't pay him no mind.

"A lot of times, for instance, in college, I felt totally invisible, and at Lakeside."

When we played basketball together, Eric seemed to adroitly straddle the two sides of the team. He could advise me on how to respond to Myran's caps, but a minute later he could be holding his own with Tyrell. Will McClain Jr. describes Eric as the "translator" between the two sides. His wife, the sociologist, using a term from her profession, calls Eric a "code switcher"—a person who can employ the language and cultural signifiers of more than one group.

At first—it had been about fifteen years since we'd last seen each other—Eric was gracious but guarded. In conversation he often seems to pause before deciding how much he wants to divulge. He tells me that he finds people are often most interested in putting their own opinions out there. In those situations, he lets them go right ahead. "I like to watch and listen a lot of times and just see what other people have to say," he says, "then go from there."

Over the course of meeting with Eric several times, I realize that—despite all the basketball games, sitting at the same lunch table, and suffering through years of German classes together—I never really knew him very well. Some of that, I think, was being stuck in the midst of adolescence—it's hard enough to figure out yourself at that age, much less anyone else. But race was its own barrier. Because Eric was black, I shied away from talking to him about some of the things I did with some other friends—I worried that I would say or do something that would offend him, although I couldn't put my finger on what exactly that might have been.

That line of separation, I think, also affected Eric. When I tell him that I felt uncomfortable at Lakeside—that playing on the basketball team was one thing that helped me feel like I fit in—Eric is surprised. "I was clueless to the fact that someone like yourself would have experiences at Lakeside that were confusing, that might not have been so pleasant," he says. "I would have assumed it was just fine for you."

"It's too bad we couldn't talk about it back then," I tell him. "I guess I just acted out by listening to lots of heavy metal."

Eric laughs. "Also, when you're living it, you're not thinking about it—you're little kids," he says.

I'd been surprised when I heard that Eric had left Lakeside in the middle of his junior year, a year and a half after I did. I always thought that he would graduate; no matter what happened, it seemed like he would deal with it stoically and move on. His feeling that he was cheated out of playing time on the football team was the catalyst for his departure. As we talk, though, it becomes clear that other issues were gnawing at him at Lakeside.

"I never felt part of the whole thing," he says of his seven years at the school. "I felt more tolerated than anything like being fully embraced, fully accepted. It was like I was accepted on the periphery."

Eric remembers that teachers would hardly ever call on him, something I observed in the classes I had with him. He felt that some didn't think he should be there, so they just ignored him. Others, he thought, wanted him to succeed but were worried they might embarrass him by making him speak in class, so they tended to look past him. At the time, it was fine with Eric, who was shy and soft-spoken anyway.

"I think maybe I was the token. I was there to a certain degree to make people comfortable to say, 'I have a black friend,'" he says. "You're dealing with a situation of people who are not used to being around a bunch of black folks, who don't know very many. And you're in a safe environment, so obviously it's an opportunity for you to delve into the world of black people, to get a little taste or a flavor of what black people are about, so you can say, 'I know this black guy, and he's my friend,' and therefore if you have any type of negative feeling about black people in general, you can always go to that as a way to say, 'Well, I have nothing against black people, see, I have this black friend.'"

After Eric left Lakeside, he graduated from Franklin, a public high school in the South End. The following year, he enrolled at the University of Washington, where he eventually got a degree in finance (though financial aid problems caused him to drop out for a while—the time period during which he briefly played community college basketball with Damian). In general, he moved on with his life, falling out of touch with both classmates from Lakeside and most of the guys from Willie McClain's CAYA team.

Damian, who has kept in touch with Eric, calls him "the millionaire next door," after the best-selling book, which describes an unassuming type of person who does his job, saves and invests his money, and retires rich even though no one around him would have thought he had done so well. I get that feeling, too, after Eric tells me he bought his first condo when he was twenty-two and still in college. To pay the mortgage, he found a roommate and worked full time while going to school, first driving a shuttle bus for a downtown garage and later working for Washington Mutual.

One afternoon, I meet Eric downtown for lunch. We walk to the Columbia Center, the tallest building in Seattle, a seventy-six-story skyscraper with a reflective black-glass surface. The bottom three floors of the building are an atrium built around a central fountain, with escalators crisscrossing at forty-five-degree angles from floor to floor. A food court with stalls such as Moghul Express, Thai Rama, and Fiesta Fiesta lines the perimeter. I grab a sandwich with Eric, who wears charcoal-gray slacks and a royal blue dress shirt without a tie.

Upon graduating from the University of Washington, Eric got a job doing internal accounting with a dotcom that aimed to create a system to place classified ads in newspapers around the country. Considering that Craigslist was in the process of killing off newspaper classified ads, it wasn't a very good idea. Eric left shortly before the company went bankrupt. In 2002 he took a job setting up customer accounts for the multinational accounting and consulting company Deloitte & Touche. Two years later, he quit to start working for the city of Seattle as an auditor, checking the books of businesses that contract with the city. His municipal job, he tells me, is the first work environment in which he's felt fairly comfortable being himself. "The culture's just different," he says. "It's more—I'm not going to say blue collarish—but it's just different."

At Deloitte & Touche, for example, Eric found it hard to adapt. In part, he says, it was just him. He's a quiet, introverted guy, not really prone to gossiping and chatting around the office. He doesn't like to drink or go out to the bar after work, which was a popular pastime with his colleagues. "That's just not my thing, and maybe if it was my thing, I would fit in more," Eric says. "I don't want to make it all into a racial thing. It's more a cultural thing, I guess. But I mean those two, a lot of times, go hand in hand. Not always, but a lot of times."

When confronted with the quiet black guy sitting at his desk, some coworkers would suddenly act as if they were tiptoeing on eggshells. "I would find a lot of people would want to talk to me about sports and that would be it. As if I couldn't talk about anything other than sports. And so, if that's our thing, then hey, whatever, you know?" Eric laughs.

"I don't want to make it seem like, 'Oh, woe is me, because I'm black, I can't . . .'" he says. "I don't believe that. No, I think it has more to do with me and my personality and the way I am, not to say that if you're black things aren't difficult at times."

Even at the city job, Eric is still the only black male in his section. I ask him if sometimes he doesn't wish that one of the kids he grew up with in the Central Area were working across the hall. "Yeah, it's lonely. It can be lonely," he says. "But I met other people. I have friends that I met in college, so I have a social network of people who are similar to me, have the same struggles, went to college, doing pretty well for themselves, but still . . ."

He pauses and then continues, "There's just not a lot of black people up here, anyway. And the black people that are up here, you know, especially black males, especially ones who are native, who are born and raised here, a lot of them just aren't doing that well. You have a lot of people coming from other states who take jobs up here and they do OK, but I don't know—everywhere I seem to go, I'm always the only black guy."

Eric wonders about his own responsibility to help African Americans who have not done as well as he has. He thinks about coaching a kids' basketball team to provide a role model—a black male who has succeeded in mainstream society. "I know I can do more," he says. "It's just this kinda thing where it's like you get so focused on trying to make a living, trying to get ahead, that that's where all your energy is. The little free time you get, because work can stress you out, you want to relax and do something you want to do. I think that's the issue for a lot of folks like myself."

Having grown up in the Central Area, he says, he feels an extra obligation. "If someone comes from the Eastside, it's great that they're trying to help, but a lot of times they can't relate," he tells me. "There is a kind of skepticism on the kids' part, like, 'What's the deal, what's really going on? Do you really care about me or are you doing this just to make yourself feel good?' And again, it's like, if you have that credibility and you come from that you'll be wise to the kids and the type of games that they play."

I ask Eric if he would consider sending his kid to Lakeside. After hearing about his experiences at the school, I expect him to simply say he wouldn't, so his answer takes me by surprise.

"I might," he says. "I struggle with that. I'm finally realizing, at thirty-something, that the most important thing is education, that's definitely the most important thing, especially in the society today. And it is more or less an equalizer. Granted, there's still other issues, but if you can get a good education, it can open some doors for you."

Eric is aware that the choices he faces now as a soon-to-be parent are similar to the ones white parents faced in the late 1970s, when Seattle enacted its mandatory busing scheme. "I saw a lot of people who were all for improving the education of these inner-city kids, but they wouldn't send their kids to the public schools," he says. "You wanna make sure that your kids get the best. I can understand that. Everybody wants that."

It is, in essence, a choice between racial solidarity and the potential for class mobility. If you send your kids to a public school, you have to worry about them falling behind their peers in private schools. On the other hand, as a black parent, you worry that they will lose touch with other African Americans. "I know I want my kid to get the best possible education," Eric says, "but at same time I hope it's in a somewhat diverse setting so they can get to know other people as well. And I don't want them to feel isolated, either.

"That's something I'm dealing with—if I would send them to Lakeside. I probably would send them to private school, but my wife thinks we probably should send them to public school and all that kind of stuff, because the fact is that what happens, most of the well-to-do, they take their kids out and all that is left is those who can't take their kids out, and, unfortunately, you see how the schools are. It's just a mess."

Eric, as he often does, bursts into a kind of rueful laughter as he finishes the sentence.

• • •

"It was like I was in a play," Chris Dickinson says. "It was almost a role. I just lived it for all it was worth."

We are sitting in the basement office in his spacious house in South Seattle, a few miles north of Eric's place. Chris, who has just gotten home from work, has thrown his suit jacket and tie over a sit-up machine in front of his desk. He sits on the other side, his feet up. Behind him, a seven-by-four-foot banner with PRINCETON written in orange on a black background hangs on the wall. Framed pictures of his wife, Ashleigh, and kids—four-year-old son Jack and two-year-old daughter Hannah—stand on the desk and on the shelf behind the couch where I sit.

On the far wall hang two framed commendations from the Lakeside School for "Distinguished Service"—one given to Chris's maternal uncle, a founding partner in one of Seattle's prominent law firms, and one awarded to Chris's father, Cal, who made partner at another of Seattle's principal law firms and served on both Lakeside's alumni board and board of trustees for many years ("Widely read and rational . . . a calm, reasoned statesman in a time of turmoil," Cal's reads).

Chris and I are speaking about his emergence as a star athlete, with frequent visits from Jack and Hannah, who poke their heads in the door, dart in to grab a corn chip from the bag Chris holds in his hands, and then, giggling, scurry out. Chris tells me that he still wonders about the change that overcame him in middle school as a rapid growth spurt transformed his body and social standing.

"All of a sudden I was perceived as being good-looking and this athlete," he says. "My dad used to talk about Rudolf the Red-Nosed Reindeer and say that it was a terrible message, because nobody liked Rudolf, nobody wanted to play with him, and all of a sudden when Santa liked Rudolf, he was the most popular guy. It was like that. Physically I changed and all of a sudden my entire life changed. But I probably carry some of the insecurities I had still today because there was such a massive perception change associated with my physical appearance."

Chris, who still looks like a movie version of a high school sports star—tall, with short brown hair, blue eyes, and a strong jaw—speaks in a deliberate, sometimes almost tortured pace. Sports and what they mean to him is a subject he has spent a lot of time mulling over. "It's like larger than life," he says. "You're a big fish in a small pond. Seattle's a small city; it was easy to take it a little too far. But literally, it was like a drug."

In the old photo taken right after we won the Western Washington AAU championship, Eric and Chris both smile and hoist the trophy and appear completely content. Looking at it now, it strikes me how rare it was to see either of them so relaxed and comfortable.

"At that age and time, my energy and thoughts were not competing," Chris says of our team. "There was joy in playing, just a visceral connection to the game. It was very pure. It just flowed. I loved those guys. If I could see them now, I'd just give each of them a big hug."

Chris and Eric both found escape and freedom on the court. Though they came to Lakeside from nearly opposite backgrounds, each struggled to fit his personality with the institution. Both of them now often refer to the "roles" people are expected to play—Eric as a black man, Chris as the son of a prominent family.

Eric is especially conscious of this process. He remembers that in ninth grade, Chris adopted a little bit of "black" style—he hung out with Eric, got into rap, and learned to break-dance. Eric noticed that some other white guys in Chris's clique gave him a hard time. Eric thought Chris's friends felt uncomfortable with someone trying to act differently— they wanted to reel Chris back in so they wouldn't feel threatened.

I also had my own memories of Chris, primarily of our first meeting, when we were supposed to fight at the eighth-grade dance. At the time, I saw Chris as my opposite, a "natural aristocrat" from the wealthy Madison

Park neighborhood who was an easy fit at Lakeside. We were in reality more like mirror images of each other, two kids hiding their insecurities with macho posturing. In my case, I was trying to blot out the thought that I was a dorky loser. Sports stardom seemed like a way to cover all of that up. But by the time I met Chris at age fourteen, I was starting to realize that I wasn't big enough, strong enough, or fast enough to go very far in athletics. My face-off with Chris brought this home—despite my bluster, I knew that there was no way I would beat him in basketball or a fistfight. It was hard for me to accept, and the reason our initial confrontation stayed with me all these years.

When I mention my memory of our first meeting to Chris, I have to laugh when Chris tells me he has only a "faint recollection." It's the first time either of us has brought it up since the incident happened. "I do remember how visceral the whole thing was, the whole Bush-Lakeside thing, and how big a thing basketball was, you know? And girls and all that," Chris says. "I bet you the exact same stuff was playing with both of us."

As Chris and I talked as adults, I realized that he, Eric, and I were all working through a lot of the same things, just from different angles. In the end, Eric and I got by for several years, but we both finally had to leave Lakeside to feel comfortable in our own skins. That wasn't an option for Chris.

Chris's family was well established at Lakeside by the time he enrolled. His older brother and sister were athletes and popular students at the school. Chris's dad, Cal Dickinson, graduated from Lakeside in 1949, went on to Harvard, a stint in the navy, and then back to Harvard Law School, where he roomed in the same boardinghouse as future Supreme Court justice Antonin Scalia. When Cal returned to the Northwest, he took a job with Perkins Coie, a white-shoe law firm.

At work, Cal specialized in industrial-labor law, handling cases for Boeing. He became known outside legal circles for his involvement in civic causes. His name appeared on committees to clean up the waterfront, develop the downtown shopping district, and build roads and parks. There were also his years of involvement with Lakeside.

Chris brings up his dad frequently in conversation—Cal's success seems to present both a model to follow and a challenge to meet. "My dad walked the walk, man," he says. "I mean, he grew up in an environment where you achieved, then you provided. Back then, that was your frickin' role. You weren't supposed to be emotional and take care of yourself and love yourself, you're supposed to go to work and be a man.

"Even if he was that guy that grew up in that culture, he always wanted to love us and take care of us and grow up to be a good husband. It's not like you're always successful, sometimes you suck, but I always perceived that he had a very loving and pure intent."

By the time I meet Cal, I expect a stern, analytical lawyer. I'm surprised to find a soft-spoken, reflective man. "I think Chris has felt a lot of pressure to live up to what he sees as my accomplishments," he tells me.

Instead of shrinking before his dad's achievements, Chris steered into them. Most notably, he was president of the Lakeside alumni board, a job his dad had held decades earlier. He laughs when he talks about it. "I just realized that I couldn't be my dad," he says. "It was funny being in that same position, thinking, 'That's what my dad did.' You find yourself just walking in your parents' footsteps. Like the first time I dropped Jack off at school it happened to be right behind my parents' house. And I remember driving up the street, turning the corner, and then being in front of my parents' house. It blew me away. It was like coming full circle. Like, I'm right back, my kids are right where I was, in the shadow of my parents' house."

That night, as we speak in his basement office, Chris buzzes with energy. He's just home from his job, where he brokers employee health insurance plans between businesses and insurance companies. At the beginning of our conversation, he takes out a yellow pad of paper and writes "Doug" on the top, but ends up doodling geometrical shapes on it. As we speak, Chris begins to stretch on the floor. I find it disconcerting at first, but then realize that this kind of multitasking must be a habit of someone driven, short of free time, and very athletic.

Several months earlier, we had met at six on a Tuesday morning at his gym in the Belltown neighborhood north of downtown Seattle, only a few blocks from where Damian and I had seen Myran. The place was one large room with a hip, industrial feel—brick walls, a high ceiling crisscrossed by exposed wooden beams and silver venting ducts. Half of the space was filled with workout machines, the other covered with mats. In one corner, a small class mimicked an instructor's yoga poses.

Chris was in the middle of training for an Ironman triathlon, which he was due to run in a few months. To complete the race, he would have to swim two and a half miles, bike 112 miles, and run a full marathon. His training regimen was intense. Before starting to warm up on the treadmill, he warned me: "Last time, I had to vomit."

It was easy to see why. After a short jog, the routine was nonstop and grueling. The exercises included jumping back and forth over a foot-high orange cone while twisting around in the air; shuffling sideways while tossing an eight-pound ball to one of the gym's trainers; and standing on one leg on an eighteen-inch-high box and then lowering himself to the mat before pushing back up. Within minutes, his face was dripping sweat. When I asked what was motivating him, he told me, "I want to see if I can make it. You're out there all by yourself. You either do it or you don't."

By the time we speak in his house, Chris has run the race. He says it's still hard to describe the experience. "There's nothing like feeling—it makes me almost emotional—like I did at different times on that race. Before it started, when I was facing all the preparation I'd done and there were fifteen seconds before the gun went off, I had tears rolling down my cheeks, and everybody else on the beach did, too. It's palpable. You don't even know what to do with it. And to be running on mile twenty of the marathon and I'd never even run a marathon before? And I'm all by myself in the dark? Man, you can't have that unless you do it."

He continues, "It wasn't like I was trying to smoke somebody. I had a little bit of competitive juice, but some guys get so attached to beating the guy in front of them. I sort of released myself a little bit, like I wanted to win but I could also see life from just, 'Screw it, why do I need to be like that?'

"And then the family was with me, they surprised me, and I ran with Jack holding hands for a while and we ran across the finish line together. I'll never experience that in my life, even if I do it again, I'll never have that first time again. It was like having a child. Nothing will be like having our first kid, but it was akin to that. It was special. Those things just define you because they are who you are and working through that adversity."

The experience stood out in part because it was something with a clear goal and a defined set of steps necessary to achieve it. In real life, Chris says, things get compartmentalized. You are a husband, a father, a worker who brings home money to support the family. In each role you try your hardest, but how do you know you're doing it right? You get in a chute and start running. Your old identity slips away. In some ways, Chris says, the Ironman was an attempt to access the old athletic drive that had been buried, but to do it for the sake of personal challenge, not to make himself feel good by beating other people.

At the race, all the merchandise on sale—Ironman biking shorts, hats, T-shirts—made Chris feel a little sick. He saw it all as another way to establish an identity and build the ego, to go around saying "*I'm an Ironman.*" Chris tells me, "I'd see people wearing that stuff head to toe and I didn't associate with that at all. It wasn't about that. I wouldn't put a bumper sticker on my car."

The discipline it takes to complete an Ironman triathlon, as well as Chris's continuing interest in Native American spirituality and meditation, seem a way to get a handle on a life that—along with the culture around it—is constantly accelerating, or at least an attempt to slow things down just a little bit.

We take a break from speaking in Chris's office to go upstairs and have dinner with Ashleigh, Jack, and Hannah. Over steak and asparagus, Ashleigh—who has taken off from nursing until the kids are in school full time—describes visiting an open house at a private school earlier in the day. She and Chris are trying to decide where to send Jack to kindergarten. They've ruled out the local public school, but are pondering options for private schools—should they send him to one with grades, or one without? How much pressure is too much for a kid?

"It's weird having a massive waiting list to a school," Chris tells me after dinner. "When a preschool has a waiting list and then you feel like you're into the club when you get in, it's weird. The politics of Madison Park are totally in play, too, so not only are you competing but you're in this weird social environment and it's just very peculiar. You have to play the game and you feel like you do, you have relationships with people"—Chris takes a deep breath—"it's all new, but it's very weird and it starts very early."

Unlike twenty years ago, when it was normal for kids like us to play several sports and have other hobbies as well, Chris says it's now common for children to begin focusing on a single sport as early as first grade. The idea is to get good enough to eventually draw the attention of high school admissions officers and college recruiters. "You get a sense nowadays of that, that it's like, Jesus, you know, the envelope's been pushed in some inappropriate ways," he says.

Still, you have to do what's necessary to prepare your kids. The reality, Chris says, is that the world has become more competitive, and the Internet is only fueling the speed of that change. "Your ability to comprehend, process, and use information is even more important than it ever was, and without those basic building blocks and skill set you are *way* behind. Unless you can learn things quickly and apply them, and not be intimidated by people that can, it's a real disadvantage, more than it was before," he says.

"It's just more and better, part of it is human nature. So say some guy has a ten-foot long jump, well, people are going to try and jump ten feet and one inch. And so if you have the school and it's competitive, people are gonna figure out better ways to get in and how to be more competitive, and the same thing with college, people are trying to get in and do more and more and be more competitive. Everybody's trying to get an edge."

There are times when Chris wants to change course—or at least slow down a bit—though it doesn't seem possible. "I feel out of alignment, I feel unbalanced, I feel like my outlook on life isn't simple, I feel like it's complicated. I don't even feel all that disciplined," he says. "Look, it's all part of growing and existing. Who's ever done this work, family, have a mortgage thing right?

"Sometimes I wish you could work in a gas station and just be happy with being you and being alive. And it's not OK. I can intellectualize it all I want and know that that's an ideal but I'm pretty far from achieving that. I'm pretty affected by it."

"What do you mean?" I ask.

"Just the need to achieve," he says. "In part, it's not just the family, it's the whole culture. If you're used to excelling, you either excel and you fit in, or you don't. So sometimes it doesn't feel like there's a breather."

I tell Chris that I'm surprised, because from the outside—high school sports stardom, Princeton, good job, Mercedes in the driveway, beautiful house, loving family—he seems to be doing really well.

"That's what I'm saying," he says. "My perception is different than that. It's hard. It's just the old saying, sometimes you need to stop and smell the roses. And if you're always looking for a bigger flower, it's . . . I'm not alone. I'm totally not alone. I think that's not an unusual thing, when you grow up in an environment like that. And it's not just my family, it's Lakeside and that culture.

"The higher your expectations are with everything, the tougher it is to reach them and therefore the tougher it is to be satisfied. It's one thing I want to do and it keeps shifting, it's like the better you do or the more you have, you can catch yourself just focusing on the next thing, or comparing yourself against a different set of expectations. . . . But if you talk about spiritual development to me it means being able to just exist right now and be happy with what's around me and not just focus on the future or the past or what didn't happen, or what I want to happen, or what I don't have. That's jail, in my opinion. And a lot of times, it's great. But it has its claws."

Lakeside Revisited

On a Friday afternoon in September 2005, about three thousand students, parents, faculty, and alums of Lakeside School mingled under forty-eight tents set up on the school's soccer field, browsing displays put up by school organizations such as the outdoor program, the athletic department, and the gay-and-lesbian student group. White banners around campus declared in cursive maroon script, LIVING OUR MISSION. A band played Brazilian music. Eventually the crowd filed into a large tent set with rows of chairs to listen to short speeches by students and alums leading to the main event, a keynote address by the school's most prominent graduate, Bill Gates.

The event marked the formal launch of a campaign to raise $105 million. That day, the school announced that the Bill & Melinda Gates Foundation had just pledged $40 million, and an additional $30 million in donations had already been lined up. The money, the school said, was being raised for two main purposes: to increase diversity by boosting the amount of financial aid available to students, and to expand the Global Service Learning Program, which would send students to places such as Peru and India to do volunteer work.

Speaking from behind a podium, Headmaster Bernie Noe announced, "This evening we say to the families of the Greater Seattle area that if you have a son or a daughter who is qualified and motivated to do the work at Lakeside School, then we want your child to apply. We will make available financial assistance so that any child can attend the school."

Gates, dressed in a dark gray blazer and blue shirt, capped the afternoon with some reminiscences about his school days. He recalled being assigned to computerize the school's class schedule and how he made sure to put the attractive girls in his classes and give himself Fridays off. He said that Lakeside was the type of place that allowed kids like him to fool around with computers in those early days instead of having teachers regulate their use, and that's how he learned to program. He was supporting the school now, he said, because he saw a "deep need for leadership in the world," something he thought Lakeside could provide. "If there had been no Lakeside," he said, "there would have been no Microsoft. And I'm here to say thank you."

In the three decades since Gates had attended Lakeside, it had become one of the most prestigious private schools in the country, its success paralleling the rising fortunes of the Northwest (which in large part were driven by Gates and Microsoft). The *Wall Street Journal* has ranked Lakeside among the most successful high schools in the country at getting its students into "selective" colleges. As Lakeside's profile shot up, so did demand—the school now receives about four hundred applications for thirty-two slots in each incoming fifth-grade class. It charges more than $20,000 a year in tuition. Its endowment has grown to more than $150 million.

Just as all the individual members of our basketball team have had to adjust to changing times, Lakeside as an institution has faced the challenge of transforming or falling behind. One persistent blemish on the school's image has been the perception that it is only for rich white kids. Over the years, Lakeside has had a consistently hard time retaining black students and faculty. As recently as 1999, every faculty member at the Upper School was white. A few years later, the school commissioned a consulting firm to conduct a survey about Lakeside's perception in Seattle, and the answer came back as "rich, white, and elite."

The fund-raising drive kicked off by Bill Gates was one of continuing efforts by the school to change its image. "I want as many students as possible, from as many different backgrounds as possible, to enjoy a Lakeside education," Gates told the crowd that afternoon. "So I think it's important to put the financial aid program at Lakeside on such a solid footing that money will never be a reason for denying a Lakeside education to a promising student."

The idea behind the event was quite radical. The school was stating that it was going to do everything it could to draw more students from minority and nonwealthy backgrounds, even if that meant fewer slots for its traditional constituency, the city's elite families. Instead of minority students coming to Lakeside in a haphazard way, as they did when I was a student there, the school was seeking to develop a sustainable pipeline. Minority and nonwealthy students who were qualified for Lakeside would be sought out and their tuition paid. This would negate the need for anyone to devise an integration program such as our basketball team—Lakeside would already have a diverse student body. In essence, the fund-raising drive was asking alumni families to donate to an effort that, if successful, would diminish the chances of their own offspring gaining entry to the school.

But besides the basic outline of the program—the idea that there would be many more students and teachers from minority backgrounds—the school had a hard time pinpointing what its diversity push would mean, though notes from planning meetings reflect that administrators thought the effort could turn Lakeside into a "rock star" school. In March 2004, as the diversity campaign was gearing up, the school's director of admissions, an African-American woman, wrote an e-mail expressing her concern about comments she'd heard from white students and families who thought that new minority teachers and students would "reduce the quality" of the school. "My first few years at Lakeside were hard ones," she wrote. "I was publicly accused of being unfair, to offering too much financial aid, to being inattentive to connected and affluent families. Each of these accusations was ill-founded and inflammatory, and it is difficult to ignore my suspicion that most of these accusations would not have been made if I had been a white male. My experiences and others I've observed make me wonder why it is okay in this community for people to attack its newest, most vulnerable members with such vigor. . . . My fear as I sit down to write this is for the new students and adults of color who will join us next fall. Will this community have changed enough by then so that they don't have to have their abilities questioned because of their race?"

More than a year later, as Gates spoke from the podium, the diversity campaign was already hitting snags that in the coming months would get worse, attracting embarrassing attention from the national media, and eventually resulting in a lawsuit that charged the school with fostering racial discrimination.

"Diversity" started to become a buzzword at Lakeside in the mid-1980s, when private schools across the United States—led by the National Association of Independent Schools—stepped up efforts to recruit students who were not wealthy or white. "Multicultural education," the thinking went, would not only broaden the opportunities available to minority students, but also aid traditional private school students in "developing respect for the immense complexity of humanity and gaining insights and perspectives into their own particular cultures," the NAIS wrote in the 1980s.

In 1987, Lakeside devoted twelve pages of its quarterly magazine to diversity. In an introduction to the set of short articles—most by staff and faculty members employing yawn-inducing jargon about things such as curriculum development and statements of educational purpose—the headmaster, Dan Ayrault, wrote that the school had not made enough progress since admitting its first black students in 1965: "Given the number of advantages and resources we have inherited, we should be a model of excellence in diversity, and we are far short of that."

Lakeside was serious in its intent to increase its diversity. In the fall of 1986—a few months after our basketball team had its run—Ayrault hired a new Middle School head who was nationally known as a leader in the diversity-in-private-schools movement. The new head began to increase the school's recruitment of minority students. At the same time, Bob Henry, an African-American teacher who had grown up in Seattle, joined the school as the Middle School's diversity coordinator. "It was a lot of work and a lot of interesting times, and not all of it easygoing and fun," Henry says of his early years at Lakeside when I meet with him in a classroom at the Middle School, where he now teaches history.

By the early 1990s, the number of nonwhite students at the Middle School had climbed to nearly 25 percent, Henry tells me, but then things got sticky. The diversity push had an unexpected setback when Ayrault, a dynamic and respected headmaster, died of a heart attack in 1990. Other hurdles were perhaps more easily foreseen, such as the zero-sum game of private school admissions. "With every diversity admit, there was a traditional nonadmit, and I think that had an impact," Henry says.

"I don't know if it was ever said, 'Hey look, you gotta get off of that case because our kids are not getting in,' but something was made known. And obviously the school has to earn its living, therefore you can't close your doors on the families that have supported the school traditionally."

The other problem that came with higher minority enrollment, Henry tells me, was a perceived shift in the school's culture. Parents began to grumble that the "diversity admits" were diminishing Lakeside's academic quality. In addition, some parents complained that a few of the African-American boys were starting fights and messing around in class. Henry says that a lot seemed to come down to the "subtle" ways people see race: Some of the black kids were aggressive, he says, but there were also aggressive white kids—that comes with adolescence. "What complicates it or exacerbates it is the color line, because the color line is a trigger for all kinds of emotions and all kinds of primal responses," Henry says. "If it's black kids bullying, then it becomes a different thing, oddly. Everything becomes different when the color factor plays in."

By 1993, the Middle School head who had been hired to increase diversity had left. Support for the diversity program had not only evaporated, Henry says, but also many of the newly enrolled black students dropped out once they got to the Upper School. Henry, a trim, thoughtful man who picks his words carefully, was chastened.

He tells me that he had viewed diversity through the lens of his own experiences in the 1960s, when his had been one of the first African-American families to move out of the Central Area to the South End. He integrated a white public middle school and found that, because he felt he was representing all blacks, he forced himself to become a "stellar student." When he came to Lakeside as diversity director, Henry looked for potential students who were not only solid academically, but who also could handle the "stress" of being one of the only blacks in a white institution. In other words, Henry says, he was looking for young versions of Jackie Robinson. "Of course, we're talking about kids. That's the difference," he says. "Jackie Robinson can make the decision on his own and stick to it."

Henry also began to question some of what he was doing. In the early 1990s, stories began to appear in the media touting the idea that "black men are an endangered species," Henry tells me. He thought that black male students at the school should have a forum to discuss issues like that, so he started Lakeside's first affinity group, the African American

Brotherhood. Now, Henry, who tells me he has been influenced by the writings of black conservative Shelby Steele, wonders if affinity-based groups—Lakeside also has groups for Asian and gay students—do more harm than good. "It's institutionalizing seeing yourself and being yourself as a racial person—as a racial identity, a sexual identity, whatever," he says. "I think that's limiting, and potentially closes one to the opportunities to experience the broader world. To really be educated is to see all those possibilities of who you are because you are so many things."

Henry left the diversity job and switched to teaching full time. "I think I did a couple good things in the role and raised some good questions, but it was draining, emotional work," he tells me. "To some extent it's what one should do and can do wherever they are, but to another extent, as Malcolm X says, you're in the belly of the beast, so you better take care of what you're doing and what you're saying and where you're saying it. That was a strain, so I chose to be a schoolteacher and have my impact in the day-to-day back-and-forth with kids."

Lakeside's diversity tide ebbed until 1999, when Bernie Noe came on as the new headmaster. If the board of trustees wanted a forceful leader, it got one in Noe, who came to the school from the prestigious Sidwell Friends School in Washington, D.C.—the alma mater of Chelsea Clinton and current school of Malia and Sasha Obama—where he had been the Upper School principal.

Noe is a short, energetic man about fifty years old. He still has a somewhat boyish look—his hair, though now silver, is parted in the middle and falls down across his forehead. His tan sports jacket and tightly knotted tie add to the preppy look. From his office windows, which offer a view over the Lakeside quad, you can see students trundling between classes with backpacks slung over one shoulder. Inside, large, framed posters of Gandhi and Martin Luther King Jr. hang on the walls. When he speaks, Noe, who has spent his career educating the children of the rich and powerful, emanates an unwavering belief in his ideas.

From the moment he arrived at Lakeside in 1999, Noe proceeded as if his intention was to raise Lakeside to the level where its national reputation would be on a par with his former employer. He started by shaking up the old guard. Noe instituted a formal faculty review process, which the school had not had before (the classrooms had been basically the fiefdoms of individual teachers). Several teachers who had been at the school for years either left or were told that their services were no longer needed.

In 2003, Noe shifted the focus to where the school was going in the next decade. "We held a retreat," Noe tells me. "All the faculty, the board of trustees, the parents' association, the alumni association, representatives from the staff, representatives from the student body, and we looked at the mission statement and said, 'What do we need to do here? What will these kids need to know graduating into this new world?' The two conclusions were: We need to be a more diverse community—at the adult and student level we need to be better at doing diversity. And we need to be teaching the kids about a global world."

After the meeting, department heads immediately began to look for teachers of color, Noe says. The administration discussed ways to make minority students feel more comfortable, such as holding "Diversity Days." They also set a goal to increase the number of students receiving financial aid to a third of the student body within a decade, a rise from about 13 percent when Noe arrived at the school. "The goal is to have everybody feel like it's their school," Noe says. "So from the most privileged to the least privileged and everybody in between, you're equally valued, equally celebrated, equally appreciated."

Of course, offering more financial aid, not to mention sending kids to foreign countries for "global learning," was going to cost a lot of money. The school launched the "Living Our Mission" campaign with the goal of raising $105 million, which Bill Gates helpfully kicked off with his $40 million contribution. In the meantime, under Noe's direction, Lakeside had already started to aggressively seek minority students and teachers to fulfill its goals.

Terrance Blakely was twelve when he came home from a basketball trip in the summer of 2000 and saw the letter from Lakeside on his bed. He was so upset that he started to cry before he even opened it—he knew that he must have been accepted.

Blakely had come to Seattle three years earlier. His father had been in the army, and the family had lived in Alaska, Florida, Georgia, North Carolina, and San Antonio before his dad's final assignment at Fort Lewis in Tacoma. Blakely's parents had decided to remain in the area and moved to Tukwilla, a South End neighborhood that has seen its African-American population balloon with the movement out of the Central Area.

In public elementary school, Blakely was put on the "gifted" track, leaving his regular classroom for special classes with other advanced students. When Blakeley was in the sixth grade, one of his teachers told his mom that she should look into Lakeside. About five times that year, Blakeley did half days at his elementary school, and then traveled the twenty miles north to Lakeside to take part in a battery of tests and interviews.

Blakely hated the idea of leaving his friends and crossing the city to go to Lakeside. He tried to bomb the entrance exam, purposely leaving questions on the multiple-choice test blank. It didn't work. When the acceptance letter came, his mom told him to go for a year and see how it went. In addition, administrators at Lakeside put on a hard sell. "In my interview, I said, 'I'm probably not coming here. I don't feel like this is really the place for me.' I was really polite about it," Blakely says. "And it was like, 'No, it would be a great place for you, we would feel honored if you came,' the whole nine yards. As a sixth-grader, some adults are completely fascinated with me? I'm like, 'Maybe there is something there.'"

The seventh grade was a shock. "The things they did for fun were not what I did for fun," Blakely says. "Kids in seventh grade were talking about going to the symphony and going out on boats. I was used to playing football in the street and having a sleepover."

For the first several months, Blakely lived "two separate lives," traveling up to Lakeside for school but then coming back to the neighborhood every afternoon to hang out with his old friends. Eventually he was caught in between—he wasn't comfortable with the kids at Lakeside, but the neighborhood kids started to distance themselves. "I now became the spoiled kid on the block, and I just ended up not really having anything to do," Blakely says.

When basketball season came around, Blakely faced a choice: If he stuck to his position of disassociating himself with Lakeside kids, he'd have to skip the season and miss doing something he really liked. He chose to play, and the kids on the team ended up as his closest friends throughout the rest of his time at the school. "I had a common bond with them," he says, "and if I was going to be friends with anyone else at the school, I figured it would be the kids I played basketball with."

Eric Hampton, when we spoke, made the point that going to Lakeside for him was a confrontation on both race and class levels—he felt he was different because he was African American, and because his family, in comparison to the average at the school, was poor. People treat you differently because of your race, and, at the same time, you don't really get their world because the financial gap means they do things that you don't.

Several other African-American alums of Lakeside I contacted expressed feelings similar to Eric's, and talked about their means of dealing with them. Stan Evans, who graduated in 1973 in the same class as Bill Gates, was still processing the experience three decades later. Evans, who got into the school through its summer program for minority students, later went on to earn a law degree. He said that Lakeside had taught him analytical skills he would not have learned in public school, but he had mixed feelings. Mainly, he thought that leaving the black community to attend Lakeside had always made him a man in the middle—it severed his relations with the kids he grew up with, but he said that when he went back to Lakeside for alumni reunions he felt that all he had was "superficial friendships." "The majority of blacks I know have a little regret that they went to Lakeside," he told me.

Ronnie Cunningham, who graduated in 1986, told me he fit in through playing sports and then "decided to get what I could" out of the school. He said that though he received acclaim as an all-city running back, he regretted that he didn't gain confidence in his academic skills until years later, when he was in graduate school working toward his Ph.D. in psychology.

Bob Henry, the Middle School teacher and former diversity director, told me that he had sent his oldest daughter to Lakeside for her freshman and sophomore years, but she had then asked to leave. "She still has painful memories of those days," he said. "It was a time where, as she looks back on it, it was formative in that she became aware of this hierarchical structure of things and how it was set. I don't know if girls are more sensitive than boys are, but she saw where the power was. She saw the whole thing lined up and she wanted to compete or to be in those roles, and she did all that she could, but in the end she didn't particularly like herself as a result."

Henry said that kids who come from minority or nonwealthy backgrounds end up in a peculiar situation at Lakeside. Because they can't participate in all the rituals that their classmates are—such as getting a new car when they turn sixteen or vacationing in Sun Valley—they often end up sharply observing everything around them. The role, Henry said, is "almost anthropological."

I contacted Blakely, who graduated in 2006, because I wanted to speak with some recent African-American Lakeside students. We meet in the summer of 2007, after he has just finished his freshman year at Trinity University in San Antonio, where he is planning to major in accounting before going to law school.

The same week, I catch up with another African-American graduate of the class of 2006, David Changa-Moon, who is a student at Whitman College in Eastern Washington, where he is studying engineering. Changa-Moon had started at Lakeside in his freshman year. Though they had played together on the basketball team, Blakely and Changa-Moon are not close friends. I meet up with both at Starbucks—with Blakely at one in the Madison Park neighborhood, and Changa-Moon at one near a shopping mall south of Seattle.

Both describe a series of challenges and choices that go unnoticed by the average Lakeside student—often in words almost identical to those of Eric Hampton, who attended the school fifteen years earlier. For example, most nonwealthy minorities in Seattle live in the South End, and Lakeside is at the very northern edge of the city. While many students with more money have stay-at-home moms who take them to and from school, a lot of minority kids come from families where both parents have to work. Coming from the South End, it's about an hour and a half bus ride each way. Not only do you have to get up much earlier, but also, when you go to a school that assigns several hours of homework a night, that means you have much less time at home to get it all done. Besides that, you might be expected to cook dinner for your siblings or do other chores to keep the household functioning.

Another complication, Blakely tells me, is that the school seems to have lower expectations for students of color. For example, he says, in Middle School most of the minority students were placed in a lower-level math class. When his parents complained, Blakely took a test and got bumped up. But for some students, it's tempting to take the easier route.

"It's like, 'If I don't try enough, they'll leave me alone, and then just let me coast along for a little bit,'" he says.

Changa-Moon often breaks into laughter when he speaks about his time at Lakeside, shaking his head at various absurdities. "It's so backward to how you're used to living life," he says. "I would sit there and eat this really good food and I would come home and have food from the food bank that the rest of my family's eating. So it's just that sort of reality, that sort of juxtaposition."

Changa-Moon continues, "You don't hear of bad things happening in the Lakeside community, you don't generally hear of deaths, things like that—it's a rare occurrence, it's surprising, it's staggering, it's a big deal. But when you come from a community in which a life where you're struggling is just normal, you can identify with people because you understand everything isn't easy, everything isn't given to you. I understand that everyone has their own struggle, but when your struggle is to just eat and live and stay healthy, it's a much different struggle."

A very basic issue is, of course, money. Not only does the average kid at Lakeside have a lot of stuff—a cell phone, an iPod, the desirable brand of laptop, computer games, a scooter, a car—but also access to money powers a student's social life, making possible things like going to baseball games, movies, or restaurants. While kids from poorer backgrounds might just hang out and watch TV or play basketball at the local playground, Lakeside kids tend to do things that require cash. "It's not like I can just go home and say, 'All right, Mom, can I have twenty bucks? I want to go to the movie.' That's not going to happen," Changa-Moon says. "When that's just assumed, it's like, 'Why aren't you doing this?' When you're young it's hard to be like, 'Well, my parents do not have money. I can't afford this.'"

Though Blakely's parents resisted at first, they eventually broke down and got him the things he felt he needed to fit in—first a cell phone, and then a car a few months after he turned sixteen. At times he felt very involved with the Lakeside social scene, and at other points he pulled away from it to spend most of his time with friends he played with on a select basketball team outside of the school. Changa-Moon felt that his large family kept him grounded. "I was in the popular group, I guess, just because I played basketball and I'm a person of color, and that pretty much locks you in," he says. "So I'd always get invited out to things, but I just didn't really choose to do that."

For Blakely, one of the biggest differences between Lakeside and public school was the level of motivation in students. In public school, he says, most kids don't really plan much into the future beyond what they're going to eat that afternoon. Unlike Lakeside, which starts prepping kids for the SAT in eighth grade, a lot of public school students don't even think about college until the second half of senior year, and then they'll likely just head off to community college, if they go anywhere.

At Lakeside, the payoffs were tangible. Kids who did well, first of all, got material rewards from their parents. Because the kids were already motivated, teachers could spend their time going through the lessons and engaging the students, which made classes more fun. Even if you didn't like doing a lot schoolwork, you could still see college ahead, which would be paid for by your parents. You knew that if you made it through college, you were going to be well positioned for life. "There are a lot more foreseeable goals at Lakeside than in public school," Blakely says. "I think that's the underlying difference."

It has been harder for private schools like Lakeside to attract African-American faculty than students. For a minority student, there is the prospect of feeling isolated or out of place, but Lakeside offers the carrot of a good education and entry to a prestigious college. A teacher of color, on the other hand, doesn't have that potential payoff and also may be in high demand at many other institutions.

Beginning in 2003, with its new mission focus in place, Lakeside set out forcefully to change the racial composition of the faculty. The search was led by T. J. Vassar, who, in 1968, was one of the school's first three African-American graduates. Vassar had returned to Lakeside in 1992 to direct the Lakeside Educational Enrichment Program, the summer course for minority students, and later became the schoolwide diversity director. At Noe's urging, the school soon hired a slate of new teachers of various backgrounds, including two Latin Americans, one of East Indian origin, and three African-American teachers: Chance Sims, who began at the school in 2003; Kim Pollock, who started there in 2004; and Novella Coleman, who began in 2005.

Sims, a history and humanities teacher in his early thirties, had been teaching at Tacoma Community College. Coleman, who hired on as a math teacher, had just graduated from Stanford University. Pollock, in her midforties, had been teaching English at Bellevue Community College, across Lake Washington from Seattle.

A short woman with a hearty laugh and a forthright manner, Pollock had long focused on issues of race. She had started the ethnic and cultural studies curriculum while at Bellevue Community College and taught a class called "White Culture in the United States." When T. J. Vassar called out of the blue to ask her about taking a job at Lakeside, telling her about the school's new mission focus, she was intrigued. "I was very committed to the idea that if I could reach the kids that were going to rule the world at fourteen, fifteen, and sixteen that I could have a shot at actually making change," Pollock says. "I was very much devoted to that idea and very much seduced by that idea."

One of Pollock's focuses had been the theory of "white privilege," which puts forward the idea that white people benefit from their skin color in countless ways of which they are often unaware. One widely distributed essay on the subject lists fifty examples, including:

When I am told about our national heritage or about "civilization," I am shown that people of my color made it what it is.

I can swear, or dress in secondhand clothes, or not answer letters, without having people attribute these choices to the bad morals, the poverty, or the illiteracy of my race.

I can do well in a challenging situation without being called a credit to my race.

Pollock says she made her stance clear when she interviewed for the job at Lakeside. "I told them that antiracism is what I teach," she says. "You can put whatever name on it you want, you can call this an English class, or a sociology class, or whatever, but I'm going to teach antiracism and I'm going to use all my tools to do that." Sims, too, focused on "social justice," teaching about things such as imperialism and colonialism in his world history courses.

Pollock, as might be expected from her track record, immediately began to talk about racial issues in a more direct manner than the school was used to. As she recalls, things began to heat up at the start of her second semester, in January 2005, when the Upper School held its Martin Luther King Jr. Day assembly. A number of teachers, both white and black, participated in a panel discussion about their experiences during the 1960s. T. J. Vassar, the diversity director, spoke about being one of the first black students at the school in 1965. A white teacher spoke about not remembering there being many black people around when he was a kid. Pollock talked about her family being one of the first to integrate a white neighborhood in Chicago. "I said something very, very controversial at that point," Pollock tells me. "I said that if someone grows up in America, I mean everybody, you cannot help but be racist, because our culture is racist, and boy, did that set off a firestorm." The reaction was immediate, with students at the assembly yelling out in protest. What a lot of white students took away, David Changa-Moon tells me, was that Pollock had just called all white people at Lakeside racists.

At another assembly, a few months later, one of Pollock's students, a girl of East African origin, gave a PowerPoint presentation that quoted various comments that had been made to her during her time at the school. They ranged from fairly innocuous to the bluntly offensive, including,

If I went down to the South End, would I get beat up by all the black people?

Is it true that black guys have big packages?

If people in Africa are starving and dying, then why don't they just eat the dead to stay alive?

We should put every AIDS-infected person on an island and burn them. That's the only way of solving the AIDS epidemic.

The next day, the school had an extended advisory period to talk about the presentation. Changa-Moon tells me, a bit wryly, that the main effect this had was keeping race front and center as a subject of discussion.

In May, an African-American student in the freshman class sent a heartrending poem by e-mail to all faculty and staff that described his feelings of isolation at home and at the school. It began: "How does it feel? I see this boy every day. He goes to school where almost everyone is the opposite color. I don't think it bothers him but I wonder how it feels. How does it feel to go to a place and know that everyone sees you as a failure?"

Pollock responded with a letter—titled "Be Ware of the Damage a Good Heart Can Do"—e-mailed to the same group, in which she admitted to deeply conflicted feelings about the diversity push: "What becomes of the community, and what responsibility does Lakeside have to those communities as we harvest their 'best and brightest'? Do other communities come and harvest the white children who are 'able and willing' to come to the top institutions which are not white and ask them to learn how to survive and function and be judged by standards that have nothing to do with their own identity?"

Pollock tells me that Noe told her to "slow down," that she was pushing change too fast. She recalls meeting with Noe in his office, under the poster of Martin Luther King Jr. "I told him that's what people said to Martin, they told him to slow down, they told him to wait, and here you are honoring him forty years later telling me the same thing," she says, laughing. "He didn't like that too much."

By the fall semester of 2005, when Bill Gates kicked off the fundraising drive, the situation at the school had deteriorated. One of the newly hired Latina teachers let it be known that she planned on leaving. Novella Coleman, the African-American Stanford graduate in her first year of teaching, was having a horrible time in her math classes, getting questioned by kids about her qualifications and her competence. In class, one kid asked if she had gotten into Stanford on an athletic scholarship. Another asked if she was from Compton, the Los Angeles neighborhood known in rap songs as the home of the Crips and the Bloods. When she said she wasn't, he pressed ahead with a series of questions about what the area was like. When Coleman was questioned by a female student about something she wrote on the whiteboard, another girl in the class turned to the student, wagged her head, snapped her fingers, and said "You told her!" in way that made Coleman think the girl was trying to imitate the stereotype of a sassy black woman. After a couple of months, Coleman announced that she would resign at the end of the year.

"I felt like students were holding me under the microscope, I felt attacked by parents, and I felt marginalized by those who claimed to be addressing my concerns. I was miserable because while I have undergone a lot of personal growth to be in a place where I viewed my race and culture as an asset, I knew that at Lakeside my race and culture were liabilities," she wrote right before she left the school. She had, she said, "been reduced to tears at the thought of returning to Lakeside or even spending another moment there."

In the meantime, a group of parents had begun to push back against all the diversity talk. Some wondered why they were spending more than $20,000 a year to have their kids take part in a social experiment. The parents also claimed that admitting more minority students to the school was lowering standards. Others objected to the political bent that teachers such as Pollock and Chance Sims were taking. Did diversity just mean left-wing political views? What about ideological diversity as well?

In an effort to address those complaints, Noe—at the suggestion of a staff member—invited Dinesh D'Souza to speak at the school's annual spring lecture, which comes with a $10,000 speaking fee. D'Souza, a former Reagan staffer who was then a fellow at the right-leaning Hoover Institute at Stanford, has long been a conservative firebrand. His books cover subjects such as the evils of political correctness, the triumph of Ronald Reagan, the greatness of America, how the depravity of the cultural left resulted in the 9/11 attacks, and his latest, *What's So Great about Christianity*. If Noe wanted to throw some red meat to conservative parents, D'Souza was certainly the guy to bring it.

D'Souza was supposed to speak about the war in Iraq, but it was his views on African Americans that attracted attention. In 1995, D'Souza published *The End of Racism*, a polemic about race in America. In the book, he asserts that slavery was not a racist institution; that blacks do not achieve as high as whites because of "cultural deficiencies"; that black "cultural pathology" has contributed to a new form of discrimination, which he calls "rational discrimination"—because some blacks commit crimes, it is logical that there is prejudice against all of them; that segregation was a benevolent system put in place to protect blacks from whites who might harm them; and that inner-city streets "are irrigated with alcohol, urine and blood." D'Souza comes to the conclusion that racism might still exist in some minor form, but it is liberals and blacks themselves who are the problem. His solution is to do away with affirmative action and the 1965 Civil Rights Act. Also, blacks should learn to "act white." "If America as a nation owes blacks as a group reparations for slavery, what do blacks as a group owe America for the abolition of slavery?" D'Souza asks.

In the book, D'Souza praises black conservatives Glenn Loury and Robert Woodson Jr. as part of a small group that consists of "the only people who are seriously confronting black cultural deficiencies and offering constructive proposals." Both men held positions at the American Enterprise Institute along with D'Souza, who was a fellow at the think tank. After *The End of Racism* came out, both resigned in protest. Loury wrote, "It is hard to avoid the conclusion that in some influential quarters, when the object of discussion is the African-American community, basic principles of decency and of scholarly and journalistic integrity no longer apply. Blacks seem to be held in such contempt that we can be slandered, defamed and insulted without remorse or consequence."

In a faculty meeting during the first week of January 2006 called by Noe to discuss issues of race on campus, Chance Sims brought up Dinesh D'Souza and spoke about how offensive he found D'Souza's views. When a white staff member took responsibility for recommending D'Souza to Noe, Sims told her, "Shame on you." That prompted a white male teacher to stand up and tell Sims he had no right to speak that way. The meeting, which had been meant to soothe nerves, only heated up simmering tensions among the faculty.

Noe tried to make the D'Souza appearance a "teaching moment." Terrance Blakely tells me that students were given eighty-five pages of *The End of Racism* to read and then discuss with their teachers. Blakely was "disgusted" by the book and by the idea that the school would consider hosting a speaker whom Blakely felt wrote hate speech about African Americans. For Blakely, it stripped everything down to reveal the power differential at the school. "You have kids saying, 'I feel offended and I feel threatened that you're bringing this guy to the school,' and they say, 'Well, he's not here to talk about that so he won't really touch on that issue, so you'll be OK.' And then it's just like, 'Well, if I had a little bit more money behind me, or if I had a little bit more power, I bet this would be different.'"

With pressure from teachers and students mounting, Noe canceled D'Souza's speech. (The school, which still had to pay D'Souza's fee, ended up substituting William Kristol, a prominent neoconservative.) The cancellation incensed many parents and alumni, who saw it as censorship. The local press soon got wind of the whole mess, followed shortly by right-wing blogs and the national media. When D'Souza appeared on FOX News's *Hannity & Colmes*, Lakeside issued a statement: "We realized Mr. D'Souza's presence could cause emotional pain to many at our school including our increasingly diverse student body." D'Souza chatted amicably with the sympathetically outraged hosts—Susan Estrich was subbing for Colmes—for a few minutes, blaming his cancellation on

Lakeside's "Kabbalah" faculty before the show cut to Greta Van Susteren, who had an update on a young, white American woman gone missing in Aruba.

The situation at Lakeside continued to worsen. A few weeks after the D'Souza uproar broke out, Pollock taught in her American Cultural Literacy class, in honor of Martin Luther King Jr. Day, King's "Letter from the Birmingham Jail" as well as the response of the city's white clergy to King's calls for desegregation. She asked the students to look at how the clergymen called blacks in Birmingham "our negroes" and labeled King an "outside agitator."

Pollock tells me that a few boys in the class began to question her. "They not only denied the possessiveness of the language, this one person and two of his friends, every word I said they argued back, every word that I said they questioned," Pollock says. "So I started talking about the concept of possessiveness, of whites possessing blacks, about how the first laws instituting slavery were laws against women, so that a white man could create his own workforce by buying a woman and raping her, and raping all of his children, raping his daughter and raping his granddaughter, and I said that directly that way, I said that's how black people came to look like me."

The boys questioned how Pollock, who is light-skinned with reddish hair and freckles, knew it was rape. Couldn't a slave love her master? they asked. Sensing that the discussion was getting out of hand, Pollock tells me, she cut it off. One of the students then told her, "By stopping this conversation, you are intellectually raping us." Pollock says she ended the class, had the students leave, and wrote up what had happened. Later that day, she says, she walked into the lunchroom and overheard the boy who accused her of "intellectual rape" bashing her to a group of students. Pollock walked up and told him, "You're not the first little white boy to challenge me, and you won't be the last."

In response, Noe placed Pollock on probation. The school's academic director arranged a meeting between Pollock and the boys. Pollock says the boys accused her of "exploiting" her students. Pollock, at that point, felt that the administration was not going to give her any support, so she resigned.

After Pollock disappeared from the school—the administration said she left for "health reasons"—Chance Sims, on February 14, sent an e-mail to the school's staff titled "A Valentine for Kim Pollock." It read, in part, "Some will say that [Pollock] was uncompromising, antagonistic, difficult and selfish but those who knew her knew that she was a rare individual with a heart and mind that was unmatched. I have heard administrators say that her departure was inevitable. After learning that the administration is spending hundreds of hours dealing with the D'Souza debacle, I'm left to wonder how this school might look if the administration spent hundreds of hours supporting retention efforts." Sims closed the e-mail by quoting Pollock's favorite passage from the Audre Lorde essay "The Master's Tools Will Never Dismantle the Master's House," which reads, in part: "For the master's tools will never dismantle the master's house. They may allow us temporarily to beat him at his own game, but they will never enable us to bring about genuine change."

Noe responded by placing Sims on a two-month probation and postponed offering him a contract for the next year. "Chance, no one has a problem with points you raise or the messages you promote at Lakeside, but rather the way in which you raise them," Noe wrote in his letter informing Sims of the probation. "It is at a point where your method of delivery is unacceptable: it undermines the sense of community we are trying to build at the school."

During all this, many alums and parents weren't feeling any sense of community at all. One parent wrote to the *Seattle Weekly*, "As for the lofty goals of Lakeside, it's getting downright creepy. Not only do kids only hear from left-leaning speakers, the constant mantra about diversity and saving the world has made many of them tune out. The lecturing about privilege, materialism, poverty, diversity and class is starting to feel like a religious crusade. And with Bill Gates' donation of $40 million to further this campaign, it only becomes more fervent." At the end of February, Noe sent a letter to parents and alumni to explain the D'Souza cancellation. "I am sorry that this proved so controversial a decision," he wrote. "I had to weigh the relative values of going ahead with the lecture—possibly bringing about a disruptive, no-holds-barred debate—and of risking setbacks to our ability to build the inclusive community we seek to be."

By the end of the academic year, five of the six newly hired minority teachers had left the school: Coleman, Pollock, the two Latina teachers, and the East Indian. Sims, who had been accepted to a Ph.D. program at the University of Washington, stayed on in a part-time position. Pollock returned to teach at Bellevue Community College.

In October 2006, Sims and Coleman filed a lawsuit accusing Lakeside of creating a racially hostile work environment. Lakeside hired one of Seattle's most prominent law firms to fight the case. It produced thousands of pages of documents, including copies of meeting notes, e-mails, and depositions. In January 2008, a federal judge dismissed Coleman's suit, writing that she offered only "subjective evidence to support her claims." Sims's case continued, though. In September 2008, one week before it was set to go to trial, Sims and Lakeside agreed on a confidential settlement. The school's problems weren't over, though. In June 2009, Regina Higgins, an African American who taught at the school for a decade, filed another discrimination lawsuit against the school. In it, she claims that she was fired after she raised concerns about the treatment of black students and teachers at Lakeside. Her case has not yet gone to court.

The D'Souza controversy hit at the core weakness of Lakeside's diversity mission. While nearly everyone agrees that "diversity," in a broad sense, is a desirable thing, what exactly that means in the real world is hard to define. Is it simply letting in more students and teachers of color and then assuming they will assimilate to the "Lakeside Way"? Or does it mean that the majority of students should somehow change to be more accommodating of students who come from different racial, ethnic, or financial backgrounds? Isn't one of the main functions of institutions such as Lakeside preparing and shaping students to assume positions of power in society? If so, how exactly does "diversity"— letting in more people of different economic and racial backgrounds— fit in with that?

One day, Chris Dickinson, who is active in the Lakeside alumni network, brings up the D'Souza cancellation. He tells me that scuttling the speech angered him. He thought the whole thing had been mishandled. A better approach, he says, would have been to do what Princeton did when he was a student there and it had invited the political scientist Charles Murray to speak. Murray had just published the book *The Bell Curve*, an extremely controversial work that includes the claim that African Americans haven't done as well because they have genetically lower IQs. In response to an uproar on campus, Princeton had an open forum after Murray's talk in which students and faculty could debate the claims in his book.

This tendency toward putting out things for "debate" is one of the defining features of an elite education. It's a great preparation for careers in law, business, or politics, in which people are expected to make decisions that affect the lives of others. To do that, you have to feel somehow that you are entitled to be in that position. The training at a school like Lakeside teaches students to talk about ideas in the abstract, at the policy level, to make the "hard choices" necessary to keep the wheels of society moving. As a result, classroom discussions at Lakeside can be brutal, with little mercy for other students' feelings. In this type of environment, it might be acceptable to ask if a slave might love her master—it's all just part of the debate. The onus is on the other person to come back with a stronger argument.

When I left Lakeside to go back to public school, one of the primary things I noticed was that as far as "intelligence," there were really no differences between my friends in public school and the people I had known at Lakeside. This surprised me, because one of the consistent messages at Lakeside was that we were the best and brightest.

The difference came as we went on to higher education. Students I had known from Lakeside tended toward law and business. Most of my friends at public school went into various fields of engineering, a career that no one I knew from Lakeside pursued. I don't think it was because everyone at public school was more inclined toward math, but that the institutions offered distinct types of training. Public school was structured around a series of exams that gauged your ability to memorize and recall facts and figures. Lakeside—which, as a private school, has been able to opt out of giving state-mandated standardized tests—structures its curriculum around the critical interpretation of theories. While a civil or aeronautical engineer works from mathematical formulas that leave little room for dispute, the career of a lawyer or a CEO depends on being able to convince other people that your version of reality is the right one.

Until you learn how to function in this world, elite institutions like Lakeside can be vicious. It was predicable that there would be a ferocious push back against teachers such as Kim Pollock, who were presenting versions of American history and society that many people at Lakeside ardently disagreed with. The school administration should have expected that at least some students and teachers would respond in the way they'd been trained.

Months later, Lakeside administrators still couldn't explain what exactly had gone wrong. "The adult community here, now that we're diverse, we don't know how to talk to one another," Noe tells me. "People kind of have retreated into these politically correct shells and they don't say anything, so we're working on that. The workshop in January is: 'How do you have a difficult conversation with a person that's different from you?'"

When I ask Noe if the school can serve its traditional elite constituency and also accommodate an influx of students from minority or poor backgrounds, he insists that the goals are compatible. "I've said over and over to the community that this is not a school that is just to preserve privilege," he tells me. "We're not here just so already privileged kids can accrue more privilege. We're here to be a great school for this area and to produce some great local leaders, national leaders, global leaders."

T. J. Vassar, the director of diversity, calls the problem one of implementation. He tells me that the school was not used to having several African-American faculty members, and the black teachers were not accustomed to the culture of private schools, so they "bumped heads."

As one of Lakeside's first black graduates, Vassar occupies a revered place in the school's mythology. He tells me about enrolling in 1965 and remembers some uncomfortable times, such as reading the books *Huckleberry Finn* and *Native Son* in English class. Vassar points out that the word "nigger" is used often in *Huckleberry Finn*, and Bigger Thomas, the main character in Richard Wright's *Native Son*, strangles the daughter of the white family that has employed him. "So the first book is about a slave, Nigger Jim, and the second book was about a black dude choking the hell out of a white girl. OK?" Vassar says, laughing heartily.

In the end, Vassar says, he found his niche playing sports—"I figured if I could kick people's ass on the sports field that was my equalizer, because I didn't realize until I got out of Lakeside that I was as smart as anybody else"—and was eventually popular enough to get elected school president as a senior. "You have to remember, why did T. J. get chosen to come to Lakeside to be one of the first black students to come here? And I know why. It was the Jackie Robinson effect. It wasn't because I was the smartest dude in the world—hell no! It was because I think they saw that I could get along with people pretty well."

Vassar went on to Harvard, came back to Seattle, and later served on the board of the Seattle Public Schools from 1981 to 1989, a period of intense friction over the city's mandatory busing program. When he returned to Lakeside in 1992 to run LEEP, part of his reasoning was that he thought maybe he could accomplish in the private-school setting what had failed in public schools.

"You know what I like about Lakeside now?" he asks. "Lakeside defined excellence and said, 'We can't have an excellent school without having a diverse school.' Lakeside said having a diverse school is a necessary part of excellence. Now, we start talking like that, even though we may catch some hell getting everything into practice, getting the job done like we want, we're going to have some failures and some things like that, but when you say that, when you commit that to paper and start spreading it around, you get a very different mind-set about what it is that we're supposed to be doing."

Vassar says that with public-school desegregation a thing of the past, private schools such as Lakeside are the only educational institutions in Seattle still making an active effort to achieve some kind of racial mix. "You know what's a travesty?" he asks, when speaking about his time on the school board. "Then I was working for a quality integrated education in the public schools, and the private schools were the way that people were opting out of integrated education. And now, if you want a good-quality integrated education, you gotta go to the private schools instead of the public schools. It's just a huge irony."

Terrance Blakely and David Changa-Moon, unsurprisingly, have the most pragmatic assessments of Lakeside and its diversity efforts.

Blakely says he felt grateful for the opportunities the school afforded, but he also realized that the institution was getting something out of him and other minority students in return. When I tell Blakely that I saw him featured in several issues of the school's magazine, he laughs and tells me that a group of minority students began to call themselves the "poster children."

"We had a little tally going among the kids," he says. "How many newsletters are you going to make this year? It got to the point where the same four kids who were a little more social with the rest of Lakeside got put in every magazine, every sports page. I mean there's a directory picture of eighty percent of the minority students in the school, but the school shows it as, 'Oh, we're a nice colorful mix of kids across the entire school.'"

Blakely says he tried to find a balance, agreeing to have his picture taken and do interviews with school publications, but also trying to get across viewpoints that he thought were not always heard at the school. "There's comes a point where I don't want to be your spokesman, because I don't agree with a lot of the things you do," he says. "But it's hard for me, and I think it's hard for a lot of kids, to sit there and say I don't agree with some of the practices you're doing, but it would also make me a hypocrite because I'm taking your education, and I know what your education is going to do for me."

Both Changa-Moon and Blakely credit Sims and Pollock for taking on issues that would not otherwise have been raised at the school and engaging in battles that students could not realistically fight. Blakely says he intentionally tried not to speak out too much in order to avoid being stigmatized. "I think that is the one fear that every conscious minority has is, 'Am I going to be that guy or that girl that is talking civil rights movement all over again and is everyone going to just go, OK?'" he says. "Because that's what they'll do. When you say something it's just like, 'Oh, you really should settle down. It's not that bad.' But these are people that don't live the same life that you do, that aren't walking in that same path. But then, it's just like, 'Do I want to be that person where it's them versus me?' So then you just get along to go along."

Changa-Moon, though involved with groups such as the Black Student Union, says he was more of a "spectator" by the end of his time at the school. He tells me that it's a big responsibility to feel you need to educate your wealthy high school classmates about life in the South End. "It's not like we're just there and going to school," he says. "It's this cultural education we're supposed to bring and provide all these students, and I'm just not that into it. At fourteen, fifteen, sixteen, seventeen, when I'm confused, and then you're tasking me with this?"

Changa-Moon says that Lakeside faces a core incongruity with its diversity program. "If Lakeside was ever to really pursue its rhetoric of democracy and all these ideas of the 'equal chance,' of everyone having an equal say in the direction of our country, then Lakeside School and other private institutions like it would not exist, fundamentally they just wouldn't be there," he says. "Because they exist to provide students a leg up and to have more influence in society. . . . It's really hard because the rhetoric that you're spewing, it's in contradiction with the actual institution that you have."

If the school was serious, Changa-Moon says, it could take the money raised from Bill Gates and others and then go to an open admissions policy, in which slots at the school would be given by lottery. Then everyone would truly have a shot at a Lakeside education.

In the end, both Blakely and Changa-Moon say that going to Lakeside will probably alter the rest of their lives. "You can find all sorts of studies and stuff about the poor and what's going on in their environment, but you don't hear one thing about the rich and what they're living like, where they go, all that stuff, you have no idea, and this was able to open my eyes and I got to see, what is it?" Changa-Moon says. "What do these people do? What are they like? What is this whole top two percent? What is that life like? And so I got to see where lots of decisions get made and how they get made and who makes them, and I got to see what that was like and I got to see what that was, and now I have friends in those places. I think that provides me a huge opportunity. I don't know if that's a good thing or not, but it's there."

With his mixed emotions about being chosen as part of the modern-day Talented Tenth, Blakely tells me he is already feeling guilty about not returning to the school to mentor other students of color. "They're going to always be Terrance Blakelys," he says. "There's going to always be Davids, there's going to always be us. We just came through the system and that's fine, but they're going to bring someone else in and they're going to be the next kid on the basketball team that gets good grades. It's not going to stop. And they're going to come in and they're going to deal with the same psychological and emotional stuff that we did. I would have loved if someone would have come back down to talk to me."

But, he says, there's a reason why very few African-American graduates stay involved with the school. For the average Lakeside alum, he says, "You go back because it reminds you of happy times—'These are kids I grew up with, this was a great place for me.' The minorities, they go back thinking, 'This is a place where I was isolated.' There's a girl that spent every lunch period by herself in one room. How is she going to go back? She doesn't have those experiences. And then, from my position, with those experiences I do have, I got them potentially because I had to sell a little bit of myself, so I mean is that something I really want to glorify? I think it's different. It's completely rational why people don't go back, because they don't have good memories."

• • •

One drizzly, gray Saturday morning, I drive to a public middle school in the South End to meet Ronnie Cunningham. Ronnie, who graduated from Lakeside in 1986, was the first black student to make it all the way from fifth grade to senior year, a "lifer." His mom had been the one who tipped off Eric Hampton's dad about the school. When I was in eighth grade, Ronnie was the star running back on the football team. I knew him from his letterman's jacket, which was gold and maroon—the Lakeside school colors—and had MR. CUNNINGHAM written on the back in cursive. He now works as a staff psychologist at a nonprofit for minority students called Rainier Scholars.

When I get to the school, I find the cafeteria, and quickly spot Ronnie, who still has the compact frame of a running back. He wears jeans and a maroon sweater, has a goatee flecked with gray and a friendly yet contemplative manner. There are about sixty fifth-graders in the room, sitting at or standing among the long lunchroom tables and chattering among themselves. Ronnie yells out that they need to get their stuff together and get ready to go to class.

As the kids file out, Ronnie and I walk to a registration table that's been set up in the hall. Ronnie introduces me to Bob Hurlbut, the founder of the program. Hurlbut is, in his own words, a "fat, middle-aged white guy." A former software salesman who was also active in Young Life, a Christian organization for youth, Hurlbut tells me that he was looking for meaning in his life when he happened to read *Hope in the Unseen*, a book by the journalist Ron Suskind that tells the story of a low-income African-American student who goes from public school in Washington, D.C., to Brown University. At Brown, the student meets some other black students from poor backgrounds who seem much better prepared for the Ivy League. It turns out that they came out of a New York City program called Prep for Prep. That sparked Hurlbut to do some research, and in 2002 he started Rainier Scholars based on a similar model.

The program, which is privately funded by donations from places such as the Bill & Melinda Gates Foundation, uses fourth-grade test scores to identify minority students who show potential. It sends letters to their parents and invites them to apply. Eventually, after more testing and interviews, about sixty kids—all students of color—get admitted before the start of sixth grade. For the summers before and after that year, they attend school every day, taking intensive math, science, and English classes. During the school year, they have classes every Saturday, and are expected to do several hours of homework—on top of their regular classwork—every night. The students have frequent one-on-one and group meetings with Ronnie and other staff members to talk about their progress and any challenges they are facing. The program also hires summer counselors—David Changa-Moon was one—to work with the students.

Nearly all of the students in the program get accepted into either a private school or an advanced program in the Seattle public schools. Counselors continue to meet with the kids once they get past the intensive first couple of years, teaching classes in leadership and helping them find internships. They also help them with college choices. The idea is to provide all the support that a "normal" student from an upper-middle-class family would receive as a matter of course. Rainier Scholars estimates it spends $27,000 on each student over the seven years they're in the program.

As Hurlbut and I stand in the hallway and talk, a stream of parents and kids enters the building. There are Somalis, Ethiopians, African Americans, Mexicans, Vietnamese, and Cambodians—the full cross section of South Seattle. A couple of staff members welcome them, hand out information packs, and guide them through the auditorium doors by which Hurlbut and I are standing. After a while he excuses himself, and I take a seat in the audience.

This is a recruiting day. The staff has sent several hundred letters to the families of minority students who scored well on the WASL standardized test. Now it is Hurlbut's job to convince them to formally apply.

Ronnie gets onstage and gives a few introductory remarks before Hurlbut takes the microphone with a burst of energy. He wears khakis and a white dress shirt. His belly hangs down over his belt, a brushy mustache perches above his upper lip, and his hair is unkempt. The salesmanlike and evangelical parts of his personality come to the surface. "If you don't believe that college preparation starts in fifth grade, you're wrong," he says.

The more Hurlbut talks, the more animated he becomes. Several of the parents around me pay close attention, nodding as he speaks. "We're developing a new generation of leaders for our country," he says. "You have talented kids, and we're going to take that talent and put it to the test. This is about choices—who they want to be and how they'll get there. It's so *you* get to choose who you will be instead of someone choosing for you. If your child gets an education, he or she will probably go on to be president and CEO of a company, not just a worker bee."

When Hurlbut finishes, the parents sit in their seats and fill out the interest form that will start the process of getting into the program. As they leave, they line up at the registration table to drop them off.

After the parents have thinned out, Ronnie tells me that after he got his Ph.D. in psychology at the University of Washington, he wanted to come back and do something in the community where he grew up. He had basically gotten into private school on a fluke—he had tagged along with his sister as she went to LEEP, the Lakeside summer program for minority students. The idea behind Rainier Scholars appealed to him as a way to institutionalize the process of identifying talented students of color and to stop them from slipping through the cracks.

His job includes meeting with administrators at private schools such as Lakeside—Ronnie tells me he is a member of the alumni board in part to "hold their feet to the fire" on race issues—and talking to them about how many Rainier Scholars they might take. He tells me that they seem to have hit a wall—the private schools took about as many in the first year as they did in following years. The problem is that there are many more qualified and talented minority kids than open slots.

Ronnie's comment raises larger questions. Rainier Scholars, in many ways, is a much more organized advance on Randy's Finley's efforts in the late 1980s—Hurlbut, with his mustache, large frame, and folksy salesmanship, even bears a striking resemblance to Finley. Hurlbut also has realized he can't do it by himself and has built an infrastructure— including a board and a staff—to help move his efforts forward. The program is designed to bridge the chasm that Finley couldn't cross—not only getting the kids into private schools, but also making sure they have the background and support they need to succeed when they get there.

At the same time, Rainier Scholars is not Zion Prep, a school that tries to accept and work with every student it can, no matter their test scores. The Rainier Scholars program, instead, enrolls sixty of Seattle's highest-testing minority students a year and looks to get them into private schools or the advanced tracks of the public schools. The idea is that without the program, the kids may fall behind and never be able to reach their potential. You have to wonder about the next sixty, who barely miss the cut. Or what about all the other kids after that? How many other talented kids lose out because their families lack the means or the background to guide them through the system? What about the students who don't score high on standardized tests, who aren't going to go to college? Have we just accepted, as Doug Wheeler and Damian both charge, that a certain number of kids just aren't going to make it? Are the Rainier Scholar kids the educational equivalents of Jackie Robinson, with thousands of others missing the chance?

After lunch, Ronnie and I climb the stairs and walk through the second-floor hallway to sit in on a few classes. There are ten to fifteen students in each class, and I'm surprised at how enthusiastic they are for sixth-graders on a Saturday morning. In a math class, they eagerly work on problems, raising their hands to shout out answers. In an English class, a young African-American teacher leads a discussion about the book *The House on Mango Street* in a style that reminds me, when I think about it, of classes at Lakeside. When he asks what a character's motivation is, several students jump in to offer answers and debate among themselves. Unlike many classes I had at private school, the students seem to be actually excited to be talking about the book, not doing it just to notch another good grade on their transcripts. The only significant difference I can see between this class and one you might see at a private school is that not a single student is white.

Part Five

Structure and Manhood

God forgive me for my brash delivery.

—*Jay-Z*

What It Means to Be a Man

Will McClain Jr. tells me that if I really want to see what his life is like, I should come down to his house on Friday night. "That's when it really gets going," he says with a laugh.

His place is about thirty miles southeast of downtown Seattle, past the city of Kent, out toward the foothills of the Cascade Mountains. The road out there runs past several large apartment complexes before the buildings thin out, strip malls giving way to dirt lots. I take a left into a development called Meridian Firs and drive several blocks past single-family homes on small lots until I reach Will's place, half of a town house duplex. I pull up in the dark, park next to Will's white SUV, and walk up to the door.

Will swings it open and ushers me in. He is a large, muscular man, standing about six feet tall and weighing about 230 pounds. In both his athletic build and his facial features, he looks very much like a younger version of his father. He wears blue jeans, a navy blue T-shirt, and black Nike running shoes with a red swoosh. A silver watch hangs on his left wrist, matching the silver hoop earring in his left ear. He has a mustache and a goatee, trimmed hair, and a relaxed manner.

We sit on a blue couch in the living room, in front of a large-screen projection TV playing the game show *Deal or No Deal*. Howie Mandel is bantering with a black woman trying to win $1 million. The beige carpet of the room matches the walls. Everything is childproofed—most breakables, such as a grandfather clock that used to sit on top of the TV, are packed away. A large collection of toys is packed in a corner across from the front door, including a basket of children's books, a plastic dump truck, and a Tickle-Me Elmo doll.

On the other side of the room, under two African masks, a small karaoke machine sits next to the wall that separates the living room from the kitchen. Next to it there's a coffee table stacked with framed photos of Will and his wife, Cheryl, and their kids. More hang above it. Around the corner, in the dining room, three of Will and Cheryl's kids—Janessa, who is eleven; Christian who also is eleven; and Kelia, who is nine—chatter as they play the board game Life at the dining room table. They dash to say hello when Will calls them.

Cheryl, a fourth-grade teacher at a South Seattle public elementary school, greets me and soon is joined by Imani, their two-year-old daughter. As we talk, Cheryl spreads a pack of cards with images of the "Bratz" dolls facedown on the floor and begins to play Memory—a game where you turn over one card and then try to flip the other card that matches it—with Imani, who has amazingly accurate recall. She jumps up and does a little celebration dance every time she gets another pair.

Seeing him in this context, I start to understand what Will had told me one day when we went to lunch: "In my younger twenties, without my first child, I could have been in the same position as James Credit and Tyrell Johnson. Settling down for me was a must, an absolute must."

Our team made as much impact on Will as anyone—through Randy Finley's involvement in his life, Will got into Seattle Prep, an elite high school, and then was courted by college athletic programs. Will also shows that the path to adulthood is not only about schools, but having the right structure in place to get through difficult transitions.

When Will quit the Boise State football team after his sophomore year and came back to Seattle, he didn't view it as the end of his organized sports career. He enrolled in community college, where he played baseball for a season. After that, Will—just as his dad had twenty years earlier—got into semipro football, which is basically an avenue for guys hoping for a last shot at college ball, the Canadian Football League, arena football, or a tryout with the NFL scout combines.

In 1993, Will took a job at Zion Prep as a preschool supervisor. He lived at home with his parents and seemed stable from the outside, but he also was drifting. "I pretty much lived a double life before I had my son,"

Will says. "With my parents, I was straight and narrow, didn't show them much of anything. But once I left the house I was completely out of control. I mean completely.

"Not being totally into a career was tough," he says. "What do you really want to do? You're in the middle, and what way do you wanna go?"

At the time, the drug economy offered a quick way to make some money. When a friend offered Will a chance to earn some cash by making a few deliveries, he grabbed it. "That was the life of my friends and my cousins that I hung around with," Will says. "It's not something I set my mind to do, but it started off with, 'Hey, drop this off for me.'"

Will was twenty-four in 1995 when Christian, his first child, was born. Shortly after the birth he was in the parking lot of a club when someone pulled out a gun and shot another man. Will realized that his involvement in the drug trade meant he might never see his son grow up. He decided to get out immediately. "After you stop, you don't have the money," he says. "But I learned to balance my paycheck. I told people, 'You can't bring it to my house.' They started dropping off one by one, and sure enough, life changes. Damian went through the same thing, but he went through the way of Christ."

In the meantime, the 1990s took a horrific toll on the kids who only a few years earlier had come over to play at the McClains' house. Tyrell was killed and dumped in the South Seattle ditch in August 1991. James Credit, who had played on Willie McClain's CAYA basketball team, was shot in front of the downtown nightclub in March 1993. Sultan Smith, another player on McClain's CAYA team and Myran's best friend, was shot and killed at Twenty-third and Union in December 1999. Of the ten guys or so who were regulars on Willie McClain Sr.'s squad, those three are dead.

For Will, it brought home how little margin for error there was between living and dying among many of the guys he'd grown up with. "You're talking about seeing James two days before his fatal incident, seeing Tyrell a week before his," he says. "It's not like you haven't seen these guys in weeks or months. It was like days. And you wonder, 'What could have happened to them when I was sitting there talking to them?' Or, 'What if this would've happened when we were at the store together?'"

In the meantime, Will's life gradually started to take direction. At Zion Prep, Doug Wheeler noticed that Will had a talent for math. Wheeler hired a specialist to train Will and eventually made him the school math tutor. After four years of semipro football, it dawned on Will that the break he was waiting for wasn't going to come. "Professional sports would have been fun," Will says. "Once I realized that wasn't going to happen, I got more into teaching and just living life."

Will had another son, D'Andre, in 1998. Four years later, when D'Andre—who lives with his mom not far from Will—was in preschool, Will chaperoned his class on a field trip to the zoo in Tacoma. Cheryl's daughter, Kelia, also was in the class, so she went along as another escort. While the kids were checking out the beluga whales, Will and Cheryl started talking. They were married in 2004.

As we sit in the living room, the TV game show *Deal or No Deal* heats up. The contestant, an African-American woman from Fort Worth, Texas, named Wynetta, eventually takes the deal from Howie Mandel, settling for $115,000. Will, Cheryl, and I groan when we see that she would have won $1 million if she had held out. Cheryl scoops up Imani and heads upstairs to bed. In the dining room, the three other kids keep chattering as they begin a game of Monopoly.

Will tells me that he loves having so many kids in the house. It reminds him of his own childhood, when guys like Damian, JT, and Myran would often stay overnight, or, in some cases, live with the McClains for weeks at a time. "If you had a situation and they could help you, and it wasn't going to put none of us out, then it was, 'Hey, we'll work with it,'" he says of his parents.

Will shares his dad's love of sports and coaching. In the summers, he plays right field for a semipro softball team. The team's sponsor, a local Hooter's, pays for the players to compete in tournaments in places such as St. Louis and Las Vegas. Every spring, Will coaches girls' fast-pitch softball at Garfield High School. This year, he tells me, he's going to coach Kelia's fourth- and fifth-grade basketball team. "Last year they were running buck wild and I was sitting on the sideline and I made up my mind, 'I'm coaching,'" he says, laughing. "I think my wife is going to help me, so it's going to be fun."

When we were kids, everyone called Willie McClain Sr. "Big Willie" and Will Jr. "Little Willie." The close identification between the two has continued. Both have worked at Zion Prep and are known for their involvement in coaching. Willie Sr.'s profile has increased over the years.

He's been a sports star at Garfield High School, vice principal of Zion Prep, an ordained minister, and now pastor of his own church.

I ask Will if it's been hard to step out of his dad's shadow. "You know what?" he says. "I'm still in his shadow, to this day. I am still in his shadow. I have the name, I have the same look, I have the same persona. And you know what? I have accepted it. I am still Little Willie. June Bug's son. And to this day, I'm grown, at Garfield coaching fast pitch, people say, 'Hey, you June Bug's son?' And then they'll tell me a story about when he was in high school."

In 2004, Cheryl was offered a teaching position at a U.S. military base in the Azores, a Portuguese archipelago in the eastern Atlantic Ocean. Will and Cheryl, who had applied through the State Department, were eager to live overseas for a few years. They thought it would be a great opportunity to see the world and to expose the kids to life outside of the United States. In the end, Cheryl had to turn the job down because she was pregnant with Imani. Though they have submitted an application every year since, nothing has come through.

To add some money to the family budget, Will worked for several years as a bartender at a nearby Indian reservation casino. He made good money—up to $700 in tips on a Friday or Saturday night—but had to quit after he developed health problems, including high blood pressure. Going from teaching to bartending meant spending up to sixteen hours a day on his feet, which was exhausting. It also took him away from the family too much.

When I ask if it's hard to build up much savings on the salaries of two teachers, Will nods. "Exactly. But we live comfortable, the kids live comfortable, we don't want for much. Just a couple hours here and there away from the kids is what we want most of all," he says, breaking into laughter. "I think we'd take a two-day getaway from the kids over three thousand dollars any day of the week!"

A little bit after eleven o'clock, the kids are still playing Monopoly. One of the last questions I ask Will before I go is what he thinks about being a father. In the several conversations we've had, Will has always been lighthearted, genial, and quick with a joke. I'm surprised at the abrupt change that overcomes him. His face turns serious, his body stiffens, and his voice drops a notch.

"You live for your kids," he tells me. "When you don't have any kids, you do what you want, even if it's harmful to yourself, or if it's unsafe, or you know it's dangerous. It's that adrenaline to do it anyway. But once you have your kids you no longer live for you. You *have* to live for your child, because if anything happens to you, who takes care of your child? If anything happened to you, how is your child's mental state going to be knowing something happened to their father? You have to make that conscious decision and it has to be the right one, because you want to be around—no, you *must* be around—to see your children grow up and live life.

"I can't wait to see my son's first dunk in high school, I can't wait to see my daughter, who I don't know if she's going to be a linebacker or a catcher in fast pitch, but I can't wait to see her hit the ball or tackle somebody. Or whatever they want to do, whatever their accomplishments. My younger stepdaughter is a phenomenal soccer player, she has skills that she doesn't know she has—I can't wait to see her score her first goal in high school, can't wait. The older one wants to be a writer. These are things you live for, and you can't go out and drink all night and drive home. You can't do those things no more, because you have people depending on you to see these events happen, to be there to make sure they're safe, to be there to make sure they do their homework. That's what papahood's about. Fatherhood is being a father to your household, it's being a father to your children. So that's what I do."

· · ·

One morning over breakfast at a South End IHOP, JT pinpoints where his childhood took a turn. "Right after our team—right after we hooked up with you guys—that's when it all went downhill," he says. "I wish we could've spent more time playing ball together, you know, kept it going for a few more years."

The team, he tells me, was like family, with Randy and Willie as father figures and us players as brothers. "Even if a guy on that team wasn't very good, we still supported him," he says. "If he messes up, or he blew the last shot, you still support him, you know? And I think that's what we did."

After many conversations with JT, I realize that our team was the last point in his life when he had been involved in a group that he felt wholly positive about. This sense of contributing his talents to a larger effort was important to him, just as it was to every other guy. As we got older, each player moved through a series of institutions and structures, some consciously chosen, some by default. These structures provided the space within which each guy would form his own personal meaning of manhood. On our team, the boundary, drawn along class lines, was stark.

When Sean, for example, decided he wanted to leave Washington, D.C., where he was a staffer for a Republican senator, he landed a job back in Seattle as a spokesman for Boeing. He found it wasn't for him. "It was so big and so bureaucratic and stifled independent thought," he says of working at the company. "You had to have ten people lined up with you in a row agreeing with any new idea to get that new idea advanced." The company did pick up the tab for Sean to go to law school at night, and he found a better fit at the prosecutor's office upon graduation. "What I do now, it's competitive but structured. In court there are rules you have to follow. You rise and fall on your intellectual ability to work with your case within those rules," he says. "You're engaging a part of our society. You're doing something that has great meaning."

After Eric found it hard to settle in at Deloitte & Touche, a corporate accounting firm, he moved on to work for the city. "I think it's a little tougher as an African American in a corporate culture," he says. "It's not impossible. A lot of things have to line up for you and you have to have a certain type of personality." Eric jokes he's thought about going back to get an M.B.A. or law degree "to keep up a little bit" with his wife, a professor. Overall, though, he says he's found his meaning outside of the workplace. "I have my family and my friends and that's what I need. Work is just what it is, it's just a way to pay for things. I'm not all super career-oriented, like my wife. I just, you know, I got bills to pay, so this is what I gotta do."

Of all my teammates, Chris is the most outspoken on trying to find a healthy masculinity—he wants to enjoy competition without letting it turn into a desire to puff himself up by beating other people. A few years ago, he left his job brokering health insurance plans and joined a start-up founded by another Lakeside grad. The firm has developed "wellness" software that companies pay to access. Employees go online and enter personal information about health issues such as how much they exercise, their mental well-being, and nutrition (the data on each individual are not shared with the employer). The software then comes up with programs that guide people toward leading healthier lives in general, or progress toward specific goals, such as quitting smoking. The payoff for companies is lower health insurance costs. Chris has found the new job invigorating—though there is more financial instability at the start-up, he deeply believes in the mission of helping people find ways to live healthier lives. As a company principal, he has a personal involvement in the firm's planning and success.

One afternoon, when we are in Oregon for a wedding, my wife and I stop in and surprise Maitland at the winery where he works. He takes us on an extensive tour through the vineyard and the production area, precisely explaining the winemaking process. It's clear that when it comes to wine, Maitland is exacting in how he wants the product to come out.

We end up in Mait's basement office, where he works at a desk laid out with the beakers, flasks, and chemistry tools he uses to monitor the composition of his wines. Mait quietly jokes with the two other winemakers who share the space. The job, I see, gives Mait the opportunity to follow something through from start to finish, make a tangible product, and work within a group of like-minded people who all have the same goal. It is, in a way, a corrective to some of his earlier experiences, such as the pressure he felt to compete in high school basketball. "You know, when I manage people on the job, I'm more concerned that we work as a team, and there's no winner and loser other than everybody," Mait says. "I don't need to prove to anybody that I know anything at all."

As we entered early adulthood in the 1990s, what had been seen as the traditional economic path to manhood for many—get a job and work at it until you retired—was no longer a possibility for most people. When my mom was a girl in the 1950s, for example, my grandfather came home every day from his job as an engineer at the Hanford Nuclear Reservation at five. He went upstairs and changed out of his shirt and tie into his leisure clothes. He then came back downstairs and read the paper until six, which was when my grandmother was expected to have dinner on the table. The gender roles in the family were very clear—for example, my grandfather mowed the lawn on the weekends while my grandmother pulled weeds. One was men's work, one was women's. When my grandmother talked about getting a part-time job, my grandfather would have none of it—he already earned enough, so why would she need to work?

For middle-class people, this had been the model for decades—men went off to the office or factory, worked as part of a team within a formalized structure (the corporation or the state), played their part, and came home to the women and children. This had been the pattern since industrialization in the mid- and late 1800s, when youth sports leagues such as the YMCA and the AAU had been established. With men leaving farms to work in offices and factories, the idea of Muscular Christianity was that boys needed organized structures in which they could develop physically and enter into competition to avoid becoming too feminized. The skills learned on the field—stamina, discipline, sacrificing for the good of the team—were supposed to translate later into success in the working world. This was still the model when we were boys, and Coach McClain picked up on its tenets, drilling into us that we needed to think about the good of the group, not our own individual statistics. Anyone who began to showboat to the detriment of the team would be rewarded with a seat on the bench.

By 1986, though, it also was clear that individual stardom could pay off very well, even if you ditched the team. That April, Michael Jordan, then in his second year in the NBA and playing guard for the mediocre Chicago Bulls, scored an astounding sixty-three points against Larry Bird's Boston Celtics in a playoff game. At our next practice, Tyrell and Will Jr. relived Jordan's exploits, imitating his moves as the rest of us formed an appreciative peanut gallery. "Bird didn't know what to do!" Tyrell said, making us all laugh by miming a flat-footed and confused Larry Bird getting juked by Jordan. (Despite Jordan's bravura performance, the Bulls were still swept by the Celtics in the series, three games to zero.)

At that point, Jordan was simply a preternaturally talented basketball player, not a global brand. The seeds had been planted, though—before his rookie year, Nike paid Jordan an unprecedented $500,000 to endorse its shoes. With their bold black-and-red design and maverick image—the sneakers had been banned by the NBA for violating its uniform regulations—Air Jordans were snapped up by both suburban white kids and black kids from the city. Nike (another Pacific Northwest company) offshored production to countries such as Vietnam, China, Mexico, and Indonesia, where workers earned dollars a day making sneakers that sold for more than $100 in the United States. Nike's payout to Jordan soon rose to $20 million annually; by 2008, the Air Jordan line was banking more than $800 million a year in sales.

Outspoken sports stars such as Kareem Abdul-Jabbar, Muhammad

Ali, and Jackie Robinson had all come up in an age when blacks were routinely excluded from the economic riches their labor produced, and corporations were hardly throwing money at them to endorse their products. Michael Jordan, on the other hand, got a cut. In addition to Nike, he did ads for McDonald's, Hanes, Gatorade, Coca-Cola, MCI, and Chevrolet, among others. With so much money at stake, Jordan studiously avoided making any political statements in a vein similar to his predecessors—he was, in fact, sometimes said to have "transcended" race. In an age where images of athletic virtuosity could be beamed everywhere, Jordan rose above not only his teammates—whom he once called his "supporting cast"—but also his sport. As one of the most famous people in the world, his shoes and apparel sold to people who knew little to nothing about basketball or Chicago—I once saw a billboard of Jordan soaring for a dunk next to the central plaza in Dakar, Senegal, not exactly a hotbed of basketball. The lesson was that the rewards went to the superstar floating over the court, not the teammates below rebounding for him.

This tension between the ideals of working as a team and the demands of the individual star wasn't lost on Willie McClain Sr. A passionate believer in using basketball as a vehicle through which to connect to young men and teach them life skills, McClain continued to coach at both public and private high schools in Seattle after our team disbanded. In 2001 he traveled to Las Vegas as an assistant coach with a team of local high school basketball all-stars who were set to play in a tournament completely funded by Nike. McClain was there to teach defense, but he found that the stars of the team weren't interested in what he had to say. There were about two hundred college coaches at the tournament to recruit. Though the coaches weren't allowed to approach players, they could speak to them if spoken to. So when sought-after players went to the bathroom, college coaches would follow them in and stand at neighboring urinals, just to give the players the opportunity to start a conversation. McClain left the tournament disillusioned. "It was just a meat factory," he says. "It doesn't give kids a sense of anything but money. There was no value system."

In the late 1960s, my grandfather took a position as a corporate vice president for ARCO, leaving Hanford to work in New York and then Los Angeles. A staunch Republican, Catholic, and member of the Elks Club, he was blindsided when he was laid off in a corporate restructuring in the 1970s. Then in his midfifties, he swallowed his ego and returned to Eastern Washington, where he went back to work at Hanford at a much reduced salary. He was probably lucky to have a job. As the 1980s arrived, corporate restructuring and downsizing increased pace. Between 1979 and 1995, about 43 million American jobs were eliminated. Although the economy was creating new employment, by the mid-1990s only an estimated 35 percent of those jobs paid as well as the ones that were lost. The reconfiguring of corporate America was joined by the movement of women into the workforce as well as vocal calls by minorities such as African Americans for inclusion. This shifting economic landscape ushered in what was labeled in the media a "crisis in masculinity," or, as *Newsweek* put it, "white male paranoia."

The feeling was vividly expressed by the 1993 movie *Falling Down*, in which Michael Douglas plays a laid-off Los Angeles defense industry worker known for most of the film by his vanity license plate, D-FENS. When his car breaks down in a traffic jam on the freeway, D-FENS abandons it. In an effort to retake his place at the head of the family he's lost, he begins to walk toward Venice Beach, where his ex-wife and daughter live. As he passes through the multiethnic L.A. that lives on ground level in sight of the skyscrapers downtown, he goes on an increasingly violent rampage, trashing a Korean-owned grocery store and tangling with Mexican gangbangers (adding to the mix, he also kills the neo-Nazi owner of an army supply store and destroys the golf cart of two white golfers on a private course). At the end of the movie, before he is shot by the detective who's been tracking him, D-FENS says, "I did everything they told me to. Did you know I build missiles? I help to protect America. You should be rewarded for that. But instead they give it to the plastic surgeons. You know, they lied to me."

The uncertainty of white males of their place in the economic and social hierarchy also seeped into music. The iconic grunge musician Kurt Cobain grew up one hundred miles southwest of Seattle in Aberdeen, a rough, economically depressed logging town that had seen unemployment balloon in the 1970s and 1980s as the local timber mills shut down. For a few years at the end of the 1980s, Cobain lived in Olympia, sixty miles south of Seattle and then the scene of the nascent Riot Grrrl movement, where he was introduced to feminist, progay, and anticorporate ideas. This mixed with his experiences of divorce, poverty, and family dysfunction to create a music that set his acerbic rage to punk-influenced melodies. Nirvana's 1991 album *Nevermind* struck a cultural nerve, selling more than 10 million copies.

The other dominant pop music of the early 1990s, gangsta rap, had its own masculinity issues. It packaged the worst aspects of poverty-riddled, postindustrial urban America—violence, misogyny, and the glorification of crime—and sold them around the globe. The iconic and enormously talent gangsta rapper Tupac Shakur charted a contradictory path between adeptly cataloging the ills of the ghetto—joblessness, the poor treatment of women, lack of educational opportunities—and glorifying the hyper masculine, relentlessly violent "Thug Life," a notion he believed in enough to have tattooed across his stomach. As the son of a mother who was a dedicated and active Black Panther, Tupac grew up steeped in the nationalistic, communitarian ideology of the movement at the time it was falling apart—many of the Panthers around Tupac, such as his godfather, were thrown in prison for street crimes; others, including his mother, became strung out on drugs. Tupac never resolved the pull between black nationalism and the individualist ethos of the new era. As he rapped on the song "Only God Can Judge Me": "Black Power is what we scream as we dream in a paranoid state/and our fate is a lifetime of hate."

Two mammoth demonstrations in Washington, D.C., in the 1990s captured the anxiety over men's roles. Though one was for black men and the other mostly attended by white men, both harked back to much older movements. In October 1995, Louis Farrakhan, the leader of the Nation of Islam, organized the Million Man March, which attracted somewhere around that number of black men to the city. It had been a hundred years since Booker T. Washington's famous "Atlanta Compromise" speech, in which Washington had called for blacks to focus on improving themselves rather than asking whites for political and civil rights. As the leader of the conservative, black nationalist Nation of Islam, Farrakhan preached a message intellectually descended from Washington, focusing on black self-improvement and personal responsibility. He called for "atonement," asking each man in attendance to apologize for his mistakes and pledge that he would "strive to improve myself spiritually, morally, mentally, socially, politically, and economically for the benefit of myself, my family, and my people."

In 1997, another million men assembled on the Mall for a gathering called by the Promise Keepers, an organization of evangelical Christian men with an ideological lineage back to Muscular Christianity (just as Muscular Christianity was led by coaches such as James Naismith, Promise Keepers was founded by Bill McCartney, the coach of the University of Colorado football team). Concerned that men were not involved enough with their kids, the core message of the group was that fathers needed to return and take their places back as the heads of their families. The Promise Keepers emphasized physical vigor and making a space for men to gather without women. Once rejuvenated, they could lead as "godly men."

The disenchantment with modern masculinity got a different spin in the 1999 movie *Fight Club* (based on a novel by Portland writer Chuck Palahniuk). The character Tyler Durden—played by Brad Pitt—proposes that the only way to attain manhood in a consumer society in which men are dominated by women, trapped in soul-crushing office and service jobs, and sedated by shopping at IKEA, is to experience physical pain through fighting. The step after that is to destroy the whole structure of modern capitalism and return to an agrarian idyll where the freeways are turned back into farms. "An entire generation pumping gas, waiting tables— slaves with white collars," Durden says. "Advertising has us chasing cars and clothes, working jobs we hate so we can buy shit we don't need. . . . We've all been raised on television to believe that one day we'd all be millionaires, and movie gods, and rock stars. But we won't. And we're slowly learning that fact. And we're very, very pissed off."

The underlying question was how a man was supposed to be a man in a time when his wife is in the workplace (and quite possibly making more money), job security has vanished, technology means that the workday never ends, and life fluctuates to the whims of the market. The traditional gender role for men was becoming less and less tenable; new formulations had to evolve.

One alternative came from hip-hop, embodied especially in the form of Jay-Z, a rapper who had grown up in the Marcy Projects in Brooklyn. His first record, released in 1996, was a straightforward tale of a dealer trying to work his hustle in the "crack game." Over the next decade, Jay-Z branched out in a way other rappers hadn't, starting his own record label and clothing company, opening a Manhattan nightclub, buying a share of the New Jersey Nets, shilling for Budweiser, and appearing in a commercial for HP computers. On his albums, he built an intellectual framework around what he was doing—he was still a hustler, still keeping it real. It was just that he'd moved far beyond crack. His new gig was hustling in the global marketplace, promoting his brand, and getting paid. In Jay-Z's formulation, the "game" was everywhere. Crack, business, politics—everything is a hustle. Global capitalism is just the projects writ large, survival of the fittest, and it's up to every individual to try to get over however he can. As he rapped, "Momma ain't raised no fool/Put me anywhere on God's green earth/I'll triple my worth."

If anyone from our team has found secure footing within this new economic world, it's Dino, who has been enabled by technology to run a hedge fund from a financial outpost as Seattle is. At the same time, anyone else anywhere in the world with the ability to raise some cash can start his own fund, whether he is in Cape Town, Moscow, or Kuala Lumpur. Against this global competition, Dino has created his own structure, consisting of his tightly knit Greek family for emotional support and his group of analysts. Dino is, as he says, the "team captain," piloting his small ship through the global markets. "If you can deliver exceptional value to people," he says, "they'll pay you."

If street hustling is a metaphor for life in the global economy, there's a lot more payoff in rapping about it than living the lifestyle. For the guys who got into the underground economy, it's a structure that's a lot easier to enter than to exit.

One morning, I visit JT at the two-bedroom house he shares with his mom in the South End. I sit in the living room on the couch facing a window that looks out on the street. A TV in the corner plays *SpongeBob SquarePants* at low volume while JT sits in a reclining chair across from me. His two-year-old daughter, Simone, perches on his chest, smiling, with her arms around his neck while we talk. JT's mom, Sharon, hurries in and out as she prepares to leave for her job as a sales clerk in the china department at a downtown department store.

On my lap, I'm holding *The Tupac Shakur Legacy*, a coffee-table book that is a cherished possession of JT's. It's a lavish production, full of photographs and little pockets that hold pullout items such as reproductions of the playbill from when a twelve-year-old Tupac landed a role in *Raisin in the Sun* at a Harlem community theater, a complete reproduction of one of his notebooks, and even a copy of his prison ID card from when he was locked up in 1995 after being convicted of sexual assault.

Tupac, JT tells me, is his favorite rapper. "He really talked about what was happening, like Marvin Gaye did," JT says. I mention Tupac's contradictions, such as singing one song lamenting the death of his friends from violence and then another with lines such as "Fuck you, die slow motherfucker/My four-four make sure all your kids don't grow." JT tells me, "That's what the streets are like. He was telling both sides."

JT says that everything he has learned to survive on the street works against him in the straight world. For example, on the street, you need to be "cool"—showing any type of enthusiasm or emotion can expose you to violence (the African-American sociologist Elijah Anderson calls this "the code of the street"). You learn to lay back and let things come to you. When you start to look for a real job, JT says, it's hard to get out of this mind-set. You still tend to just sit around. And without ever having learned to read very well, JT is totally blocked off from modern technology. He tells me he has never used the Internet. "If you can't spell, you can't use a computer," he says.

Two decades after going to the streets, JT says, he's got nothing. The money comes and goes, and is impossible to hold on to when you do get it. Without a steady income, you can't support your family, which makes you question your own manhood. You see your friends go to jail or die. You find that others will double-cross you. Eventually you feel trapped. "It's like a drug, man, it's an addiction," JT says. "I fight every time somebody's talking to me about the game or they're making this money, or they got this plug, and I get that idea, 'Shit, maybe I should jump back in the game, maybe I'll be successful again.' But then again I think about, 'What if I do it just one more time and I get popped?' Like *Blow*, you see that movie? When he's older and fat, and he's got the hookup, and that one time cans his ass. That could be me."

For Damian, the church and his faith in God have provided an alternative structure to the streets. In Sam Townsend, his pastor, Damian has found a mentor who provides advice on things such as work situations, marriage, and buying a house. "He's this stable male figure that leads by example, somebody I can look at whose life is one of stability, a life of love and care for others. I can look at that and say, 'OK, that's the way a real man's supposed to be.'"

Damian also has longer-term plans to build a foundation for his family. In addition to his job as a teacher, he has started a number of businesses, though he's found that it's difficult when you don't have much capital to invest. One was selling suits—Damian got catalogs from wholesale suppliers, found customers, took measurements, and then ordered the clothing. He did this for a couple of years, but the margin on each sale was tiny. When a discount clothing warehouse opened in a shopping complex south of Seattle, offering brand-name suits at slashed-rate prices, Damian couldn't compete. He moved on to a few multilevel marketing ventures, including one that involved loan origination—basically, finding people who wanted mortgages, doing the paperwork, and passing it on to a lending company. The housing crash ended that line of work. To increase his income, Damian has decided to leave Zion Prep—as I write this, he's applying for a teaching job with the public schools. His goal, he tells me, is to build some generational knowledge and wealth, so that younger family members, such as his nephew David, won't, like him, have to start from zero.

After my visits with him in jail, Myran ends up doing a little over a year and a half of time (vindicating Myran's delaying tactics, the prosecution eventually dropped the charge that Myran had involved a minor in a drug transaction and reduced the sentence it was seeking). One afternoon, after his release, I meet him at a public housing complex in South Seattle, where he is staying with his girlfriend of fifteen years, who works nearby as a coordinator for a food bank distribution center. The development, tucked behind a Safeway, consists of rows of town houses along tree-lined streets. It's a warm, late summer day, just before the start of school, and a group of kids is running around, playing in the street. Myran stands behind them and waves to me as I drive up. He wears jeans and a green golf shirt, and has sunglasses pushed back on top of his shaved head. He looks healthy, though he also carries a noticeable air of uncertainty.

We drive to a pizza place for lunch. Myran tells me he's trying to keep everything cool, to avoid losing his temper or getting knocked off balance, because the addiction is always there. When he starts to feel frustrated, he tries to do something positive, such as going out and washing the car. When he looks back on his life over the east decade, he tells me, he is ashamed. He thinks of all the things he could have been doing, and the time lost with his kids. As he talks, an image sticks in my mind. Before we left the housing complex, Myran called out to his eight-year-old daughter. She dashed out of the group of kids and grabbed on to his leg, smiling. He introduced us and told her we were going out to get lunch but would be back soon, so she shouldn't worry. As he spoke, he rested his hand on her back, a man trying to grasp a stability that has often eluded him.

Play Hard and Keep It Clean

From my very first trip back to Seattle, the idea of getting the team back together for a reunion comes up as I speak with my teammates. At first, when it isn't apparent to anyone—certainly not me—how far I'm going to pursue finding everyone, it's idle chatter. As time passes, though, and I keep coming back, I find myself relaying information about each player to every other one. The talk of the reunion becomes more consistent, though it's always in the vein of "Wouldn't it be great if we all got together again?" I realize it's going to be up to me to organize it.

There are a few practical matters I fret over. The first is whether we should just meet somewhere like a pizza place, or actually play basketball again. Most of the guys on the team remain in good shape, and when I put the question out, it's unanimous that we have to play. If a guy wants to sit it out, that will be fine, too.

The second worry is logistical: I don't know where to have the reunion. Sean, who has stayed active with Lakeside, tells me he could get the school gym on a weekend. That would have a nice symmetry, as we always practiced at Lakeside. But it strikes me that once again it will require the black side of the team to travel up to meet the white side. It doesn't seem quite right. When Damian tells me about a South End community center that rents courts by the hour and is only a few blocks from Zion Preparatory Academy, it seems perfect.

When I send out an e-mail suggesting a date, Damian, Chris, and Dino all answer within a few minutes: They're in.

"I guess I'll have to work on my game," Eric Hampton chimes in to the whole group.

"I'll see you all there . . . with my ¼" vertical. Down from ½" in the 8th grade," Sean adds.

JT, who has been one of the most insistent about having a reunion, is not on e-mail. I call his house and speak with his mom. "I'll make sure he gets his ass down there," she says.

I fly back to Seattle a couple of days before the date and drive down to the community center to pay $50 for two hours of court time. On the morning of the reunion, I wake up feeling nervous. Although most guys have said they're coming, I wonder if they'll actually show. I'm curious how everyone will get along. Though I've spent significant amounts of time with everyone individually, the group as a whole hasn't been together in two decades. Many of my teammates haven't seen each other since high school.

I throw on some old black gym shorts and a faded maroon T-shirt. As I pull up my socks and jam my feet into my basketball shoes, I feel the calmness that comes from slipping into a familiar costume.

I'm staying at my brother's house in Ballard, a neighborhood on the north side of the city. Before I leave, I make a few calls. Sean picks up and we chat for a couple of minutes. He asks who else is coming and assures me he'll be there. JT doesn't answer; I leave a message telling him to call if he needs a ride. I reach Damian as he's getting ready to head out and pick up a new pair of basketball shoes. He says he's worried he's packed on too much weight to play at top form.

Finally, I try the home of Tyrell's parents. The last time I'd seen them, I'd mentioned the plans to have a reunion. They asked me to let them know if it came together. When I call, Tyrell's mom picks up. I fill her in on the location and time. She tells me they'll be out doing errands, but they'd like to come, and takes my cell phone number.

I leave my brother's house and drive over to Interstate 5, merging into the southbound lanes. It's a crisp, bright spring day. The Space Needle juts up before me, the downtown skyscrapers arranged beyond it. The sunlight reflects off Lake Union, which is dotted with sailboats. Farther south, the symmetric cone of Mount Rainier, its sides covered with snow, rises on the horizon. I realize as I'm driving that I'm trundling the same length of freeway that Willie McClain and the black half of the team drove in the opposite direction twenty years earlier to get to our practices at Lakeside. On the way, my mind returns to Tyrell. His death had been the impetus for going back and finding everyone else, and, in the end, this reunion. Over time, I had pieced together the story of his murder.

During the summer of 1991, Tyrell spent a lot of time with his best friend, a kid named Mike Scott; people who knew them called them "T-Baby" (hence Tyrell's tattoo) and "G-Money." Like Tyrell's older brother, Donnico, Mike was fairly active in the drug game. He was running up monthly mobile phone bills of about $1,100 and owned two cars, a Thunderbird and a white Buick. Tyrell, then nineteen, was more of a friend and sidekick—still living at home, he showed no inclination for getting into it like Mike, Donnico, and JT had at that point. "He was just the mellow guy," says Donnico, who, after serving more than five years in prison on drug charges, is working as a water-meter reader in Portland, Oregon, when we speak. "Every now and then he'd get some dope from somebody, just enough to get him some money. I can tell you my brother probably never had more than a thousand dollars cash in his career—I think I seen him with maybe six or seven hundred at one time. Tyrell, he wasn't really into anything heavy, as far as drugs or crime. He was just a guy who enjoyed life, smoked some weed now and then, and just liked to look good."

That summer, Mike and Tyrell often ended their nights at the 24 Social Club, an after-hours joint in the Central Area, on Jackson Street two blocks east of the intersection at Twenty-third Avenue, where there is now a Starbucks. The club had two rooms: a bar out front and a gambling room in back, with one table for dice and one for cards. Maybe forty people could jam into the backroom, drinking, smoking, and talking, some at the tables and others hanging back to watch sports on TV. Things got going at about midnight and went on until six in the morning, seven days a week. Mike liked to throw dice. Tyrell usually just chilled out, unless Donnico gave him some money to gamble. Early in August 1991, Mike had a run of luck at dice, pulling in, according to the club's owner, $19,000.

After Mike won the money, Donnico tells me, he called Donnico and told him he had a deal set up to buy a kilo of cocaine for $14,500. He asked Donnico if he wanted to go in on it. "Back then [a kilo] was going for eighteen, nineteen all day. So that was a red flag for me off the top," Donnico says. "It was way too cheap." He told Mike he wasn't interested. The last time Donnico spoke to his brother, Tyrell was out riding with

Mike. They talked about meeting later at the home of a girl Tyrell was seeing. Donnico didn't hear anything from his brother that night. A day or two later, his mom called, asking if he'd seen Tyrell. Donnico told her they'd just talked and everything was fine. A day later, he was at Longacres, a horse track south of Seattle, when his pager started to blow up. One number was from a guy Donnico hadn't heard from in ages. Donnico called and asked what was going on. He said, "Man, call home. They found your brother dead."

On August 12, two days after Tyrell's dismembered body turned up in the ditch in South Seattle, the *Seattle Times* published a brief article identifying him as the victim. After it ran, someone called the newspaper and told an editor that Tyrell wasn't just some kid, but that he'd been a star basketball player who was known and liked in the community. That piqued the editor's interest; he assigned a journalist to look into it.

The reporter, Elouise Schumacher, a white woman then in her thirties, had been covering the controversies over nuclear contamination at the Hanford Nuclear Reservation and the disastrous health effects it had on people living in the area. It was her first assignment involving black Seattle. "There was a lot of violence around that time, an extra wave of crime," she says. "We were not out covering it too much. It was maybe us saying, 'Oh, maybe we should pay attention to this one, not just do it in a paragraph or two.'"

She headed to the funeral, a dispiriting affair in which the mourners were flanked by a phalanx of Seattle police officers. She visited Tyrell's parents, interviewing them in Tyrell's spotlessly kept room, with his athletic shoes neatly lined up, his trophies and basketball posters on display, and his oversized stuffed Mickey Mouse. At the time, the police didn't have any leads they'd talk about, or much to say, except that they thought the murder was related to Mike Scott's lucky night at dice (Mike has not been seen or heard from since Tyrell's killing). Coach McClain told her about our team and the efforts he and Randy Finley had made to place Tyrell in a good school. "He had enough talent, enough gifts in sports to soften the blow of being in a private school," McClain said. "He was a smart young man; there wasn't any [school] work he couldn't do. We put a lot of pressure on him, and we actually tried to force him to go."

Schumacher framed her article around Tyrell's friendship with John

Doces, the white kid from Bellevue who had met Tyrell through the Adopt-a-Family program. "Their friendship had all the makings of a clichéd movie script: rich, white suburban kid befriends needy, black inner-city youth," it began. "Only this time there's no happy ending."

When Schumacher turned in the story, the front-page editor rejected it, telling her he thought it was "racist." "I guess he thought I was portraying him as a dumb kid," Schumacher says. After spending nearly two weeks gathering the details of Tyrell's life, Schumacher was distraught—she'd come to feel a personal connection with him. Schumacher left the office and walked around for an hour. Upon her return, she went to the paper's only black editor, told him the story had been spiked, and gave him a copy to read. He liked it enough to champion it onto the front page, where I saw it on August 26, 1991: Tyrell, smiling on one knee, cropped out of a larger group photo of our team, tucked into the bottom left hand of the paper, right under the news of the disintegration of the Soviet Union.

The break in the case came when the Seattle police got a copy of Mike Scott's cell phone bill. The detectives found that calls had been made late into the night on August 7 and then stopped for a few hours. Then, on the morning of August 8, two calls were placed to a number in Los Angeles, at 7:02 and 7:28. The cops got Mike Scott's girlfriend to call the number. She told the person who answered that it was her phone, and she wanted to know who had been using it. The man on the other end was named Harold. He told her that his cousin who lived in Seattle, Trenino Rollins, had called him the morning in question.

Trenino "Reno" Rollins also hung out at the 24 Social Club in the summer of 1991, though he wasn't friends with Mike and Tyrell; at thirty-one, Rollins was more than a decade older than G-Money and T-Baby. About five-foot-ten and 150 pounds, he had hair down to his shoulders in braids, a beard, and a mustache, and was known as a ladies' man. Rollins was new to Seattle. He later testified that he'd been born in Winnsboro, Louisiana, and, in 1985, had gotten a job installing TV towers that took him around the country. In 1990 he settled in Seattle, where he worked as a welder. When he was laid off, he began selling cocaine. When the Seattle Police later ran checks on Rollins, they did not find any evidence of a prior criminal record from other states.

At eight in the morning on September 17, 1991, Seattle police detective Hank Gruber and his partner met Rollins coming back from the mailbox at his apartment and told him they wanted to ask him some questions. Rollins lived in the Marina Apartments, a complex near Lake Washington in the Rainier Beach neighborhood in South Seattle, a quarter mile from the spot where Tyrell's body was dumped.

After Rollins allowed the cops into his studio, the first thing Gruber noticed was a "super-single" waterbed—an odd size, about four by seven feet. Tyrell's body had been wrapped in sheets made for just that type of bed. Upon seeing it, Gruber advised Rollins of his rights. He asked if there was a gun in the apartment. Rollins told him there was one under the couch cushion. It was a .22 semiautomatic pistol; ballistic tests later determined that it was the weapon used to execute Tyrell with a bullet to the back of the head. The homicide detectives placed Rollins under arrest.

When the case went to trial the next year, Rollins maintained his innocence. When first questioned, he told the police he knew nothing about Mike Scott, Tyrell, or the cellular phone, and that he had gotten the gun from his brother. He changed his story in court, where he testified that he didn't know Tyrell, but that he had bought cocaine from Mike several times. In addition, Rollins said, he had purchased the gun from Mike. He claimed that in the early hours of August 8, Mike had knocked on his door, asked to borrow the gun back—Rollins said Mike told him he had to meet a guy to do some business—and left his cell phone as collateral. In the morning, Rollins said, he used the phone to call his cousin. Later that day, Rollins explained, Mike returned the gun and took his phone back. At the time of the trial, Mike was still missing. Rollins clearly meant to create the impression that Mike had killed Tyrell and then fled Seattle.

Whatever his story, there was too much evidence against Rollins, who, after all, had handed the detectives the murder weapon. The pattern on the sheets wrapped around Tyrell's body was the same as that on some that were still in Rollins's apartment. Forensic investigators also found fibers on Tyrell's corpse that matched the carpet in the apartment. Finally, the police found Mike's and Tyrell's rings in Rollins's closet—Mike's a gold band with three diamonds in the middle, Tyrell's also gold, but with a dollar sign on it. The jury found Rollins guilty of first-degree homicide; the judge sentenced him to twenty-three years in prison.

After the conviction, Hank Gruber, the detective on the case, went into the King County Jail and asked Rollins to take him to Mike Scott's body, just to clear things up for Mike's family. He checked Rollins out and Rollins guided him to another wooded road in the South End. Mike Scott's body had been dumped down a hill, where it had lain undiscovered. Unlike Tyrell, Mike was still in one piece.

His murder is still technically an open case. The investigation is the responsibility of the cold case unit, which has the task of looking into unsolved murders—mainly through using advances in DNA technology—committed between 1969 and 1999. The unit started in 2000 with three hundred homicides to investigate; so, far it has cleared about twenty-five. Mike Scott's is one of the approximately 275 remaining.

One case the unit has solved is the 1990 murder of a thirty-eight-year-old Central Area woman who worked in the produce section of a grocery store. She was found on her couch, her dress pushed up over her stomach, stabbed thirty times with a pair of scissors. DNA technicians, working at the request of the cold case detectives, matched semen found inside her body to Trenino Rollins. In 2006, Rollins went on trial in King County Superior Court for first-degree homicide. It ended in a hung jury after a ten-to-two vote to convict. Rollins eventually pled guilty to second-degree homicide, for which he received an additional fifteen years on top of the time he was serving for Tyrell's murder.

While Rollins is still in King County Jail awaiting transport back to prison in Tucson, Arizona, where Washington State has farmed him out to a corporate-run penitentiary, I go to visit him. When he comes into the visiting area and takes the phone on the other side of the bulletproof glass, he looks almost dignified—pushing fifty, he has a shaved head, round face, and a goatee flecked with gray.

He nods when I tell him I'm writing a book about a bunch of guys I once played basketball with, and that one of them was Tyrell Johnson. I tell him I want to know what happened on the night of the murder. Rollins nods again, and then tells me he doesn't want to talk about it at the moment. He says to try him again when he's back in prison. "In a couple of years, the truth about this whole thing is going to come out," he tells me.

For the next few years, I send Rollins an occasional letter asking if he's willing to talk, but hear nothing back. In the fall of 2009, I contact the public information officer of the prison in Arizona. He relays my request for an interview to Rollins, who tells the prison officials to let me know he has "no intentions" of talking to me, ever.

One Saturday morning, I sit in the gallery of a King County courtroom. On the other side of a panel of bulletproof glass, a judge is arraigning a black teenager accused of auto theft. I've arrived a few minutes before the morning break, and when the judge finishes with the alleged car thief and steps down from the bench, the courtroom guard rushes out and greets me. A tall, slender, middle-aged man with a broad smile, he enthusiastically shakes my hand and ushers me through the court and into a tiny breakroom. We sit at a table topped with gray Formica, the smell of percolating coffee mingling with the cigarettes on his breath. Now retired from his job as a detective, Hank Gruber tells me he works part-time as a bailiff because it lets him keep his health benefits and still have enough time to go deer hunting.

Gruber sets a thick, black binder on the table. The case, he says, was one of those that just stick in your head. On this type of thing, the family doesn't expect much from the police, so you feel good if you can nail somebody. "You come out and you're white and you solve the murder and they think you're a hero," he says.

Gruber tells me the likely motive was to steal the money that Mike Scott had won gambling. The police, he says, think that Rollins did the murder with a partner and mentions the name of the other suspect, who was later convicted of murder and rape in a separate case and is now serving a life sentence in prison. There wasn't enough evidence to press charges against the other man, Gruber says, but it was a "two-person-type murder."

The binder holds a collection of murder scene photos that Gruber used when he taught about crime-scene investigations at the police academy. A remarkably chipper man, he opens the book and takes on the air of someone showing photos of his grandchildren as he flips the pages, which display snapshots of suicides, accidental deaths, and murders. Each one evokes a memory—the particulars of the case, the challenges, how it was eventually solved.

Eventually Gruber gets to Tyrell's section. He opens the book to a photo of police and forensic investigators gathered on a wooded road.

They hunch over something swaddled in white sheets. Gruber flips a few more pages. Each photo shows another layer of the bundle removed— the sheets are unwrapped to expose a couple of black garbage bags, which are pulled away to reveal a blue blanket. "You sure you're OK with this? I know this guy was a friend of yours," he asks before turning the page one more time.

Tyrell is lying on his back. He wears black briefs. His left leg is sawed off just above the knee, the right leg amputated a bit higher. There is a red crease in his left shoulder where it was partially severed, too. "They were trying to dismember him but they were too lazy or it was too bizarre," Gruber explains. It happens more often that you might think, he says—a killer starts to hack up a corpse to get it into manageable pieces but then quits halfway through.

There's not much to connect this body to the kid I once knew until I notice something around the neck. At first it looks almost as if they tried to cut his head off, too, and I begin to ask Gruber about it, until I see that the thin line is actually a gold necklace. I remember Tyrell flipping one just like it out from underneath his undershirt years before, a bit of flash to add to his basketball game.

• • •

I exit the freeway in South Seattle and drive east a couple of miles before pulling into the parking lot of the community center, a boxy, concrete building that sits next to a complex of athletic fields. I arrive fifteen minutes early. As I get out of the car, a dark green Ford Escort station wagon with a dent in the passenger-side door parks a few slots away. Damian climbs out in a black nylon sweatsuit and his just-purchased white high-tops. We walk into the lobby of the center, which is crowded with kids, all of them African American. A couple of teenage guys standing around the pool table call out and greet Damian as we pass.

The gym has red cinder-block walls, a sign listing rules of conduct, and a clock over the door with the requisite metal grille. On the sideline stands a row of portable aluminum bleachers.

The rest of the team begins to show up a few minutes later. Sean walks into the gym in maroon shorts, a gray T-shirt, and flip-flops, grabs a ball, and begins shooting. A few minutes later, Dino enters with Willie McClain Sr., who wears a red nylon track suit and carries a camera in his right hand. Sean walks over, gives McClain a hug, and shakes his hand.

"How you doin'?" Sean asks.

"I'm great," McClain says.

"You look great."

"You too."

Sean rubs his head where his hair has receded and tilts forward to show McClain, who laughs and says, "That's all right. Better you than me."

Sean moves over the bleachers and sits down to put on his shoes as McClain keeps talking.

"I just had a breakfast meeting and I was bragging to them about 1986 and all that we accomplished," he says. "That should go down someplace in the books."

Randy Finley arrives next, his bushy hair and mustache now white. He is followed by Chris Dickinson and Eric Hampton, who, when he enters the gym, throws his arms in the air in a Rocky-like gesture. Maitland, who has driven up from Oregon, walks in wearing khaki pants and a muted, green-and-yellow Hawaiian shirt. Coach McClain's youngest son, Demetrius, shows up with a friend. Eric's younger brother, Joe, also comes with a friend. Joe Miller, who was Willie McClain's assistant coach, shows up, as does Doug Thiele, a former Lakeside teacher who was hired by Randy to tutor Damian, Will Jr., and JT. Maitland's younger brother, Rob, who used to tag along to games, has flown up from Los Angeles for the reunion.

As the guys drift onto the court, the sound of basketballs thumping on the floor begins to reverberate off the walls. Willie McClain and Randy Finley huddle and talk while we warm up. Chris and Eric get together in a corner to loosen up.

"Is that going to do any good?" McClain shouts over at them. "All that stretching?"

After about fifteen minutes of chatting and shooting around, we gather in a circle at center court to reintroduce ourselves.

"I'm Doug. I'm a journalist," I begin.

"I'm Chris Dickinson, I've got a couple kids, and I work in employee benefits."

"I'm Eric Hampton. I am married now. I work for the city of Seattle."

"I'm Maitland Finley. I've been working in the wine industry in Washington and Oregon. I live in a town called Yamhill down south. I'm single, and, uh, I just have a dog. That's it."

"I'm Coach Willie McClain. I have three men now, they're not boys.

I'm still in the ministry, still working with youth. I'm glad to see you all, you men, back from '86. All right!"

"I'm Damian Joseph, I am a teacher and a preacher. I'm a teacher at Zion Preparatory Academy, and it's wonderful. I love helping kids. And I'm a preacher at Greater Glory Church of God in Christ."

"Dino Christofilis. Married with two kids. I have my own investment firm. Glad to be here."

"I'm Sean O'Donnell. I'm a lawyer with King County."

"I'm Randy Finley. I was the auditioning guy. I just had a wonderful time doing it. And when the basketball season was over, it was hard to let go. That's why we started the tutoring class and got almost everybody off into high schools. Got 'em graduated and I've been hearing all kinds of wonderful things. And Willie, it's wonderful to see you again."

"It's good to see you, too, Randy," McClain answers.

Everyone claps after the introductions. To choose teams, we pair off, roughly by height, picking up the younger brothers and their friends to fill out the sides. McClain says, "My advice to you all: Play hard and keep it clean!"

The game starts. Chris takes the first shot. He misses, and Eric's younger brother, Joe, grabs the rebound and kicks it out to Damian at the top of the key, who nails a jumper.

Chris hits the next shot from far out on the left side of the basket.

When Dino gets the ball, just beyond the three-point line, he rises and fires a jumper that pops down through the net. He has exactly the same form he had as a kid, and, as usual, no hesitation in shooting it.

There might be an undiscovered gene that determines your basketball skills, because everyone plays in almost the exact same style he did twenty years earlier.

Even though he's gained some weight, Eric still has a rattlesnake-quick lateral step he uses to throw off defenders, drive by them, and then put up a high-arcing shot that seems to slide straight down through the basket.

Chris's shirt is soon soaked with sweat as he bangs away against Sean for position under the basket. When a teammate shoots an air ball that bounces on the floor, heading out of bounds, Chris leaps after it in an attempt to keep possession for his team.

Sean would get the prize for most improved. Still thin and with the same long limbs and wingspan, he has grown into his body and crosses the court without the awkward, robotlike movements he had as a kid.

When Damian dribbles, he pounds the ball into the court like he's trying to punish it. As soon as we start the game, he also gets deadly serious. He wants to win.

Maitland sits it out, watching from the top row of the three-level bleachers, his elbows on his knees. Later, he grabs a ball and shoots on one end of the court when everyone is on the opposite side.

Coach McClain sits on the first row of the bleachers, leaning forward, studying every play, looking totally content. As he always used to do, he occasionally erupts with admonishments: "Cut the baseline off! Step up and play defense! Come on, Damian, you gotta get that!"

My only reliable play remains the outside shot. At one point, Damian gets free at the top of the key and drives toward the hoop. I am standing a few feet away from the basket and come off my man to pick up Damian, who is barreling straight down the lane. He begins to jump, the ball in his right hand as his arm rises toward the hoop. I leap and try to block his shot. We collide in midair, both of us stopping cold, my head jolted back as I absorb the force of Damian's momentum. Willie McClain emits a loud groan from the sideline. Next time, I think, I'll let Damian have the two points.

We take breaks between the games. Players gulp from their water bottles and rest on the bleachers. Chris, smiling, comes up, knocks me on the shoulder, and tells me he loves being back with the guys. Damian makes motions like he's practicing his jump shot and calls out, "Hey Coach McClain, you were right, too! I missed him underneath."

Dino asks Eric where his office is. "Your e-mail's on that list?" he asks. "You're working downtown? I'll hit you. We can get lunch."

During one game, I sub out and sit on the bleachers. It's impossible not to notice that all the white players from the team are here while several of the black guys aren't—Will McClain Jr. and JT, who'd both said they were coming, haven't shown up. I miss Tyrell's smile and the suspense of knowing he might at any point pull off an outrageous, behind-the-back move. I miss Myran's running commentary and jokes.

After several games, when everyone's had enough, we head over to Zion Preparatory Academy, where we have pizza and soda in the cafeteria under the framed pictures of the Tuskegee Airmen that hang on the walls. There is a lot of catching up and reminiscing about things such as listening to Run DMC and ranking on each other during the van rides.

(Rob Finley)

(Rob Finley)

Eventually we settle into chairs and form a circle. Randy Finley kicks things off by talking about his motivations for forming the team. "What I wanted out of this was a group of kids to learn from basketball just how much bigger the world is," he says.

Willie McClain speaks next. "My motivation was selfish," he says. "The purpose for me was to give an opportunity to the players that I had been bringing up in athletics, the opportunity to go to the Lakesides, the Seattle Preps, and things like that."

As we talk, Sean leans forward, following each comment. Maitland and Eric both say little. Damian maintains a focused look throughout.

"The cool thing about the team was that it was different from the way I was brought up and where I came from," Chris says. "Nobody remembers any of the games, we just remember what it felt like to be with everybody."

When the conversation comes around to him, Eric says, "It was a great time and I'm really glad Doug did this and I got a chance to see all you guys again. I'm touched and I'm just happy to see everybody again and I don't know . . ." Eric chokes up, holding back tears. "I don't want to get too deep," he says and stops.

At one point I mention the old Lakeside chant, "It's all right, it's OK, you'll all work for us someday."

"I think they did at Seattle Prep, too," Sean says.

"This was against Rainier Beach," says Damian, who was the first to remind me of the chant.

No one else wants to pick it up, so Coach McClain jumps in: "You're talking about two worlds, spectators and players, people who come to the game and watch, and people who will unite and fight at the drop of a hat for every player on that floor."

"On the floor, the power's with the coach and we have a united goal, and that's to win the game," Sean says. "That's what Coach was saying, the basketball court is sort of, I don't know, it's not the sanctuary . . ."

"That's the word," Willie McClain answers.

Damian says that after Randy Finley got him into Seattle Prep, he saw that even some kids who were rich were still adrift because their parents fought or were gone all the time. He was poor, he tells the group, but he always knew his mom loved him. Everybody has problems, he says, not just people who happen to be poor and black. "It's not just us having the issues, it's everybody having the issues. It's just in a different area. So that's why the whole experience works for everybody," he says of playing basketball together.

In the middle of the conversation, JT walks up to the glass doors of the school. He wears black pants, tan Timberland boots, and a long-sleeved black T-shirt with G-UNIT written on the front in silver cursive. Randy Finley gets up and rushes over to greet him. As JT enters the circle, Willie McClain says, "Hey, JT!" and stands to hug him. After grasping McClain, JT makes his way around the circle, hugging each player one by one before he sits down next to me.

When it comes around to him, JT is the first to bring up Tyrell. "I'd just like to talk about T-Baby," he says. "You guys probably already did that . . ."

"Just a bit," Willie McClain says.

"Man, I can't understand why he didn't take that chance," JT says about Tyrell's opportunity to go to private school through our team. "I don't know what he said to you. He should have just tried. He could have gone back to Garfield."

"I think for Tyrell there was a lot of outside pressure for him to be in the local high school, Garfield. I think a lot of coaches, parents, people that had tradition with Garfield, did not see," Willie McClain says. "There was no doubt that T was going to go to Garfield and private school wasn't an option."

Coach McClain has told me this before. His hope for Tyrell was that he would take the chances offered him and get away from the streets. He didn't, and he died.

One, of course, doesn't necessarily follow the other. But in speaking about it with Coach McClain, I realized that he saw the team in life-and-death terms—at the time we came together in 1986, some of his players were facing futures that would considerably darken over the next few years. He had seen the chance to get his guys into private schools as an alternative track that might well keep them alive. For Coach McClain, Tyrell's refusal to embrace opportunity revealed an unwillingness to change the direction of his life.

Other guys had their own thoughts about Tyrell's life and death when I first spoke with them. Sean, the prosecutor, told me that what happened to Tyrell was tragic, but that when he worked in the juvenile court system, he saw a lot of cases that also were tragic. He says that, if anything, having known Tyrell made him more dedicated to his work—if people know there are consequences to their actions, he says, they'll be less likely to commit crimes. If they don't commit crimes, they won't place themselves in danger, as Tyrell did.

Damian, who also had sold drugs, distanced himself. He thought that Tyrell had gotten in way too deep and been set up by a group such as the Black Gangster Disciples. "The last time I saw him, I was at a skating party or something, and he was *gone*, to where he almost didn't notice me," Damian says. "He was gone. So he probably knew that something was happening. It was shortly after that that he ended up dead."

JT saw his own alternative fate in Tyrell. "It could have been any one of us," he says.

Tyrell's death, though, fails to provide much meaning at all. He was a kid who grew up in the neighborhood and went along with what people around him were doing. He hadn't shown any particular ambition besides trying to get enough money together to have a good time. He died at age nineteen—not even really out of childhood—because, it seems, a couple of men wanted to get a piece of some gambling winnings. "Tyrell was at the wrong place at the wrong time," his brother, Donnico, says. "I'm not a hundred percent sure, but I got a real good feeling. It wasn't for him. They didn't know him, he wasn't doing the drug deal—he was just with his friend."

Donnico says his family has never gotten over Tyrell's death. "My mom and dad, and my little sister, every now and then they'll just start staring at me, you know, and they'll be, 'Man, your brother's supposed to be here right now.' Just certain things, right? And like, my little sister, we'll all be somewhere and she'll just start crying."

Even now, Donnico tells me, Tyrell still sometimes visits him in his dreams. Every time it's as real as if his brother were sitting and talking right there next to him. The visions always end the same way: As Tyrell gets ready to leave, Donnico becomes frantic, begging him to stay a little longer. Tyrell looks at his brother. "I gotta go now," he says, fading away as Donnico tries to hold on to him.

I'd been trying to hold on to Tyrell, too, or at least a memory of a time long passed. On some deep level—I certainly was not entirely conscious of it—I'd thought that by finding out what happened to Tyrell and my teammates, and getting everyone back together, maybe I could regain some of that sense of being part of a team with other guys at your back, believing that you could conquer the world, that the security of the court was going to extend off of it. It was as futile as calling Tyrell's parents to invite them to the reunion and thinking they might come.

Tyrell's story is done. He will always be that kid on the front page of the paper, taking a knee and smiling at the photographer. The rest of us, cropped out of that picture, have gone on.

In the more than twenty years since we played together, we've made our ways through a changing era whose contours were apparent in the front-page coverage of the Soviet Union's collapse on the day Tyrell made his headline. The end of the Cold War and advancing technology has ushered in an ever-faster, more competitive world. Seattle has adjusted about as well as anyplace else in the country, retooling the local economy toward high-tech, white-collar work. Those of us in private school back in 1986 were getting a much better preparation for this new reality.

Within this larger context, everyone from our team is an individual with his own aspirations, hopes, and struggles. The reason I was able to work for so long on this book was that I immensely enjoyed speaking with each of my teammates. Each guy, as an adult, has his own special qualities.

Eric struck me with his wry sense of humor and a deadeye analysis that I hadn't known as a kid. He may be quiet, but nothing escapes his observation.

Chris and I talked intensely about the way boys (and men) use sports to shape their identities and hide insecurities, something that has troubled both of us since the evening we met at an eighth-grade school dance.

Willie Jr. made me laugh with his lighthearted sense of humor and quick turns of phrase. He delights in the presence of his kids.

Sean fascinated me with tales of grisly crime cases and the way the prosecutors approached trying them. As always, Sean sprinkled his stories with incisive stabs of humor.

Dino is committed to his family, loves his work, and is truly gifted at it. He has a deep sense of his own identity that allows him to thrive in a cutthroat industry.

Maitland, when you sit and speak with him, radiates a thoughtfulness, intelligence, and essential kindness that is hard to get on the page.

Every time I visited Randy Finley at his winery, he was the same whirlwind as ever, telling jokes, pouring me glasses, and regaling me with digressive stories that almost always, eventually, wound back to make a point.

I'd hardly known Coach McClain as a kid. After spending time with him as an adult, I came to see him as an amazing man—his life spans from pre–civil rights, segregated Mississippi to tech-era Seattle. Along the way, he's found a calling—in tandem with Diane, his wonderful wife—by being a solid source of support for other people who need help. In his own, humble way, he's lived a life to emulate.

Of course, when you spend so much time with people, there are those you become especially close with. For me, that happened to be Damian, Myran, and JT.

Damian and I hit it off from the first evening we sat down at his kitchen table. We both share an abiding interest in the vagaries of race and class. Countless times, we talked for hours on end, each of us making our points, finding agreement, and challenging each other where we disagreed. We don't find accord on everything. I know that in my case, at least, our jousting has made me rethink a lot of my own assumptions.

I walked back into Myran's life during a very rough time. As always, he made me laugh with his string of jokes, some fairly outrageous. Beyond that, though, there were times when the kid I once knew was right there in front of me, trying hard to make a connection. When I saw his situation, I realized that he didn't exactly need someone to drop in, take notes for a book, and then disappear. He needed a friend who could try to provide some support and encouragement. I hope I will be able to do that.

JT is simply one of the most openhearted, enthusiastic people I've ever known. Given the reality of street hustling, these are qualities he often has to cover up. But away from the streets, he is always a joy to be around. We met many times early in the morning to walk the two-and-a-half-mile loop around Seward Park in South Seattle. Along the way, JT would always jauntily greet our fellow walkers, black and white, exclaiming, "It's a beautiful day!" On a deeper level, from our very first meeting, JT identified the team as a "family." While I might have been embarrassed to use that exact formulation, I had the same feelings myself. We had both been boys looking to salve our insecurities, a place to feel safe. When sports ended for JT, he transitioned into the streets. With my background, I was fortunate to have many more options.

I chose to get far away. I didn't want to deal with things falling apart, especially the pain of my own family coming undone. I saw distance and separation as means to escape. But to wall yourself off from hurt is also to block out much of being human. In the end, the championship moments are brief. Everything in between comprises the brunt of life. People—whether collected in teams or in families—are imperfect. You invest in them and they disappoint. You get ground down, and you let yourself down. You try and you fail. If you're lucky, you get another chance to try again.

Coach McClain was right. Basketball welded the two sides of our team. Playing on a team excused us to give ourselves wholeheartedly to a cause and a group of people in a way we otherwise couldn't. Without the structure of a team, it's almost impossible to keep it going. As men, we get pulled apart—even before the divisions of race and class are factored in. As Eric says, you get caught up in the hustle of life—you focus on your job, your family, paying the mortgage, and you lose track of the other things you could be doing.

Jackie Robinson, later in his life, recognized that sports are an imperfect vehicle for achieving equality. In fact, celebrating people on the athletic fields can be a substitute for real equality. It's one thing to give up a position in the starting lineup of a basketball team, and totally another to lose a slot at a prestigious private school. In Damian's words, there was a reason why the Lakeside kids used to chant "It's all right, it's OK, you'll all work for us someday": It reflected a truth that insisted on being spoken.

Our team was never going to do more than paper over this rift and perhaps give a few of the black players a shot at bettering their positions in life. There were really no demands on the white side except to simply show up. Lasting friendships can't be built when the power differential flops onto one side. To really work, the group with the advantages—money, position, status, education—has to let down the armor of superiority, has to give up its edge.

It always struck me, when I spoke with my teammates about our time playing together, that the dominant memories were of joking around during the van rides. No one had clear recollections of our games—it would have been very hard to write about them if Maitland's brother, Rob, had not unearthed a couple of old videotapes. I think those rides, though so brief, showed us possibilities for something different, what we could be—just kids having fun and forgetting, temporarily, Lakeside, the Central Area, whatever individual ruts we were in at school and at home. I've come to see why Coach McClain said the team "worked," even if the later outcomes for some players have been so sad and tragic. Those moments showed him something that he hadn't seen in his life before, and hasn't seen since. It was a vision of transformation, of our better selves.

A lot of years have gone by. We are all now in the same age bracket as Randy Finley and Willie McClain when they formed our team. There are no more AAU tournaments, no more games, no more van rides. Nothing to bind us together. All we have is us.

In the cafeteria at Zion Prep, the conversation begins to wind down after a few hours. Guys need to get home to their wives and kids. Before we leave, everyone gathers at one end of the room, where there is a stage about eighteen inches high. We arrange ourselves for a photo.

On the floor, from left to right, stand Dino, Mait, JT, Coach Mc-Clain, Chris, and Sean. Coach McClain holds the plaque we received for winning the 1986 Western Washington AAU championship, the same one that Chris and Eric had once lofted above a crouching Tyrell.

On the riser, in the back row, stand Damian, Randy Finley, Eric, Coach Miller, and me.

Mait's brother, Rob, tells us to get ready. We smile at the camera. JT—just as he often did two decades earlier—holds his right hand in front of his chest and raises his index finger in the "Number One" pose. Everyone begins to laugh as the shutter snaps.

(Rob Finley)

Twenty Years Later
Front Row: Dino Christofilis, Maitland Finley, John Thompson, Willie McClain, Chris Dickinson, Sean O'Donnell
Back Row: Damian Joseph, Randy Finley, Eric Hampton, Joe Miller, Doug Merlino

Acknowledgments

One of the main pleasures in writing this book was getting to know my teammates again. To a man, they were incredibly patient with my habit of popping up every few months with a new set of questions. I have tried my best to reflect their voices in these pages.

My family in Seattle and Australia have given essential support throughout: Gene and Inky Merlino; Kay Harvey; Michelle Merlino; Jim and Lynn Merlino; Jean Merlino; Dave and Carlene Merlino; Nik Merlino; Paul, Cheryl and Roman Merlino; Dina Potter; Mary Harvey; Lexi Rado; Noel, Mary and Julie-Ann Gurd, and Kerry Gurd.

Friends have been steadfast with moral support, encouragement, commiseration, and as drinking companions. In no particular order: James Sandler, Brandon Sprague, Alisa Weinstein, Jim Rudd, Millie Org, Robin Shulman, Jessi Hempel, Alida and Rupert Bale, Sunil Abraham, Glenn Gordon, Faye Lane, Charles Hack, Austin Ramzy, Chris O'Connell, Steve Fyffe, Gerasimos Rigas, Amparo Anguiano, Gavin Simpson, Ben Naimark-Rowse, Matt Rodriguez, Roxanne Bartlett and Charlie Frey, Ralph Bruksos, Peter Molnar, David Hill, and Marton Dunai.

Gerald Vandeboe helped me see, many years ago, that writing could perhaps be a worthwhile pursuit. Brendan Koerner, Josh Prager, Tom Zoellner, and Paul Hendrickson gave invaluable professional advice. Jessica Blanchard explained the Seattle school system. Professor Quintard Taylor helped orient my thinking about Seattle's history. The *Seattle Times* gave me a job and experience when I needed both. The UC Berkeley journalism school provided the necessary foundation to build on.

Rob Finley saved the day by digging out some old videotapes of the team and went even further by transferring them to DVD. Minky Worden has been the perfect mix of friend and drill sergeant. Bob Bernstein has been a continual source of inspiration, ideas, and jokes of varying quality.

Todd Dayton, Rob Gunnison, Adam Hochschild, and Nigel Hatton each took the time to read early drafts of this book. They provided insights that helped to reshape and sharpen the story.

My agent, Zoë Pagnamenta, has been a steady hand on the tiller, a calming influence, and the perfect guide through the world of publishing. Pete Beatty, my editor, saw the promise in the proposal and helped to midwife this book into being, from top to bottom. He also flies the flag for Cleveland with flair.

Every sentence of this book was written and rewritten while listening to Thelonious Monk, John Coltrane, or Miles Davis.

Finally, it would be impossible to ever fully express my debt to Tracey Gurd. She has been my editor, motivator, and best friend for over a decade. Everything would be different without her.

Notes on the Sources

The majority of this book is derived from dozens of interviews with my teammates, almost all of which were recorded and transcribed.

I also relied on the work of scholars and other journalists. The following are some of the works that I found most influential and useful.

Books

Seattle Specific

Cayton, Horace R. *Long Old Road: An Autobiography*. Seattle: University of Washington Press, 1974.

de Barros, Paul. *Jackson Street After Hours: The Roots of Jazz in Seattle*. Seattle: Sasquatch Books, 1993.

Lyons, James. *Selling Seattle: Representing Contemporary Urban America*. London: Wallflower Press, 2004.

Morgan, Murray. *Skid Road: An Informal Portrait of Seattle*. Seattle: University of Washington Press, 1981.

Mumford, Esther Hall. *Seattle's Black Victorians, 1852–1901*. Seattle: Ananse Press, 1980.

Taylor, Quintard. *The Forging of a Black Community: Seattle's Central District, from 1870 through the Civil Rights Era*. Seattle: The University of Washington Press, 1994.

Sale, Roger. *Seattle: Past to Present*. Seattle: University of Washington Press, 1978.

Spiedel, William. *Sons of the Profits, or There's No Business Like Grow Business: The Seattle Story 1851–1901*. Seattle: Nettle Creek Publishing, 2003.

Others

Abdul-Jabbar, Kareem, and Peter Knobler. *Giant Steps*. New York: Bantam Books, 1983.

Baker, Brian. *Masculinity in Fiction and Film: Representing Men in Popular Genres 1945–2000*. London and New York: Continuum, 2006.

Baldwin, James. *Collected Essays*. Edited by Toni Morrison. Library of America, 1998.

Cobb, William Jelani. *The Devil and Dave Chappelle: And Other Essays*. New York: Thunder's Mouth Press, 2007.

Cox, Harvey Gallagher. *Fire from Heaven: The Rise of Pentecostal Spirituality and the Reshaping of Religion in the 21ˢᵗ Century*. Cambridge, MA: Da Capo Press, 2001.

Du Bois, W. E. B. *The Souls of Black Folk*. Library of America, 1986.

Cassidy, John. *Dot.con: How America Lost Its Mind and Money in the Internet Era*. New York: Harper Perennial, 2003.

Cookson Jr., Peter W., and Caroline Hodges Persell. *Preparing for Power: America's Elite Boarding Schools*. New York: Basic Books, 1987.

Cross, Charles R. *Heavier Than Heaven: A Biography of Kurt Cobain*. New York: Hyperion, 2002.

Dyson, Michael Eric. *Holler If You Hear Me*. New York: Basic Civitas Books, 2003.

George, Nelson. *Elevating the Game: Black Men and Basketball*. Lincoln, NE: University of Nebraska Press, 1999.

Gorn, Elliott J., and Warren Goldstein. *A Brief History of American Sports*. Urbana and Chicago: University of Illinois Press, 2004.

Joseph, Jamal. *Tupac Shakur Legacy*. New York: Atria, 2006.

Joseph, Peniel. *Waiting 'Til the Midnight Hour: A Narrative History of Black Power in America*. New York: Henry Holt & Co., 2006.

King Jr., Martin Luther. *A Testament of Hope: The Essential Speeches and Writing of Martin Luther King, Jr.* New York: HarperOne, 1990.

Lusane, Clarence. *Race in the Global Era: African Americans at the Millennium*. Cambridge, MA: South End Press, 1999.

Messner, Michael. *Power at Play*. Boston: Beacon Press, 1995.

Miller, Patrick B., and David K. Wiggins. *Sport and the Color Line: Black Athletes and Race Relations in Twentieth Century America*. New York: Routledge, 2003.

Musto, David F. *The American Disease: The Origins of Narcotic Control*. Oxford: Oxford University Press, 1999.

Rader, Benjamin G. *American Sports: From the Age of Folk Games to the Age of Televised Sports*. Lincoln, NE: University of Nebraska Press, 2006.

Rampersad, Arnold. *Jackie Robinson: A Biography*. New York: Alfred A. Knopf, 1997.

Reich, Robert. *The Work of Nations: Preparing Ourselves for the 21st Century*. New York: Vintage, 1992.

Reinarman, Craig, and Harry G. Levine, eds. *Crack in America: Demon Drugs and Social Justice*. Berkeley: University of California Press, 1997.

Robinson, Jackie, and Alfred Duckett. *I Never Had It Made: An Autobiography of Jackie Robinson.* New York: Harper Perennial, 2003.

Wallace, James, and Jim Erickson. *Hard Drive: Bill Gates and the Making of the Microsoft Empire.* New York: Harper Business, 1993.

Western, Bruce. *Punishment and Inequality in America.* New York: Russell Sage Foundation Publications, 2007.

Wiggins, David K. *Glory Bound: Black Athletes in White America.* Syracuse, NY: Syracuse University Press, 1997.

Wilson, William Julius. *The Declining Significance of Race: Blacks and Changing American Institutions.* Chicago: University of Chicago Press, 1980.

Articles

Much essential research was drawn from several hundred newspaper and magazine articles I collected over the course of several years. The archives of the *Seattle Times,* the *Seattle Post-Intelligencer,* the *Seattle Weekly,* and *The Stranger* were especially fruitful. Articles of particular interest are, for the most part, referenced in the text.

Web sites

BlackPast.org, the Free Online Encyclopedia of Washington State History

Frontline, "The Two Nations of Black America" (www.pbs.org/wgbh/pages/frontline/shows/race/)

HistoryLink.org, an Online Reference Guide to African American History

In Motion: The African-American Migration Experience (www.inmotionaame.org)

The Seattle Civil Rights and Labor History Project (http://depts.washington.edu/civilr)

Index

A Note on the Author

Doug Merlino grew up in Seattle. He began working immedi-ately after college as a reporter for a community newspaper in Seattle before moving on to report for the *Seattle Weekly* and the *Seattle Times*. He lived in Budapest, Hungary, for three years, where he edited the *Budapest Business Journal*, and he has reported from Rwanda for the PBS show *Frontline/World*. After earning master's degrees in journalism and international affairs from UC Berkeley, he moved to New York, where he lives with his wife. Merlino has contributed to magazines including *Slate, Wired, Men's Journal,* and *Legal Affairs*.